FREE E-BOOK OF THIS TIT… PURCHASE

INCLUDES 100 PERSONAL PHOTOS OF LIFE ABOARD A… K

SEE BACK OF THIS PAGE TO DOWNLOAD

The Lauren Bruner Story - Memoir of a Sailor

SECOND TO THE LAST TO LEAVE USS ARIZONA

DECEMBER 7, 1941

EDWARD J. McGRATH & CRAIG O. THOMPSON

HOW TO DOWNLOAD YOUR FREE E-BOOK OF "SECOND TO THE LAST TO LEAVE"

1. **Save your receipt** of "Second to the Last to Leave" from the retailer where your purcharse was made. Your FREE E-Book will not be able to be downloaded without this receipt.

2. **Print your name** on the top of your receipt. Then Take a photo of your receipt with your phone **or** scan your receipt once you are home.

3. **Send your receipt** to **ebook@memoirofasailor.com** and the download link for your FREE E-Book will be emailed back to you. Alternatively, you may upload your receipt by visiting **MemoirOfASailor.com.**

IMPORTANT NOTE:

If you do not receive the E-Book link in your email, please check your mail account's "Spam" or "Junk" folder.

Thank you for your purchase. Should you have any questions or concerns, please email **info@ussaz.org** and someone will get back to you as quickly as possible.

MemoirOfASailor.com

WHAT READERS HAVE TO SAY ABOUT "SECOND TO THE LAST TO LEAVE"

Second to the Last to Leave is the most dramatic story of World War II that I have ever read. Although I have spent my life reading many stories about America's history and its continued fight for freedom, I have seldom read anything so up-close and personal that describes the action of war like this story does. It allows you to stand beside a young man who came of age and became an American hero on the same day.

Walter L. Beyer, QM3/c, Eyewitness to History
Navigational Quartermaster, Submarine USS *Bowfin*

======

My name is Lou Conter and like Lauren Bruner I was a crew member of USS *Arizona* and today am one of its last survivors. Lauren is my friend I have read his book from cover to cover, and I know how difficult some of its chapters were for him to write. I want to assure anyone who is considering to read **Second to the Last to Leave**, that Lauren's story is exactly how it was, and a Hell on Earth for every crew member.

Lou Conter, QM3/c, Eyewitness to History
Quartermaster, USS *Arizona* Crew Member & Survivor

======

Reading this book was a profound experience and it made me laugh and cry. I particularly liked Lauren's sharing his experiences of old Honolulu before the war. What can I say about his falling in love with a Japanese Barmaid named Nikki, other than it broke my heart when they were torn apart? His story is amazing and as a Hawaiian and Military historian, I whole-heartily recommend this book to anyone.

Jessie Higa, Pre-WWII & 7 December 1941 Historian

WHAT READERS HAVE TO SAY ABOUT "SECOND TO THE LAST TO LEAVE"

This is one of the most powerful World War II books I have ever read. Gripping in its detail and both heroic and horrific in its storytelling. It is one of the most complete stories ever written about the experiences of those aboard USS *Arizona* on December 7, 1941. This book is a must-have in every family's library in order that it might be handed down from one generation to another. It is that good.

Tim Gray, Chairman- The World War II Foundation

======

Lauren Bruner's book is a fast read and very realistic . It is filled with action and vivid details from its first page, and brings to life a young man's story of growing into adulthood under the most horrific of conditions. My father, DeWayne Barth (BM1/c), was a fellow crew member of Lauren's and an *Arizona* Survivor who never wanted to discuss December 7th. Until I read **Second to the Last to Leave**, I had no real idea as to the hell my father went through during the Attack on Pearl Harbor. Thank you, Lauren, for this gift to future generations.

Margaret Beth Ambroson
Daughter of DeWayne Barth, Boatswain's Mate
USS *Arizona* Survivor

======

The way Lauren tells his story is pretty much exactly the way it happened and the way I remember it, and I have never read a better account. I've read a lot of books over the years about Pearl Harbor by writers all trying to tell the same story without ever having been there. That's why they get it all wrong. But I'll tell you, Lauren's book tells it like it really was.

Howard Kenton Potts, COX, Eyewitness to History
Coxswain, USS *Arizona* Crew Member & Survivor

WHAT READERS HAVE TO SAY ABOUT "SECOND TO THE LAST TO LEAVE"

Lauren Bruner's book on the living and dying on USS Arizona came alive to me more than any other book that I have read on World War II. It is well written and makes you feel like you are standing alongside Lauren while he fought for his life. Lauren's vivid description of the "Lucky Bomb" hitting *Arizona* was powerful; similar to his descriptions of his fellow crew members being killed by splinters from the ship's teak deck after machine gun rounds continued to strafe the ship. It leaves you wanting more.

Jeff Pantaleo, Cultural Resources Manager & Archaeologist
Joint Base Pearl Harbor-Hickam

======

I have read tons of books in my life on American Military history, and have written many reviews on my military blogs. In all the reviews I have ever written, I have never had such a hard time to write this one. But then again, I have also never read a book like this, that had such a profound impact on me. While reading it, I had a hard time putting it down. Not because I didn't want to keep reading, but rather because I didn't want it to end.

This book is masterfully written with seamless transitions from first to third person and back and forth multiple times. Between the smoothness of the transitions and the content itself, the reader can easily get lost in the book and forget that Lauren is not sitting in his kitchen telling you the story himself. While I read this book, I actually felt like he was talking to me and nobody else. I have never had this perception in any book that I have ever read, and it is one of the book's key characteristics.

Troy Steward, Army Infantry First Sargeant
Operation Enduring Freedom (Afghanistan)
Military Online Radio Host

WHAT READERS HAVE TO SAY ABOUT "SECOND TO THE LAST TO LEAVE"

It is one thing to see movies or study the history books about the events that occurred on 'the day that will live in infamy.' Reading Lauren's book is quite a different experience. It must have been difficult for him to relive the horrors of what he saw done to his ship and shipmates over the course of that fateful morning and the remainder of the war. This book serves to remind us about the Hero Next Door and his huge personal sacrifice made in defense of our country."

Sheryl Comon

======

This is a really good book and more than any other book that I have ever read shares the full story of the Attack on Pearl Harbor. I was there and had a ring side seat to History and saw first hand what Lauren Bruner shares in his memoir. No other story that I have ever read shares this kind of detail about living through battle, much less America's greatest defeat. I was at Pearl Harbor as a Medical Corpsman aboard the hospital ship USS *Solace*, where Lauren and Alvin Dvorak arrived near death's door.

Jim Underwood, Eyewitness to History
Medical Corpsman- USS *Solace*

======

This book is a thrilling read that draws you into the life of Lauren Bruner, a 21 year old crew member of USS *Arizona*. My father Joseph Leon George was the sailor from USS *Vestal* who saved the lives of Lauren and his crew during the attack, and I have always searched for closure to my father's heroics, but never have until I read Lauren's book. I had no idea that I would find this story so compelling or be so proud of my father.

Joe Ann George Taylor, Daughter of Joseph Leon George

WHAT READERS HAVE TO SAY ABOUT "SECOND TO THE LAST TO LEAVE"

Lauren Bruner's Memoir of a Sailor is the most powerful account of the attack on Pearl Harbor that I have ever read. Never once did I hear him talk about the Attack on Pearl Harbor or the sinking of USS *Arizona*, as we served together throughout the rest of the war aboard the destroyer USS *Coghlan*. To know this about the man tells you how painful his memory wounds are and what a great gift to America's future generations this book is.

Joe Mamola, Helmsman, Eyewitness to History
USS *Coghlan*, WWII Veteran & Survivor

======

Lauren Bruner shares the most harrowing experience I have ever had as a reader, and I felt inserted into every second of the action. I wept with terror and sorrow as I read; it is amazing that he lived to tell the tale. Not only does this book have enormous historical value but it also serves as a testament to why Lauren Bruner's generation is called "The Greatest Generation."

Sharon Insalata

======

I have never read a better story that keeps you on the edge of your seat. Its detail of battle and the personal tragedies that Lauren fought through to survive is an example to anyone never to give up on life. I can truthfully say, for many reasons, this is my favorite book.

Dwight Lockwood, Veteran
Owner Smith's Union Bar

To read the full reviews from Eyewitnesses to History who have reviewed this book and to view their personal photographs while serving in WWII, visit:
PearlHarborReviews.com

SECOND TO THE LAST TO LEAVE
USS ARIZONA
12.7.41

THE LAUREN F. BRUNER STORY
MEMOIR OF A SAILOR

EDWARD J.MCGRATH / CRAIG O. THOMPSON

COVER ARTIST / ED MELL
PORTRAIT ARTIST / KARIN ANDRINO
COVER DESIGN / PAUL HEWITT

Bruner · McGrath · Thompson

LIMITED EDITION

This Limited Edition second printing of "Second to the Last to Leave" is being offered by the Lauren F. Bruner USS *Arizona* Memorial Foundation.

Lauren Bruner co-founded his nonprofit foundation in 2015 for the purpose of honoring his ship and its crew for future generations.

"Second to the Last to Leave" was written based on the remembrances of Lauren F. Bruner, one of the last survivors of USS *Arizona*. Interviews with Lauren during weekly visits over a four-year period provided Ed McGrath with the material to create this book. Characters are based on historical facts and events. Additional research and interviews were used to help create a more detailed story.

350 Ward Avenue, Suite 106 Honolulu, Hawaii 96814
Published in Association with Pearl Harbor Press.

ISBN: 978-0-692-98003-3

Printed in the United States of America.

To my friends,
my buddies, and
my fellow crew members
of USS *Arizona,*
in hopes
that they think
I've done them proud.

HISTORICAL IMPORTANCE

The original artwork of Crew Members and friends of Lauren Bruner that are displayed at the end of each chapter are significant, especially those of his crew.

In each case, the signature appearing under the artwork is original to the person. As well the age of that person has been calculated to the day of the Attack on Pearl Harbor and USS Arizona.

It is Lauren's and his friend Ed McGrath's goal through the foundation they have created together to have an individual portrait like those you see of each of USS Arizona's 1512 Crew Members aboard the ship on 7 December 1941.

Once completed, this special collection will be made available to the National Park Service at Pearl Harbor to share with future generations.

TABLE OF CONTENTS

TABLE OF CONTENTS CONTINUED

TABLE OF CONTENTS CONTINUED

Bruner · McGrath · Thompson

FOREWORD

Lauren Bruner & His Friend
Rear Admiral Frank Ponds, Retired
USS *KIDD* 9.9.14

While attending high school in a small rural town in southern Alabama, I read and studied the accounts of the Second World War (WW-II); specifically, the attack on Pearl Harbor and the sinking of USS *ARIZONA*.

Throughout my 33-year career in the United States Navy I studied world events leading up to that dreadful day and of the tragedies that occurred on the morning of December 7, 1941.

During port-calls to Pearl Harbor, I, like many others, was privileged to render "appropriate" honors when we passed the *Arizona* Memorial.

In 2011, my first "Flag Officer" assignment was as Commander, Navy Region Hawaii. During that assignment, I had the distinct honor of co-presiding over the 70th and 71st Commemorations of the attack on Pearl Harbor, an honor that left indelible memories of the faces of a heroic generation and of the emotional stories that they shared with profound detail and clarity.

However, it would not be until June 6, 2013 that I would have my most moving and memorable experience. It was on that day that I met Mr. Lauren Bruner and that is when my journey into naval history truly began to take on a deeply personal meaning. That is why this opportunity to contribute to such a timeless piece will forever be special to me.

Lauren Bruner is an American Legend and Naval Hero. I am proud to call him my friend. His book "Second to the Last to Leave USS *Arizona* 12.7.41" is one of the most authentic pieces of American history you will ever have the opportunity to read.

It is written as Lauren speaks, and you will be able to feel both the excitement and pain as you move through its chapters. I had been stationed at Pearl Harbor for three years, which is when I came to meet Lauren. I considered it an honor to have met him. Now I consider him my friend, my shipmate, and a part of my family.

The chapters in this book where he shares his experiences during the attack on Pearl Harbor are the most detailed that I have ever read. When you consider that what is written was taken from Lauren's own first-hand account, this makes the story that much more compelling, real, and authentic.

"Second to the Last to Leave USS *Arizona*" is a gripping read, and one that you would not want to put down. It is that good.

Although I have never recommended a book before, Lauren's book, I believe, is a must read by anyone committed to a deeper understanding and appreciation of that tragic day and the courageous hours of those who have been called our greatest generation.

I whole-heartedly recommend it to anyone who loves America, her Military, or just simply a thrilling story. It is the story of the attack from someone who was there and continues to live and share his experience in a very personal and profound manner.

Thank you, Lauren!

Fernandez L. Ponds

Rear Admiral Fernandez "Frank" Ponds
USN, Retired

Bruner · McGrath · Thompson

WELCOME

Commander Jeff James & His Friend
Lauren Bruner Saluting The Crew Of USS *Arizona*
At The Memorial Shrine Wall 6.7.13

In "Second to the Last to Leave," Lauren Bruner shares a very uniquely personal and compelling glimpse into one of history's most gruesome and costly wars. His vivid first-hand account of the attack on Pearl Harbor and its impact on those who endured it is told in a manner unlike any I've ever read.

It is rich with adventure, sacrifice, and a commitment to our nation told in the voice of a young sailor; you can almost close your eyes and be transported back in time.

Lauren talks about "fate" almost like a friend or a shadow that has followed him throughout his life. It has dealt him blows and almost killed him during the Attack on Pearl Harbor, but has also kept him alive so that he can share this cornerstone of American history.

It is seldom in life that one is afforded the opportunity to meet a true American hero and Naval legend, but I was blessed on both accounts when I met Lauren.

I've had the great pleasure to get to know him for several years, and now call him friend and shipmate. I visited the USS *Arizona* Memorial with Lauren twice, and it truly stands out as one of the highlights of my naval career.

I most strongly urge you to read this book and truly get an inside understanding of how America's "Greatest Generation" was formed. It is well worth your time.

Jeffrey W. James
Captain, USN (Retired)
Commander, Joint Base
Pearl Harbor-Hickam 2011-2014

SECOND TO THE LAST TO LEAVE

PREFACE

For over 75 years, Lauren Bruner did his best to suppress thoughts and memories of his fight for survival at Pearl Harbor during the morning of 7 December, 1941.

Common to many who have served our country in battle, Lauren and his fellow sailors suffered tremendous physical and mental pain as a result of the attack. Lauren *never* spoke about his memories of the actual events of that day; not with his closest relatives or friends, nor with those in the media who sought out his story.

In particular, relating the story of the actual attack—as recounted here—was always, and continues to be, almost too painful for Lauren to endure. To allow him to further recall what occurred that day would not only guarantee episodes of contiued night sweats, but nightmares as well. Readers can only imagine the effort it took to describe his experiences for this book.

What Lauren and his fellow sailors witnessed and experienced that morning is considered to be one of the most terrifying events in human history.

Strong-willed and determined to never talk about the horrors of war, Lauren chose to suppress what his eyes and mind found difficult to comprehend—man's inhumanity to man.

For those who lived through that day, the attack pummeled and shocked the base roots of human sensibility. Lauren Bruner, and thousands of sailors and Marines became victims in, and witnesses to, a macabre drama that unfolded before their eyes. In Lauren's case, he experienced grisly injuries and observed horrific sights, most of which were sickening and beyond comprehension.

As a young man who had recently turned 21, he witnessed wholesale murder; shocking atrocities; heads and limbs separated from torsos; a sea of dismembered bodies—flesh and limbs in ribbons—all part of an orgy of destruction and intentional killings that were indiscriminately inflicted on military and civilian personnel alike.

For Lauren, it sent him into what today is understood to be Post Traumatic Stress Disorder (PTSD), which caused decades of nightmares, visions of dead bodies, and memories of the stench of burning human flesh—including his own. One does not have to wonder why he no longer desires to speak about this particular chapter in his life.

Despite all this, Lauren Bruner—by sheer determination— survived. And very late in life, he came to the decision that his story should be told, once and for all. But to do so meant reliving the assaults on his memories, at least one last time.

Through the tears, through the heartache, Lauren's story has been offered up to history with only one request. In order for Lauren to live out the remainder of his life in peace, his wish is that no one—whether they be from print or electronic media, the public, or even close friends—ever ask him to describe what happened on Sunday, 7 December, 1941.

To put it simply, please do not ask Lauren about the attack on Pearl Harbor because he will not answer. He will not discuss what he has described as the "death of *Arizona*" again.

"This is my request," said Lauren. Anything beyond that, he is still pleased to explore.

As co-authors of Lauren's story, Ed McGrath and Craig Thompson ask that this request be honored, out of respect for what Lauren has endured. To do otherwise would be to dishonor not only Lauren's service to our country, but would dishonor his fellow crew and their service, as well. Each suffered the indignities of war, so that all who followed could continue to live out their lives as free Americans.

"Although I am happy to have shared my memories in this book," said Lauren, "I do not want to further discuss or answer any questions concerning the actual attack. If you wish to ask a question concerning the attack on Pearl Harbor itself… and what I experienced, I direct you to my friend Ed McGrath."

"As you read these chapters," he said, "know they were real and that it was truly Hell on Earth. The horrors of what I witnessed on that morning have kept me from sleep for many years after."

Despite all this, Lauren has some advice.

"Distant memories of what I've shared have cooled down the nightmares and cold sweats. They still come into my mind on occasion, but by discussing them with Ed and by writing them down, it's as if I've gone to a confession. A great weight has been lifted off my shoulders."

"For those who serve in the Military and have fought in battle, reading my book may give you hope… perhaps even a road map on how to exorcise your own demons."

"I chose to face the future and not let my past dictate what might lie ahead. And I decided to not let my mind's wounds stand in the way of a full life."

"If you feel that heavy weight from having a story to share, find a person you can trust, as I did. Allow a friendship to develop. Then, when you feel comfortable… just begin 'talking story', as the locals say in the Islands of Hawaii."

"I believe it may help. It has for me."

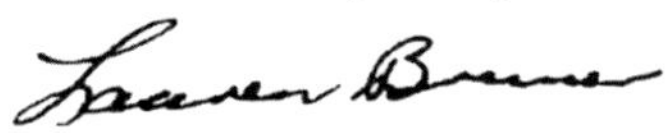

Lauren Bruner Today

"This is pretty much how you will find me today as I approach the centennial of my life. Five years ago, my life changed for the better when I met my friend Ed McGrath, who came to interview me and, true to his word, has come back every week ever since.

It is also important for me to take this opportunity to thank Dyanne McGrath, Ed's wife, who makes me homemade dinners every week. For someone who lives alone like I do, I can't thank Dyanne enough for her thoughtfulness and homemade meals."

"Second to Last to Leave"
Today

U.S.S. ARIZONA

These are my words and this is my story.

Lauren F. Bruner

PROLOGUE

Pearl Harbor - Territory of Hawaii TH
Approximately 0840
Sunday, 7 December 1941

A cool spray of water hit Fire Controlman Third Class Lauren F. Bruner's burned torso as the saltwater bit at his exposed nerves.

More important concerns arose as the Navy motor launch navigated through oil-fueled fires, dead and dismembered bodies, and sharks.

Early in the morning, USS *Vestal's* launch had been a simple Liberty boat for sailors. That designation had ended in an instant, less than an hour after the attack on Pearl Harbor.

Orders from *Vestal's* captain had been to "…get these two burnt bastards to *Solace,* straightaway!"

"Doesn't look like either will make it."

Adrenaline pumped through Lauren's veins. Burned over seventy-three percent of his body, he knew death was closer than life. But pain was the last thing on his mind. Fellow crew member Alvin Dvorak was seated next to him. They had just escaped off USS *Arizona.*

Bombed and still being strafed, their ship had already sunk into the shallow depths of Pearl Harbor's Battleship Row.

The coxswain maneuvered his rescue launch through turbulent waters. He quickly read and reacted to every twist and turn the Japanese fighter planes hurled at them. His hook-man, pole in hand—stood sure-footed at forward while he called out and pushed aside obstacles and bodies in the water.

With the strength Bruner had left, he used his charred fingers to grip at the wooden bench seat.

He hung on while the launch's coxswain deftly evaded errant torpedoes and bomb geysers on each side of the channel. Machine gun fire and the whine from Zeke fighter planes and Val dive-bombers were relentless from above.

Lauren focused on the all-white ship with the giant Red Cross painted on its side—dead ahead. He turned to his crewmate, Alvin Dvorak, Boatswain's Mate Second Class.

"Alvin... they're taking us to *Solace*."

Dvorak simply answered, "Yup."

Like Bruner, Dvorak was badly burned, with over eighty percent of his body scorched. Each man had the skin on their hands, arms, legs and faces "blackened like charbroiled chicken."

"Both of us had our hair burned off. But Alvin was worse. Both ears completely gone."

To reassure himself, Lauren reached up to touch his own.

Thank God…

They were still there.

A new wave of enemy fighters returned up the West Channel, banked directly over hospital ship *Solace,* then came south down Battleship Row. They strafed anything dead or alive that moved—or floated—in the water.

Lauren felt certain he was headed to his own funeral.

Is this an honorable way to die? Barely twenty-one, he'd never given any thought to death.

He'd offered his life to the Navy for his father's desertion, and he was determined to get through whatever was thrown at him.

His lungs were seared from fire and smoke; Lauren choked as he took a breath.

I can get through this.

Only a hundred yards to *Solace*.

"Alvin… we're gonna' make it. Don't give up…"

"Yup."

Having been out on liberty only twelve hours before, Lauren changed his mind about life. *Life is a shitty and dangerous place.*

"I wanted to puke my guts out."

As though to avoid the horrific sights, the coxswain sped up the boat. Lauren became even more nauseous. "I couldn't hold it in any longer." He gagged, dry heaved and finally retched over the side.

He turned back. It was all he could do to keep his eyes on *Solace*'s red cross.

The launch inched closer toward its hull.

Other launches ferried more wounded Sailors and Marines toward *Solace*. Each competed to get in line for the starboard gangway—first-come, first-served.

All medical personnel were engaged in triage on deck. Only one was at water level to help victims come aboard and to climb the steps of the gangway once they arrived.

"His name, as I remember it, was Jim Underwood."

"So many dying," Lauren said. "Most picked up straight outta' the water."

Still, Lauren felt relief wash over him as the launch approached the mercy ship—so far untouched by Japanese invaders.

It appeared they were within reach until, at less than twenty-five feet above the water, a new lone-bandit Zero headed straight for them.

— —

Lauren's Purple Heart

"My Purple Heart was awarded to me for my wounds suffered during the attack on Pearl Harbor, but I would be surprised if you have ever seen one exactly like it before.

The uniqueness of my medal is that an Admiral's Silver Star is pinned to its ribbon, which was given to me by my friend Rear Admiral Fernandez 'Frank' Ponds on the day we met years ago.

At our first meeting, which was scheduled to last only 5 minutes but ended up being more like 30, Frank took a silver star off of his uniform and pinned it to the ribbon of my medal as his way to pay me honor.

Along with our friendship, his star has always meant a great deal to me, and I wear it with pride."

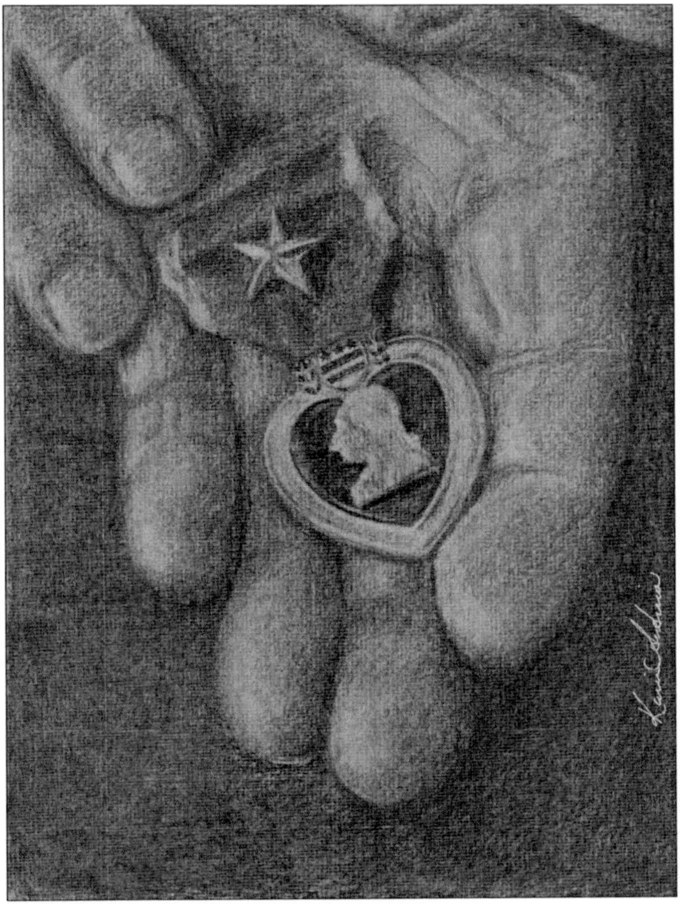

My Purple Heart

Awarded for Wounds Suffered
During the Attack on Pearl Harbor
7 December 1941

Bruner · McGrath · Thompson

Chapter 1
LUCK OF THE DRAW

15 November 1938

A blustery Seattle morning followed Lauren when his mother, Lucille, and step-dad, John Kellerman, dropped him off at the downtown Navy recruiter's office. As usual, the rain poured in proverbial buckets. Lauren glanced up at the black clouds.

Nothing new for Washington State.

He looked forward to the start of basic training in cloudless Southern California. His initial designation during basic would be "Seaman Apprentice."

Lauren had been to the recruiter's office once before, when they first encouraged him to enlist. But when he visited the office right after graduating from Elma High School, he was still seventeen and the Navy turned him down.

He recalled a short, pudgy recruiter, telling him he was sorry, but they had enough "kiddie cruisers" already. He'd have to wait until his eighteenth birthday to join up.

Shit. This was not what they told me the first time I talked to them. That sonovabitch lied.

"Now, six months later, I was ready to set off to see the world on my own. Excited? All I really wanted was for my parents to drop me off and go on home."

Lauren's wish was not to be granted.

"No such luck," he recalled. "My mother cried as she hugged and kissed me goodbye. Would've been a hell of a lot worse, except most of the other recruits, who left that morning, went through pretty much the same damn thing."

Shortly after the Kellermans left, Lauren received his first taste of a long-time tradition in the Navy: "hurry up and wait."

"It took all morning to fill out my paperwork, get fingerprinted, and have a Navy mug shot taken."

By late afternoon, recruits boarded the train in Seattle for the trip south to San Diego. Lauren sat by a window, ready to begin what his recruiter had promised as "his new, great adventure."

He had plenty of time to think while the modern steam engine pulled the train down a soothing, hypnotic path—distracting him from distant conversations and other muted sounds. It brought back memories of Washington and the mill trains that followed tracks between Elma and McCleary.

It was a good time to think back on his youth. But the steady, muffled clickety-clack over the steel-belted wooden ties allowed him to doze off.

Now, Lauren's mind wandered and dwelled on two thoughts, in particular: *I can't believe this day is finally here, and I wonder if the Navy knows about my arrest record?*

As a kid of eight, Lauren had been caught running moonshine for Burgess Dairy in Tenino, Washington, where he worked for food and clothing.

"Hell," he said, "It was the depression."

"Old man Burgess had attempted to supplement his dairy income by distilling liquor through his creamery inside the barn. And he used us kids as 'slave-labor' to milk the cows at three-thirty in the morning, then muck the barn… seven days a week. I was assigned to seven cows.

"I swear, though… I *never* knew about the moonshine. There were six other kids around my age, and we were sorta' ram-rodded by a sixteen-year-old kid who drove the dairy truck. Name was O'Shea, as I recall."

On what would turn out to be Burgess' last drop-off, the farmer had given instructions for Lauren to accompany the sixteen-year-old driver to transport fifteen stainless steel "milk cans" to a retail dairy in Aberdeen, about ten minutes up Highway 101.

While off-loading the "milk cans" from the old pickup, a half dozen guys in suits—FBI—deftly swooped into the delivery barn and surrounded the two boys.

Young Lauren was startled. He saw a gun holstered on an agent's belt. "I'd never seen anything like this before, and was scared as hell."

An agent looked at Lauren, then the milk cans, and then to the teenage truck driver. "What d'ya have there?" he asked.

"What d'ya think?" the kid retorted. "We're makin' a delivery… of milk."

Without another word, the agent moved to the truck bed, removed a canister, pried off the lid, and dipped a finger through the opening.

Lauren looked to the truck driver, but got no sign anything was wrong.

"The kid was cool as a cucumber."

They both watched as the agent put his finger to his tongue, and displayed a wry smile.

"This isn't milk," said the agent. He threw a stern look at them. "You're both under arrest."

The boys protested, but the man was unforgiving.

He nodded to the other agents; they immediately split into three groups.

The first surrounded the boys and held them in place; another quickly began to impound the truck and tag the evidence; and the third group headed out the door for the retailer—and to arrest Burgess back in Tenino.

"They completely shut down the dairy," said Lauren.

"I later heard Burgess and his other runners were all arrested… along with me… and the truck driver kid.

"Never went back to the dairy, not even to get what few things I had.

"To this day, I don't know if O'Shea, the driver, had any knowledge of what we were carrying. We were taken away in separate cars. When we arrived at the jail, they separated us from the others."

"Hell, I spent most of that day in jail… in a real cell, to boot. They tried to scare the shit out of us, and it worked."

Fortunately, his mother and Lauren's cousin, Flora Troxell, bailed him out. Lauren neglected to list the incident when asked about prior arrests in his enlistment papers.

—

16 November 1938

Nearly twenty-four hours passed before the group of enlistees reached San Diego. Several stops were made along the way "to pick up other recruits and add them to our brood, all of us mother-henned by a heavy-set petty officer."

The enlistees arrived at the train station "…at the end of the tracks. Go any further, and you'd run into Mexico," said Lauren.

Their next form of transportation was "a big old, battleship-grey Navy bus, takin' us to basic training camp."

"Some smartass enlistee… a member of our group, said something like 'This bus looks like a beat up old Battleship'—and that didn't set well with the Chief in charge. I'd see that same kid, all through basic. Instructors were *always* on his ass."

"There's somethin' to be said about opening your mouth when not asked."

Immediately upon arrival in San Diego, Lauren and his fellow enlistees received their shots, buzz cuts, uniforms, and gear. That was immediately followed by three months of intensive, "hard-ass work and exercise—grinding on the parade grounds and learning 'the Navy way'. Do what you're told, shut up and don't ask questions."

17 February 1939

His first true opportunity to relax came at the end of basic training. Lauren had earned a ten-day leave.

"Hell," he said, "I had nowhere else to go but home."

"When I entered the Navy, I'd have never guessed I'd look forward to going home. But there I was on a Greyhound bus. And the lull of the ride was soothing after all the crap during basic."

They passed through the Siskiyou Mountains, and Lauren recalled "the incredible height of the snowpack… higher than the bus, on both sides of the road."

"But throughout my trip, back to Washington, all I could really see in my mind was mother's home cookin'."

Upon arrival at the Greyhound Station in Olympia, his brother Clarence hadn't yet arrived. To pass some time, Lauren stopped in on his cousin Flora, who owned the beauty parlor located inside the depot.

"Flora was shocked when I walked in and… I'd say, she was pleased to see me."

Lauren had worn his uniform home and was struck by how happy and proud Flora was when she saw him.

Looking around the shop, memories returned of cleaning the beauty parlor every Saturday morning for whatever loose change she happened to have in her purse.

"Usually paid me between fifteen cents to a quarter for cleaning up the parlor."

"I mentioned it to Flora and we both had a good laugh."

"After my dad died, times got tough for mother. So I lived with Flora and her husband Burton… from about age eight to thirteen. Those years were much better times for me."

"Since cousin Flora ran the shop and her husband Burton sold used cars, they'd bring me into town to help out… and to keep me busy while they worked."

"After helping in the salon, I'd go next door to the little candy store and help the old man, the owner, clean up and make signs for his shop. He'd pay me a dime, but I'd always give it back to buy a bag of candy… almost always jawbreakers, 'cause I could suck on 'em all day at the cinema. There'd be enough to last through most double features, a newsreel, and one or two cartoons."

Eventually, it was off to the movie theater, located in the same block, "…on the other side of the old man's candy store. And I'd be set for the day."

As Lauren got older, he graduated from buying jawbreakers to eating the new Big Hunk candy bars. They were pretty chewy, and I could make a couple of 'em last through most of the matinée."

Lauren would spend each Saturday afternoon, with his candy, watching double features—sometimes twice—and return to Flora's shop, "…usually with money still in my pocket.

"Of course, I worked out a deal to earn my 'free' second round of movies by helping the theater manager clean up trash between shows."

"I think Burton had secretly arranged for the manager

to keep an eye out on me, as a young kid. He and Flora always warned me about the occasional seedy-lookin' character who'd kill time at the movies instead of waitin' at the Greyhound terminal for a bus to leave town."

"Worked out great, though, 'cause I could keep watching the films until Aunt Flora and Burton got off work."

"My all-time favorite movies were the 'Lone Ranger' serials starring Lee Powell... couldn't wait for the next episode to come to the cinema... and 'Tarzan the Ape Man' with Johnny Weissmuller. Boy, they really made an impression on me."

"Maybe even gave me my sense for adventure, later in life. Wanted to see the world, and all that."

That afternoon, back from Basic, Lauren's older brother Clarence eventually showed up at the bus depot,and found him at the salon.

Lauren couldn't leave for home, though, without first stopping by the candy store. "I wondered if the ol' man still ran his shop. It'd been nearly six years since I'd left Aunt Flora's to move back home to McCleary. I'd enrolled in Elma High School, then joined the Navy after graduating."

"Sure enough, the ol' man was still there... even older than what I remembered from my younger days."

"But he sure remembered me, and I was proud to show off my uniform. Made him proud, too. I'll never forget... he wouldn't let me leave without a parting gift, for the trip home. A bag of jawbreakers."

"Clarence and I bid goodbye to Flora and made the thirty-minute drive to my mother's home in McCleary."

Lauren laughed, "The jawbreakers kept us busy ridin' back."

"More memories flowed," said Lauren, "as we drove the winding roads of the Capitol State Forest. What a beautiful sight it was. There I was in the middle of a forest of tall trees, again… something I really didn't realize I'd missed so much, during basic."

"When I was really young, before dad died, he'd always point to the trees and tell me, 'that's what puts food on the table, Lauren. If it weren't for those trees, we wouldn't be here'."

" 'Proud' seemed to be the word of the day, as we arrived back in McCleary. Mother just couldn't stop declaring—over and over, again, how proud she was of me."

"Have to admit... Made me feel pretty damn good. Don't think she ever told me that before… though I'd been waiting all my life to hear her say so…. And my step-dad, Kellerman, even chimed in, too."

During basic, Lauren had put on thirty-two pounds of muscle. "Even my brother Clarence admitted I looked good. Trouble was… none of my old clothes fit me anymore. So, I borrowed a shirt from Clarence and went shopping for a new pair of dungarees."

The only reminder Lauren retains, to pinpoint the date of his trip home, is a photo of him sitting out in front of the Kellerman house, in uniform. His 5 foot 11 1/4 inch physique—at a hundred fifty-three pounds when he enlisted—was now a sturdy one hundred eighty-five. If the photo had been in color, it would have shown a healthy red complexion, highlighted by wide-set blue eyes, thick brown hair, and bushy eyebrows.

"Mother captured me with her Brownie camera. Still have that photo. Stands in a frame… in my living room.

Reminds me of my mother… and how young I was, at the time. Thought I'd grown up, was on my own, from then on, and didn't need anyone's help anymore."

"After I got in the Navy… at least in my younger years, before the war… girls, drinking beer, and getting in trouble was my life."

"But my real coming of age was still three years down the road. And I was unaware of…" He stopped mid-sentence. It was difficult to speak of past atrocities.

Lauren had no idea of what was to come. Or of the destiny he would fulfill. An attack on an American Naval base? It was beyond anything a newly minted sailor might have conceived could *ever* occur.

"Besides, we'd all been reassured during basic, that we had the strongest Navy in the world."

Although the Japanese attack would come, Lauren had a lot of living to do before death would knock at the door.

"…. And I'd have to grow up real quick, that day, or die trying."

"At my age, now, I have a different perspective than when I looked for adventure… beyond my doorstep, as a young man. Once you cross that make-believe threshold into adulthood, you can never step back again, no matter how much you want to."

"Coming of age happens under the most unforeseeable circumstances…. And when you get that damn slap in the face like I did, you begin to realize what truly matters in life."

"My suggestion to anyone who hasn't crossed that line, yet… Don't rush it. Slow down, take a deep breath, and understand that growing up isn't necessarily all it's cracked up to be. Be ready for whatever comes… the good *and* the bad."

———

27 February 1939

Following his ten day leave—enjoying mother's cooking—Lauren returned to San Diego, refreshed and anxious "to learn what ship I'd be assigned to."

To his dismay, he hadn't yet been assigned to *any* ship.

"I'll tell you, goddamn it, that was a big letdown. Worse than waiting for grades. This wasn't just killing time for test results. It was finding out what the Navy thought you could handle."

For weeks, Lauren would check the Assignment Bulletin Board, daily. Names were posted and matched against ships with holes in their crews. But his name was always missing. In Lauren's mind, it became apparent he'd more likely end up on an oil tanker, cargo ship, or possibly a Navy tug—referred to by officers as a "safe ship."

For a young man of eighteen, a safe ship was not where Lauren wanted to end up. "It was no fun," he said. "It lacked adventure and came with no bragging rights to the girls… or so my young mind convinced me, at the time."

Each day for a month, following Kitchen Patrol, or "KP," duty, Lauren checked the board, and found nothing.

"I was sick of peeling potatoes and getting damn sick of waiting for the Navy to make a decision. It was holding up my life."

1 March 1939

By the end of his third month in San Diego, Lauren reached the point where he nearly gave up. *Why bother to check the list? It'll just be a waste of time.*

Then, "…one morning… for the hell of it, I checked the Assignment Board… and sonovabitch… couldn't believe it."

Lauren stood in front of the board, exhilarated. He let out a whoop, and nearly jumped up and down for joy.

One of his instructors, a chief petty officer, approached. Suspecting why Lauren was so excited, he inquired about his ship assignment.

Lauren looked back to the board, not certain if his eyes had tricked him, then turned to the chief and reported, "… *Arizona*… USS *Arizona,* Sir!"

"I'll never forget that moment.

"That guy was the first to offer me congratulations, and the first to tell me that, from then on, I could call myself a Battleship Sailor."

"Is *Arizona* a good ship?"

"Kid," said the CPO, "it's a *great* ship. And you've just won the 'luck of the draw.' "

——

Lauren F. Bruner

Lauren Fay Bruner was born on 4 November 1920 in Shelton, Washington to LeRoy Clarence and Lucille Iowa (Smith) Bruner. Lauren endured many hardships in his life, including the death of his father when he was only six years old.

Lauren graduated from Elma High School in Elma, Washington in June of 1938 and enlisted in the Navy on 15 November 1938 for a four-year period. USS *Arizona* was his first ship, and he joined its crew under the command of Captain Isaac Kidd on 11 March 1939.

"The photo from which this portrait was drawn was taken by my mother on my first leave home after basic training. I was sitting on the steps of our front porch when my mother took this photo with her old Kodak Brownie camera.

My brother Clarence, who was driving me back to the bus station, was standing behind Mother trying to make me laugh. At least he got me to smile."

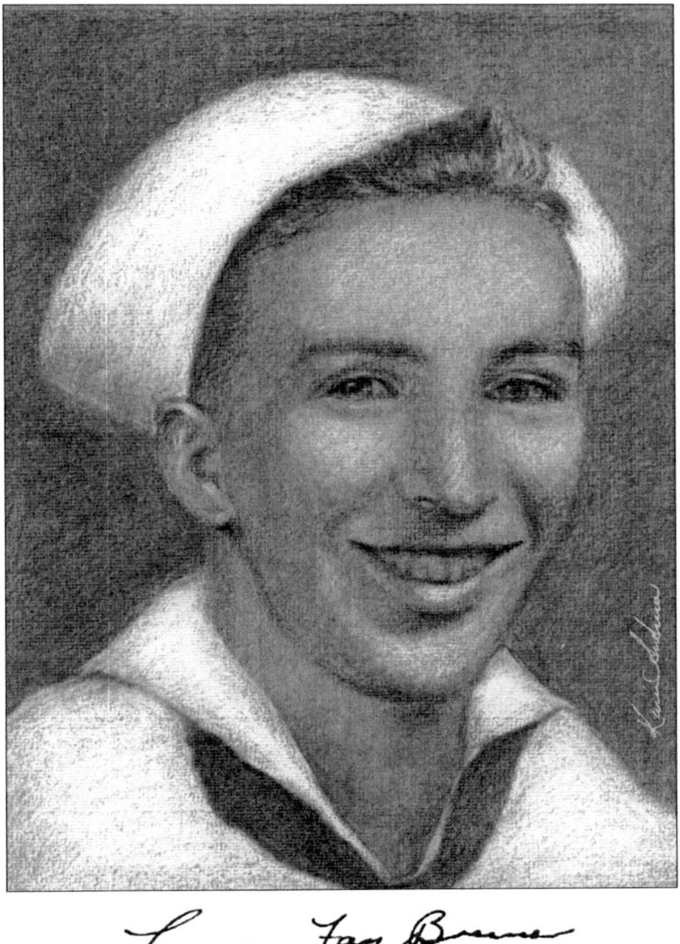

Lauren Fay Bruner
Seaman Apprentice
USS *Arizona*

Chapter 2
MEETING *ARIZONA* VIA MIDNIGHT EXPRESS

1 March 1939

USS *Nitro* (AE-2) was the first Navy ship to which Bruner was transferred, following basic training. To reach his assigned ship—*Arizona*—his ride from San Diego, California, to the Naval shipyard in Bremerton, Washington, was aboard the Pyro-class ammunition ship.

Nitro's mission was to transport live munitions, including tons of black powder, to ships located primarily on both the east and west coasts of the United States. One of her scheduled rearming sites would be at the Bremerton Ship Yard's dry dock in Puget Sound, Washington. USS *Arizona* was one of several ships dry-docked there.

Beside *Nitro's* crew of 300 enlisted men and officers, she could take on a compliment of up to 250 additional "quick trip" troop transfers.

"My boarding *Nitro* would allow me to meet up with USS *Arizona,* while it underwent retrofit at the Bremerton shipyard."

Lauren admitted he felt a degree of anxiety, when he first learned the names of his transport ship—*Nitro* and her sister-ship, *Pyro*. He had heard about the AE-2 class of ships, responsible for rearming destroyers, battleships, carriers and cruisers—sometimes while performing side-by-side and stem to stern "underway replenishments" at sea.

Nitro and *Pyro* were the only two active auxiliary ships of its class, at the time. Constantly moving between ports around the world. Ironically, *Nitro's* sister ship, *Pyro,* would later find itself moored in the West Loch of Pearl Harbor, on 7 December 1941.

"Over the ten-day trip up the coast, I got to know one of *Nitro's* crew, Gunner's Mate First Class C. J. Sickert. I came to respect how professional these guys had to be. Especially when you consider they often handled highly explosive replenishments, in good weather and bad. Sickert sometimes told me stories of full operations carried out in high seas."

"Imagine fifteen to twenty foot waves, with water washing across their decks, as they transferred thousands of pounds of munitions from *Nitro* to another ship. To an eighteen year old sailor, these guys were tough."

"C.J., as he liked to be called, had served in the Navy for a dozen years or so, and had been aboard *Nitro* for about a year. He and Seaman Bennett Landry… who I met while chipping and painting together, both filled my mind with harrowing tales."

"Considering *Nitro's* mission, they felt it was one of the most comfortable and safest ships at sea. Though I hadn't yet been on my first assignment, I had to agree that it was not bad. Even the food was better than what I'd had during basic."

"These guys worked their butts off, considering the high explosives stored in the hold… I sure as hell felt they deserved hazard pay."

"To me, every day had to be a dangerous mission, aboard *Nitro*. It seemed the Navy provided comfortable billets, and better food, to make up for the daily hazards they faced."

Bruner learned that the Pyro-class ships had refrigerated holds to keep their deadly cargo—referred to as "popcorn" among the crew—from detonating in equatorial climates. But one other term was bandied about, and its meaning was confirmed by his new friend Landry.

The ship's common moniker was "The Midnight Express." Lauren had heard it tossed about on a regular basis.

"Turns out the 'Midnight Express' title came about because there wasn't much normal about *Nitro's* schedule. Other than rotating crew shifts, for loading or unloading the hull, *Nitro* was constantly in a state of loading and off-loading… often during the late-to-midnight, and beyond, hours. Or the ship would be on it's way to another destination to perform the same tasks."

"They'd load or offload munitions and supplies, sometimes to multiple ships in a harbor; then, in the middle of the night, get underway again, only to start over with another vessel."

"One night, still in transit to Bremerton while I slept, *Nitro's* munitions crew pulled an all-nighter, when they offloaded munitions for a couple of ships, at the Mare Island Navy Yard in Northern California."

"For me, as a lowly 'pollywog,' my daily schedule was routine. After breakfast, at 'oh-eight-thirty,' I'd muster with the whole crew, on stations. Then, it was back to chipping and painting for the rest of the day."

"As an ammunition ship, *Nitro* was scheduled to supply munitions to *Arizona's* new guns being installed, and supply other war ships at the Navy yard with shells, black powder, and other explosives, as well."

"I'd find out later that dry dock was not considered a 'loading port' for exchanging freight, of any kind. So *Nitro* would service other ships first, before *Arizona* left dry dock for its official loading port."

At eighteen years old, just out of high school and basic, Lauren was ready to see the world, "…just like my Navy Recruiter promised. Trouble was, he never explained that, for a sailor, 'seeing the world' included one hell of a lot of chipping and painting."

Bruner spent his entire ten day trip up the west coast, en route to Washington, doing just that. He learned, quickly, that this was the Navy way, "…which was the only way. Didn't take me long to figure out this would include enough chipping and painting to last me a lifetime."

"Twelve 'new boots' or 'pollywogs,' as they called us, were aboard *Nitro*. All were assigned to *Arizona*. And because *Nitro* was a munitions ship, there were places on board you could go, and other areas that were off limits."

"Prohibited zones were designated with large red and white signs. Most of them simply read, 'DANGER'. To be expected, regulations included basic rules about where crew and transport sailors could and couldn't smoke."

But like so many young men throughout the ages, some couldn't read, "…or they were just plain careless. And what happened aboard *Nitro,* about half way to Washington scared the hell out of me."

"One afternoon, some idiot recruits, traveling with us, were smoking on the main deck. Against all regulations aboard *any* Navy ship, instead of extinguishing and stashing their cigarettes, some jerk tossed a butt overboard.

"Wind blew the cigarette back aboard ship and it ended up where it shouldn't have… down the stored ammunitions hold."

"Several hours later, smoke began to drift from the red zone."

Bruner was below when sirens and bells went off, and the ships fire crew immediately took over.

"From the loudspeaker, the entire crew including us 'new boots', were ordered to '…proceed to *Nitro's* aft deck, double-time.' "

"No one had to tell me twice. I was one of the first to arrive, and wondered if our next orders would be to abandon ship."

"My imagination went wild. Would *Nitro* blow up? Would my Navy career be over, before it started?"

"Fortunately, the fire was quickly doused. And it gave me a new respect for *Nitro's* crew. But the Captain? Shit… C.J. told me he was pissed. At Captain's Mast, he informed the crew, that he was pretty sure he knew the group of irresponsible sailors that caused the incident."

"The Captain added… and I'll never forget this, 'I guarantee, at the least, there will be a summary court martial of the guilty parties once an investigation has been completed.' "

"Not knowing if our *Arizona* recruits were responsible for the fire was a heartache. After that episode… narrowly escaping disaster, I was ready to just chip and paint, and happy to be alive."

"Can laugh about it now, but back then, it was dangerous and serious business."

Five days later, *Nitro* made an early morning approach into Puget Sound.

11 March 1939

"A heavy, persistent fog slowed us down on our heading into Bremerton."

Bruner's arrival back in his home state felt ironic. "Thought I'd waited all my life to get out of Washington,to see the world. And there I was, right back *in the soup*… what locals called thick fog. And thick as soup, it was" said Lauren.

USS *Nitro* navigated its course toward Bremerton Ship Yard and arrived by midmorning.

Upon docking at the Navy yard, Bruner was more than ready to leave the munitions ship for his first assignment and officially meet USS *Arizona.*

Following basic training, Bruner's "luck of the draw" assignment and his arrival back in his home state that morning combined to cause a rush of feelings. There he was, in Washington State "…ready to meet my new ship, just a crow's fly from my mother's home in the village of McCleary."

"Where *Nitro* put in was a good mile or so from the dry docks." And it was difficult to make out where *Arizona* was setting. "About all we could spot over the tree tops, from the water, were a sea of masts from ships."

On his paperwork that morning, Bruner noticed that *Arizona's* captain was named I. C. Kidd. But Lauren gave little thought as to how their lives would mesh together over the next two years, eight months and 27 days. He just wanted to board his ship and get his life in gear.

Permission to cross Nitro's gangplank was given, and Bruner's assigned group made their way on to the pier. It would soon be followed by a walk to *Arizona…* about a mile away.

"Wasn't long before a gruff crew chief showed up where we waited. Name was Callaway. Didn't waste a breath, while he instructed the twelve *of us* to 'fall-in' and follow him."

"No introductions, no Howdy-do's, just, 'If your orders are to join *Arizona's* crew, grab your sea bags, get in line, and follow me.' "

"How funny it seemed… to be so close to my mother's home, as I followed that Navy mother hen. Some called him by worse names, depending on how they wanted to describe him."

"Callaway was an 'old salt,' according to Navy lore. Covered with tattoos. I'd learn later, most of 'em were picked up during tours in the Far East."

"But there I was… hell, as the crow flies, within 80 miles of my home town of McCleary, Washington."

"Even walking at a brisk pace, it took about twenty minutes to reach the dry docks. Us carrying our fifty-pound sea bags, trying to keep up with that meet and greeter. Him carrying nothing but a clipboard."

As Bruner's group moved toward their ship, he was struck by how typical Puget Sound was for the state of Washington. Fir trees lined the streets and paths, and ran almost to water's edge.

"These forests were the same as where I grew up. Although I was keen to see new sites, it was a comfort somehow to be back home, with the smell of fir and ocean air mixed together."

"Turned out... once the fog began to clear, that morning, the skyline was pretty darn beautiful."

A combination of ships centered against the sky and the welcome scent of fir trees triggered memories of family stories Lauren had heard years before.

"I figured it was somewhere along the coast, full of Navy Yards, that my father LeRoy Bruner-Daniels first served in the Navy."

"Truth be told, I have always held a more romantic memory of what happened after that. The Navy? Well, they justifiably had a different story."

"My father met my mother while on leave attending a barn dance."

"According to mother, it was love at first sight. Dad made the decision, then and there, to marry my mother and ditch the Navy. That's the romantic part... at least as far as I can stretch it."

"Of course, the Navy called it desertion."

"All that occurred long ago... years before I was born. Since my dad died when I was six, twelve years before I joined the Navy, it only seemed right for me to make up for his mistake by enlisting. Or so I thought, at the time." Lauren was intent on repaying the Navy for what his dad had first promised.

"Wasn't long before our recruit's walk brought us to the gates and security fence that surrounded two huge sets of dry docks... both filled with battleships."

Bruner's group approached the guard shack.

Chief Callaway passed his clipboard to the guards. They checked out the paperwork and, soon after, initialed the papers.

Then Callaway shouted, "Well, assholes, meet your ship, *Arizona,* on your right. Hope y'all like the smell of dead fish and red paint."

Having recently come out of basic, remarks from Callaway just slipped off Bruner's shoulders. He knew there was more of that to come.

As one of the 12 assigned to *Arizona,* Lauren found himself looking at "...a monstrous ship, sitting high and dry."

Bruner considered the size of his ship. When he first laid eyes on *Arizona,* she was "...an awful big bugger."

"And it gave me great comfort to know, since I wasn't a very good swimmer... there was no way she could ever be sunk."

Bruner considered himself lucky, following all the shit he'd faced, as a kid. "Fate was finally on my side. From that day on, I could call myself a battleship sailor."

At age eighteen, the thought occurred to him: *Being a battleship sailor came with bragging rights... to all the pretty girls I'd meet.*

Bruner's group was eventually turned over to *Arizona's* Master of Arms. "It was then, for the first time in the Navy, I felt I was home.

"No more chipping and painting for me."

"Oh how wrong I was."

The men stood alongside *Arizona,* looking down into the hole, which was a world of activity. A gang plank, with rope railings, connected the dock to the main deck. As I waited to board *Arizona,* I was locked in place, somewhere near the middle of the line, as those ahead of me got checked in and had their paperwork processed.

"Gave me a few minutes' rest from our double-time walk to the ship. More important, I had an opportunity to look over the rope-railing to see what was going on, down in the dry dock's hole."

There sat *Arizona* atop hundreds of keel blocks, fore to aft, down the center spine. The dock and ship was awash with areas marked off with red tape, to signify dangerous areas for "hot work" welders, especially around fuel-oil and aircraft gasoline containment tanks. Scaffolding and platforms, ladders and other equipment filled the space stem to stern.

"Hundreds of sailors were down in that hole... all working their asses off, as the ship sat high and dry."

"It was a hell of a long way down. So far down, in fact... it sorta took my breath away. Normally not afraid of heights, I pulled back a little, for fear of falling in."

Bruner's line inched closer to the Officer of the Deck. Lauren continued to be amazed at all that was going on at the same time. He couldn't comprehend how hundreds of sailors could work in a setting that appeared to be an absolute mess.

"Everywhere I looked, the ship was cluttered with cables, ropes, winches, and electric wires. Welders were working alongside sailors who performed other duties."

"Though I wasn't bothered by the noise, what was going on was a mixture of loud sounds... from those who yelled orders, to the sounds of metal against metal, of hull scrapers, and popping electrical welder's arcs. And the sounds reverberated from the dry dock's concrete walls, back to the steel hull."

"It was pretty exciting to watch. But not for long…"

"Bruner, Lauren F."

"Welcome home," the officer of the day said.

He flipped through Bruner's orders and, in a detached voice, shouted back information as if he'd said it hundreds of times before.

"You're in Deck Force 4. Have a nice time. Follow that sailor. He'll show you where to stow your things. Then report back here, on the double. And wear something you don't mind getting dirty."

"Next."

"That was it. That's why I'd waited all that time in line."

"Come to find out, when I returned, my first afternoon's battleship sailor duty was to work on the exterior of *Arizona's* hull, below… way down in 'the hole.' "

"Not counting hundreds of railroad tie-like oak keel blocks the ship rested upon, bow to stern… looking straight up from dry dock's base to *Arizona's* upper deck, was the equivalent of over two hundred feet… or twenty stories high. Dry dock was one massive hole."

"I was told to report down at dry dock's base. Once there, someone shoved a wheelbarrow and shovel at me. My first job was to clean up mussels and barnacles being scraped from the hull."

"The sailor in charge said, 'Start shovelin.' When the barrow's full, follow the line to dump this shit in the baskets.' "

"Damn, that crap smelled to high heaven. Trick was, to not get hit by loosened shit on it's way down."

"Made me wonder if I'd ever get that rancid odor out of my head, or off my clothes. Fact is, it only took a day or two for me to get used to it. Can't remember smelling it anymore after that… though memories do bring it back, occasionally, when near a harbor."

Before moving up in rank, "…from shit sweeper to wire brush man, I must've dumped a hundred or more wheelbarrows, full of dead and dying mussels, into large baskets. When full, they were winched up and out of the dry dock's depths."

"I asked one of the fellas where they dumped that shit after they pulled it, up top."

He laughed. "Are you kiddin'? That's tonight's dinner. They'll throw a little tomato sauce on 'em and call it Mussels Marinara."

"Have to admit, I had to look long and hard at the guy before he broke into laughter."

To be certain, Bruner was one of many scrub sailors assigned to what he called "the shit job." "About all we could do was smile, and talk trash to one another, just to keep our minds off of what we were doing."

"One of the recruits who came up aboard *Nitro* was also assigned a wheelbarrow and shovel. At one point, he said, 'I thought we joined the Navy to see the world, *not* clean the trench of an outhouse.' We both laughed and realized we'd just have to grin and bear it, as they say."

"*Arizona* had already been in dry dock for a couple of days before our group of recruits arrived. I figure we stayed in dry dock nearly ten more days. During that time, I spent every day in the hole… closest to the ship's heart and its four giant propellers. Together, those three-bladed props stretched over fifty feet across."

Twice, while on breaks from cleaning and painting, Lauren and a couple of buddies he'd met placed themselves at the bottom of the ship's steel hull. At that point, they reached up to touch it.

"After that, I had bragging rights for years, telling the girls how I 'held up *Arizona* with one hand.' Woulda' helped more if I'd had a Kodak down there."

At the end of each shift, Bruner returned to crew quarters to fight his way through a long line of sailors waiting to take a shower. "Can't remember ever smelling as filthy as when I lined up with others who smelled as bad as I did."

"Early on, my clothes were covered in red paint and all kinds of shit. But advice from others in my division who'd been around a while taught me a quick lesson."

"So I wouldn't ruin my other dungarees and t-shirts and have to switch out garments, the trick was to wear the same clothes every day. Then, wash the clothes while they were still on my back… *as* I took a shower."

Following the routine others had shared, Bruner lathered up his clothes, while still on, stripped each piece off, and then "…while in my birthday suit, scrubbed, rinsed, and rung out the garments."

He would then take his shower, grab a towel, and head back to quarters.

"The easiest solution for drying my work clothes was to drape them over the ropes of my hammock. That meant I could put on a clean, unstained set of clothes and sit down for mess. Later, I'd often head out on deck for a smoke… in an area where it was legal, then I'd hit the sack."

Having grown up in Washington, Bruner and his high school friends had sometimes ventured from McCleary to Seattle. "I'd been close to some big ships in the harbors around Seattle and Tacoma. But *Arizona* was, by far, the biggest ship I'd ever seen. Especially from the bottom looking up."

"Before *Arizona,* I'd only been on *Nitro…* smaller in comparison by almost half a football field. Before that, the largest boat I'd been on was a rowboat out fishing with my brother Clarence."

"If I play back that period of time in my mind, I can see *Arizona's* hull transform itself. When we first arrived, it was still a barnacle-encrusted piece of steel. At completion of dry dock, it had been turned again into a sleek battleship, with a fresh coat of red lead paint covering her hull like a blanket.

"Despite all the complaining while scraping, shoveling, and painting, I felt damn proud of my share of the work that turned *Arizona* back into a sea-going beauty.

21 March 1939

"By the time hundreds of work orders were completed, and checked off by the dry dock manager... which included our cleaning and painting *Arizona's* hull... all cables, wires and welders had been cleared from the ship. She looked damn beautiful."

Every shore connection was detached, along with the water supply lines and fire hydrant lines that had been brought aboard for 'hot work'.

A crane lifted the gangway back to the dock and the first warning signal sounded to make certain the dock's floor and surrounding levels were clear of personnel.

Soon after, *Arizona's* ballasting began in preparation for 'lift-off' from the blocks. It would take several hours before the dry dock water level matched sea level.

"But truth be told, all of that was topped by the thrill I felt the day dry dock was filled, and we were pulled out into the water. Nothing much compared to the adrenaline rush I got as I watched from a railing that overlooked the hole being filled."

Shore leave had been canceled in order to get underway. Most crew, not assigned to make *Arizona* ready for sailing, observed all the action from the main deck as Captain Isaac Kidd and the Dry Dock Manager performed a final inspection.

The day selected for undocking had decent weather. Despite a slight mist, the heavier fog had lifted and tidal changes, wind, and currents were calculated to be at levels safe for the process to begin.

"That's when it got exciting," said Bruner. "At first, there was near-total silence. But as soon as a 'go' clearance was received from the dock authorities, someone opened the sluice gates to the flooding tunnels… and tons of water began to rush into the giant hole."

"Those of us not assigned to duty cheered as we watched over twenty million gallons of seawater race in to fill the void."

"They called it 'putting water on the hull and floating the ship, and it was a hell of a sight."

"When sea level was matched, another warning was sounded, the gates slowly opened… and our ship was pulled out, stern first, by a couple of Navy tugs."

"We felt the sensation of movement, as we watched the dock begin to slip away."

"It was my first ride on *Arizona*, or on any warship, for that matter."

"After adjustment, the tugs pulled us about a quarter mile out into the Sound."

Eventually, all ropes were released, the tugs pulled clear of the ship, the Captain ordered to start the propeller, and *Arizona* was back on its own.

"We spent a couple of days performing a series of sea trials… cruising, and testing equipment and procedures aboard ship."

"Before leaving Bremerton, *Arizona* met up with *Nitro* to pick up our supply of munitions and, finally, we sailed out of Puget Sound. Our heading… south to Long Beach to rejoin the Seventh Fleet."

As a result of these experiences, Lauren has always thought of his first meeting with USS *Arizona,* "…as the moment when he became a battleship sailor."

— —

USS *Arizona* At Full Dress

"This artwork of USS Arizona was drawn from one of the most beautiful photos of the ship that I have ever come across. The fact is, I was most probably on Arizona this very day. The captain of the ship at the time was Isaac C. Kidd, and I remember that on one day, he arranged for a Navy photographer to photograph the ship in all its glory.

As we prepared to sail out of Puget Sound, all the ship's pennants and flags were strung stem to stern (I remeber a chief telling me they called it "At Full Dress"). It was the first time that I had ever seen anything like this before, and Arizona sure looked beautiful.

Although most of the world thinks of USS Arizona from photos of her wreckage, or as she sits today as USS Arizona Memorial at Pearl Harbor, those of us who still remain and others of our crew who have gone before us will always think of her as she is here: a great and beautiful war ship."

"My Ship" — USS *Arizona* At Full Dress

Chapter 3
GIRLS, GAMBLING, & TOMMY GUNS

1 March – 11 April 1940

Following Lauren's assignment as a crewman aboard USS *Arizona* as Seaman 2/c, his Navy test scores and credits for longevity presented an opportunity to attend Rangefinder and Fire Control School.

"The Navy school was located in Vallejo, California. I was pretty excited about the trip... and the new responsibilities it'd give me. The training would prepare me as a Rangefinder Operator."

"In the Navy, they tell you where they want you... and you go. I worked hard and kept studying to advance in rank. Sixteen months in the Navy, combined with my test scores, helped me along."

The 7th fleet was anchored, at the time, off the coast of Long Beach. "And that's when my high school buddy, Billy Mann, showed up back in my life. Of all things, he was assigned as a fellow crew member on *Arizona*."

"According to my instructors, my eyes were spread out wider than most guys. And that was to my advantage. I'd never thought about it before, but it allowed me to better use the Rangefinder optics. This factor helped qualify me as a Rangefinder Operator."

Lauren and nine other crew members from various battleships, destroyers, and cruisers, were transported by bus to Fire Control School. "Only one other crew member from *Arizona* was chosen to attend," said Lauren. "His name was Albert Schreiner, but I just called him Al."

"The two of us talked throughout most of the long bus ride, and pretty much agreed that we'd both enlisted in the Navy to 'see the world.' We hit it off real good,and from that point, and throughout the rest of our lives, we became close friends."

It was Al who introduced Lauren to Marcella Stapleton—a pretty Irish-French girl.

Within the first week of their arrival at Fire Control School, two events occurred that would define the next six weeks—and eventually Lauren's life.

Shortly after training began, Lauren and Al were notified that *Arizona,* and the entire 7th fleet, had been reassigned to Pearl Harbor, Territory of Hawaii (T.H.).

"Just what we wanted to hear," said Lauren. "One of the class instructors had referred to Hawaii as 'paradise.' "

Immediately, they both felt the pain of missing out. But the sailors were told not to worry. They'd catch up to their ship at the end of training.

"You gotta' remember… there I was, a nineteen year old sailor… a kid back in school, so-to-speak ….And all I could imagine was my high school buddy, Billy Mann, arriving in paradise ahead of me… with all those girls in grass skirts. Without me!"

"Of course, there was nothing I could do except plug along… learn everything I could. I didn't want to return to *Arizona* as a Seaman again … still assigned to Deck Force Four. Had enough chipping and painting of the bulkheads and hull five days a week, not to mention holystoning the deck barefoot, with a holystone brick.

"I was determined to rise in rank, no matter what it took."

The weekend following their arrival in Vallejo, Lauren's new friend, Al, left base on a bus for Los Angeles. He returned on Sunday in his own car—a 1934 Plymouth Coupe.

"Pilot blue. Boy, was it a beauty," said Lauren. "Had wide whitewall tires and a fully padded outside rumble seat."

Rangefinder School was a small part of a larger Navy Base and ammunition depot, with the school being a "six-week deal."

"But once Al had his car at school, he'd take off each Friday afternoon... and drive down to Los Angeles to see his girlfriend, Lillian Dobbins."

On the second Friday after Lauren and Al had arrived, Al suggested Lauren ride along to L.A. Lillian wanted to introduce him to her best friend Marcella Stapleton, who lived in an apartment next door.

Marcella's parents owned a home near downtown Los Angeles on San Pedro Street. At the back of their property, her father, Patrick, had built five apartments. Three were used by each of his daughters; another by Lillian; and the fifth was vacant.

On their first weekend in L.A., Lillian and Al introduced Lauren to Marcella.

"She was an attractive girl," said Lauren. "Tall with shoulder-length, dark brown hair, and I always thought she had blue eyes that sorta' just glowed."

"She struck me as a girl who was pretty sure of herself. Liked to talk about everything. Kinda made it easy for me to like her, since I used to get a little tongue-tied when it came to conversations with girls."

"You might say she helped break the ice. And we got along well."

That first weekend, Lauren and Al took the girls out for a nice dinner. And with Al and Lillian sitting up front inside the coupe, Marcella and Lauren had to ride in the rumble seat.

"It was a tight fit..." said Lauren. "A little uncomfortable, but sure cozy."

This was the beginning of a relationship that could eventually lead somewhere, if Lauren ever decided to settle down. But that spring, the only thing on his mind was getting back to USS *Arizona*.

"Truth be told… all I wanted was to get on over to paradise and chase some girls in grass skirts… with Billy."

"Al and I slept in the car that first weekend. Eventually, we moved up in the world… to sleep on an old mattress in the one empty apartment."

There was no way Marcella's father, Patrick, would ever allow the boys to sleep anywhere near the girls. Patrick was about as Irish as you could get," said Lauren. "And sprinkled heavily with the blarney."

The fact that the family was Catholic only added to the mix.

For their trips to Los Angeles, the two sailors shared gas money. And it helped that they could fill Al's car at the Navy base for eleven cents a gallon.

Most every Friday afternoon, as soon as classes let out, they'd head south. "Though we'd usually arrive just before midnight, the girls waited up for us, every time."

After nearly four weeks of training, they took off for a weekend to meet the girls. "Problem was," said Lauren, "we didn't have more than two dollars between us after filling the car with gas."

"At the time… we were really down to bare bones. So we decided to stop at a local gambling den. We knew the old guys that hung out there were gamblers. We figured maybe… with luck in a card game, we could turn our last two dollars into enough to take Marcella and Lillian out on the town the next night. So we stopped."

As usual, they were both in uniform, and eventually left the bar believing the local guys took pity on them.

"Especially after we told 'em we were on our way to L.A. to see our girls. We played it for whatever we could get… and it worked."

"After we'd spent a couple hours playing poker, we'd earned an extra five dollar bill each. Of course, I still believe they helped us along at winning… just to get us out of there and on our way."

That particular night, Al took Highway 80 across the cantilevered Carquinez Bridge toward Oakland. He planned to drive down highway 101 to Southern California.

"We crossed the metal bridge, but hit a sharp lip at the beginning and again at the other side. I heard something fall off the car as we left the bridge, and had Al stop to see what was wrong."

Al backed the car up to the end of the bridge. Lauren got out to investigate.

"At that hour there wasn't much traffic, so it wasn't difficult to look around. I walked back toward the bridge and found Al's license plate nearly hanging off the edge."

"Must've been loose and had rattled off, when we hit those bumps. One more bounce and it've gone into the water."

With no tools or good light to repair it, Al propped the plate up in the back window.

"Soon we were back on the road, trying to make up time lost at the card game… and with the license plate."

For the rest of the trip, Al drove with one eye on the road in front, and the other eye on the rearview mirror, looking for local speed traps.

"I guess you'd say we were haulin' ass. That car ran real smooth."

They'd switch off driving and consistently drove at speeds higher than the posted limit.

"In those days, little towns we'd pass through rolled up their sidewalks around eight in the evening. Even if they had a traffic light… it only flashed yellow.

"Once we got outside any town, we'd run that baby up between sixty and seventy miles an hour. I'll tell you… we thought we were in the Army Air Corps moving so fast."

Al was behind the wheel when, suddenly, all hell broke loose. Multiple cop cars—with red lights flashing and spotlights aimed at the Plymouth—closed in on the boys from all directions.

"Two patrol cars even came at us from across opposite fields."

Oh Shit!

Al pulled over.

We're in for it now.

Before his thoughts left him, they were immediately surrounded by uniformed cops and G-men in suits—all holding Tommy guns "…the big machine guns of the day."

"And I'll tell you, it was pretty damned scary."

"The sons a' bitches surrounded us, screeched to a halt and, at once, jumped outta' their cars. They shined big flashlights in our eyes, and around the inside of Al's car."

"I was convinced… if we'd moved anywhere near the wrong way, we'd have both ended up deader than a doornail."

"The lead officer—the one who did all the talking—said that a bank had been robbed in the town we'd just passed through, and that "…the crooks had made off in a car just like ours."

Are you kidding? Lauren and Al were dumbfounded.

"Both of us had to turn over our licenses to the talker with the flashlight."

"To make matters worse, only Al had a California license. Mine was from Washington. And the patrolmen gave me a lotta' shit about it, too."

"Kept talking about how they were gonna' take us back to the town we'd just passed through and throw our asses in the hoosegow."

"But it was the Tommy guns, by far, that worried us the most. Any minute, a cop might have an itchy trigger finger."

Lauren imagined the headlines: *Two USS Arizona Sailors Rob Podunk Bank – Shot Dead.*

After fifteen minutes checking out Al's car and grilling the two sailors, another officer with a Tommy gun whispered something to the head cop. He then turned to the boys.

"Did you know your tail lights aren't workin'? Pretty convenient, if you robbed a bank… and didn't want anyone to watch your get away."

Come on… Are you kidding? Lauren was getting pissed and "…had just about enough of their bullshit."

He asked the lead cop, "Do you think we're so dumb to rob a bank carrying our Navy IDs… and in uniform?"

The patrolman didn't answer but, instead, got all the cops behind a patrol car; "…let us sweat for a few more minutes; then returned. They decided we weren't the bank robbers and said we didn't look much like thieves. But I swear, that top cop did nothing to conceal the smirk on his face."

The lead officer released Lauren and Al, but warned them to "get the taillights fixed... first thing in the morning, and put the license plate back where it's supposed to be."

The officers returned to their cars, turned off the flashing lights, and screeched away.

No sooner had the patrol cars left, than Al and Lauren sat dead quiet, staring straight through the windshield, then glanced at each other.

"We couldn't keep a straight face any longer," said Lauren. "We exploded with laughter. I mean, broke up laughing and cussing all through the night. Never stopped 'til we reached Los Angeles… and the girls."

"They waited up for us. And boy did we have a story to tell."

Other than the Tommy guns, Lauren found the experience hilarious. Even today, he laughs about the incident.

"Afterwards, Al and I figured they just wanted to scare the hell out of us."

"Well… they sure as hell did."

— —

SECOND TO THE LAST TO LEAVE

Marcella M. Stapleton

"**Marcella Margaret Stapleton** *was a pretty French-Irish brunette who I first met when I was 19. My friend Al Schreiner and his girlfriend Lillian Dobbins introduced us. Al and I had been selected from the crew of USS Arizona to attend Fire Control School at a Naval Base in Vallejo, California, which is up near San Francisco.*

Al had a car and coaxed me into spending the weekends with him in Los Angeles, with the promise of introducing me to Marcella. Sounded like a good idea to me!

Marcella's eyes were blue and her hair was a pretty shade of brown, which she wore in a style of the day down to her shoulders. About 5'3½", she was slender 'and plain good-lookin' all over. Most often she would wear a flower in her hair, which made her look even prettier.

When Fire Control School ended, Al and I were raring to go to meet up with USS Arizona, which by that time was already in Hawaii. The day we left Los Angeles I remember giving Marcella a kiss goodbye and she promised that she would write."

Marcella Stapleton was 20 years, 3 months, and 25 days old on the day of the attack on Pearl Harbor.

Marcella Margaret Stapleton

Marcella Margaret Stapleton

"A Very Close Friend"

Chapter 4
PARADISE FOUND

11 MAY 1940
Pearl Harbor
Territory of Hawaii (T.H.)

There are three world-famous travel experiences of which passengers by air and sea often speak—whether tourists, sailors, or immigrants. The first, being that of sailing into New York Harbor past "Lady Liberty," the most recognized symbol of freedom from tyranny and oppression, and the reason why America's servicemen have always been willing to lay down their lives on behalf of those who seek that freedom:

"…. Here at our sea-washed, sunset gates shall stand
A mighty woman with a torch…"
Emma Lazarus
The Statue of Liberty Sonnet, *New Colossus*

The second, which can be found on the U.S. mainland's west coast, would be the iconic art deco Golden Gate Bridge—a nine thousand foot engineering marvel and symbol of American enterprise—considered to be among the seven wonders of the modern world. Sailors entering Golden Gate Bay via the Pacific Ocean by ship view this American icon… and know they're home.

For Lauren Bruner and countless others, the third and most awe-inspiring landmark has always been the sheer, natural beauty and grandeur of Diamond Head. Known to Hawaiians as Le'ahi, as it is probably the most famous volcanic crater in the world.

The first time any Sailor or Marine sees Diamond Head, jutting out to the sea, it instantly becomes an impression to last a lifetime.

And for much of Lauren's eight years in the Navy, it was his own sign that he was home.

On April 11, 1940, Lauren, and his friend, Al Schreiner, completed their six weeks of intensive training at Fire Control School. The Navy immediately ordered them to report back to *Arizona*. This followed their ship's reassignment in April 1940 from the Seventh Fleet, based in Long Beach, California, to the Pacific Fleet at Pearl Harbor T.H.

"But I have to tell you," said Lauren, "Fire Control School was one of the many events that would, for the next eight years, transform my life… and save it more than once."

One month before Lauren had earned his Fire Control certification, *Arizona* was already berthed at Pearl. This resulted in Lauren and Al having to hitch a ride across the Pacific aboard USS *Cimarron* (AO-22), the first of many *Cimarron*-class "underway replenishment" oilers, launched only 14 months earlier.

Lauren was impressed with his incidental introduction to this "fast class" of oilers, with twin-screw speeds that took them to 18 knots, versus previous tankers whose speeds only hit 12 knots. They were used mostly to replenish fuel for ships at sea, while underway between ports, maneuvers and, eventually, in battle.

Cimarron had a capacity of over six million gallons of fuel that could be offloaded under most any conditions. To protect its cargo, the AO-22 was fitted with armaments that included four 5-in/38-caliber guns, four 40mm AA guns, and four 20mm AA guns.

"For a tanker," said Lauren, "it was one sleek ship. And it was from her rails Al and I witnessed our arrival at what was promised to be paradise."

There before them rose Diamond Head. The sea, and miles of pristine beaches, provided a pedestal for its majestic cone and ridgeline that resembles a tuna's dorsal fin.

"When I first saw Diamond Head from aboard USS *Cimarron,* I overheard a few sailors on the ship, refer to it as 'paradise.' "

"From then on, each time I sailed by that famed landmark, either on *Arizona,* or later aboard USS *Coghlan,* my thoughts always returned to my first arrival in the islands. That afternoon, on my way into Pearl, it was pretty special."

"Even now, when I see Diamond Head from a plane, I recall it as if I were a nineteen-year-old seaman again."

Lauren and Al stood at *Cimarron's* starboard rail as it passed a long, sandy beach. Al said it was called Waikiki and was famous. Hundreds were out on the sand having fun, swimming, and sunbathing.

"I was determined to visit that place as soon as time permitted... especially after Al pointed out the Royal Hawaiian Hotel—a big, pink colored building on the shore."

"Sailors," he said, "refer to it as the 'Pink Lady'... because it sounds sexier."

"Still call it the Pink Lady even today."

Less than an hour later, *Cimarron* steamed into Pearl Harbor's entrance up through the West Channel—past Pearl City Peninsula—and circled around the northern tip of Ford Island toward Battleship Row.

The sight before him, once again, took Lauren by surprise.

"If I'd, by any stretch of the imagination, thought that seeing Diamond Head for the first time was something special… coming into Pearl that same day was at least a hundred times more so."

In 1940, long before hotels, restaurants and condos took over Hawaii, pineapple farms and sugar plantations created a carpet "…almost as green as my forests of Washington."

He laughed. "Just… not as tall. But it appeared to climb from the sea, and went on forever."

Lauren's eyes feasted on the hundreds of ships moored throughout the harbor.

"The first thing I noticed was all the ships and their crews. Every kind, every size, every shape. Battlewagons to tin cans; transports to fuel tankers like *Cimarron*."

"Truthfully, up to that moment, I'd never been in such a busy and bustling Navy base. Quite a sight to see. And I knew then I was a part of it all."

As *Cimarron* rounded the northern tip of Ford Island, in the East Loch, Lauren caught his first glance at another magnificent view—what he'd come to know as Battleship Row.

"Finally, as we moved up the row, just past the Southeast Loch and second from the end, was our ship… *Arizona.*"

Guided by a Navy tug, *Cimarron* moved past *Arizona,* which was moored at Quay Foxtrot 7. He wondered where Billy might be.

"I was determined, when we had our first Liberty together, we'd head to the hotel that Al had called 'The Pink Lady.' We'd have a beer and meet some girls down on Waikiki beach."

Gliding past *Arizona,* Al and Lauren continued to stand at the rail while they compared their ship to the other battleships "…and what a beauty she was, together with the rest of the battlewagons."

"Guess we were a little prejudiced. Honestly, if I'd thought it were possible at the time, I'd just as soon dive in the channel and swim to my ship. Fortunately, my better senses were in control."

Cimarron docked on the other side of Ford Island.

"We had to wait over an hour for a launch to take us back around Ford Island to *Arizona's* gangway. That wait seemed like forever."

The Master of Arms checked in arriving crew. Then Lauren stowed his gear in his quarters below deck. He was relieved to see everything, including what he'd left in his locker, just the way he'd left it in Long Beach two months prior.

Lauren had the rest of the afternoon off. He set out to get an ice cream bar at the Gedunk—the ship's snack bar, where sailors always lined up eight to ten deep.

"Figured I might find Billy there," said Lauren.

"He sure liked his ice cream… but he wasn't there." So Lauren continued to search various decks until he eventually located him.

"He'd just got off duty. So we found an outta' the way place to sit, up on deck. We talked and caught up on just about everything until we had to head down for mess with our own division crews."

"Even as we walked, we kept talkin'… with so much to catch up on. And we agreed to get together right after mess."

Later, they were on the stern reminiscing. A slight evening breeze cooled the ship's surface and both men kicked back against a bulkhead.

The sky was ablaze with searing reds and oranges. It shimmered off the water and cast a glow across the harbor.

"It was my first Hawaiian sunset," said Lauren. "And if anyone would've compared it to a spiritual experience, that could've been it. Hawaiians refer to it as where the sun, sea and water become one."

"Musta' made Billy a little homesick, 'cause he told me he'd been writing to a brunette we'd met back in California at the Long Beach Pike."

Lauren glanced out over the channel toward the distant mountains. There, before him, were the endless fields of pineapple and sugar cane turning purple as twilight set in.

"They serve free ice-cold pineapple to sailors," Billy reported. "At the Dole cannery.... on the way into Honolulu. We'll head over there sometime."

"The closer fields are pineapple," he continued, "... those, farther out... sugar cane."

Lauren pointed out plumes of smoke in the distance.

"They're burnin' off the leaves and crap from the sugar cane stalks," said Billy. "Before the plantation workers harvest them."

"As you get to know the place," he went on "you'll see the Japanese work most of the sugar cane fields, while the Chinese run the shops and markets."

Hell, Lauren thought, *Billy got pretty damn smart, for only being here a few weeks.*

"This territory's a whole new world, Lauren. It's pretty much everything that the recruiter and the postcards described as 'paradise.' "

"Although I'd only been there an afternoon," said Lauren, "I was already convinced. This *was* paradise."

— —

SECTION TO THE LAST TO LEAVE

Albert A. Schreiner

Albert Aloysius Schreiner was born to Joseph and Margaret Kuhn Schreiner on 23 July, 1912 in Collyer, Trego County, Kansas . Al completed eight grades of school then began working on his father's farm.

He enlisted in the Navy for four years in Wichita, Kansas and at that time was 6" tall, weighed 165 pounds, had brown eyes and brown hair, and had a burn scar on his left forearm. **On 7 December 1941, Albert Aloysius "Al" Schreiner was 29 years, 4 months, and 14 days old.**

"Al was a crew member and good friend of mine aboard USS Arizona, until he was mustered out in October of 1941. After the war ended and we'd be sitting around drinking beer, he would often get melancholy about having left me and the crew before the attack. I would always tell him that he was crazy, because if he had stayed, there was a better chance than not that he wouldn't have made it."

Albert A. Schreiner

Albert Aloysius Schreiner, Cox
Mustered Out 11.15.41
USS *Arizona*

Chapter 5
SORTA' LIKE FAMILY

FALL, 1940

Prior to the war, living aboard *Arizona* was always "good fun"—a term the Hawaiians used when life went well.

"Sure," said Lauren, "like anything else, we'd find something to bitch and moan about... especially in my early days as a seaman... chip 'n paint, chip 'n paint, holystone the deck, clean the yardarm, then chip 'n paint, again. But we still had good fun."

For Lauren, being a crew member of *Arizona* "...was one hell of a great time."

"Ironically," he said, "it all proves the ol' saying, 'life's a circle.' 'Cause one of my other assigned jobs in the early days, was to help clean the number four gun turret. And wouldn't 'ya know... that's exactly where I'll be interred someday, back on my ship with my buddies after I pass from this life to the next."

"Living all these years as one of the last crew members of this great warship has been an honor I've taken seriously."

Yet it's an honor for which Lauren has no idea why he was chosen.

Friends weren't difficult to make, if you wanted to, with so many sailors on board. Considering *Arizona's* size and aside from the occasional loner "like Ronnie Lott... most everyone in our crew had a close group of friends. Those you knew, and those you worked with, although both were seldom the same."

That is, unless a fight broke out in a bar on Hotel Street.

To Lauren, the ship was "...sorta' like a family. You didn't have to like 'em... or maybe weren't particularly close to all your siblings. But woe to anyone who picked on 'em, called 'em out, or hurt their feelings."

In the language of the Old West, "Those were fightin' words." And sailors from any ship at Pearl would come to the aid of another from the same ship "...anytime, anywhere."

"On one occasion, a friend named Casper Ehlert joined in with me and Billy Man on a fight to help out an *Arizona* Marine. It was over some girl our Marine swore he was in love with. But we called that 'drunk-in-love,' 'cause we knew that gal worked in a cathouse over on Canal Street. She was seein' just about everyone in the harbor on the side."

"You know, *that* was ship loyalty... when a sailor helped a Marine. The poor bastard was by himself... and from *our* ship. So we jumped right in. Hah! Was he ever glad we did."

"*Arizona* had over fifteen hundred men," said Lauren. "Personally, I didn't know a fraction of 'em... especially by name. But I always considered us shipmates. Still do, today."

All sailors slept in close crew quarters with men of their same division. Bruner's was known as Fire Control—the division of sailors responsible to sight targets for all the guns, and determine and communicate coordinates to the plotting room located in the bowels of the ship.

"The only sailor from my crew quarters who worked and ate with me was Fred "Zeke" Zimmerman, a Gun Trainer in our port-side anti-aircraft director."

Zimmerman came into the service about two years after Lauren, in early 1940—from Cleveland North Dakota—a tiny farming town of less than a hundred, between Bismarck and Fargo.

Since enlistment, Zeke had put on an additional thirty pounds of lean muscle, coming in at 5′ 9″ and around 172 pounds. Described in his official papers as having "medium brown" hair and a "ruddy" complexion—a general designation that seemed to describe most Caucasian enlistees, in those days—Zimmerman was known by bar maids as the one with "sexy blue eyes."

"Zeke and I slept in our hammocks, about twenty feet apart. At meals, we'd pull tables down from our quarter's ceiling and chow down together."

"Now, this guy'd take three showers a day. One in the morning, another around lunch, and still *another* at night. We'd always laugh and swear the sonovabitch was tryin' to get out of work… but, he was a good guy just the same."

Occasionally, Zeke would accompany Billy and Lauren to Smith's Union Bar, "…our ship's favorite 'watering hole.' "

Continuously in operation, since 1934, it became Lauren's favorite place to hang out.

"I still go there anytime I return to the islands," he said.

When sailors weren't on maneuvers, or on special duty, they'd pass the time in various ways. Sunbathing or playing cards on deck were two favorite pastimes when stuck onboard.

"Over time, we discovered certain areas of the ship that couldn't be seen by Sunday guests or VIPs on tours. Those hideaways allowed us a little relaxation… with a hell of a lot less rules."

Often in the afternoon on Lauren's days off, he'd climb five flights of ladders and a short flight of steps from the superstructure deck to his battle station, and take a nap on the port side director's floor.

"Few were willing to climb that high, so no one disturbed me. Occasionally, though, I'd meet an officer up in the director napping as well. Just like enlisted men, they knew a good thing when they found it."

"Kept an old blanket up there to nap on. Ya' had to have a blanket, 'cause the floor was covered with hard, raised diamond-plate, to keep our footing in high seas."

"So, I'd rotate napping outside on the sky control platform… to get some sun, or go inside where it was cooler, with a bit of a cross breeze comin' through the hatches."

"I recall Matson's SS *Lurline* cruise liner used to dock every week at the Aloha Tower in Honolulu. If the *Lurline* had advertised a 'no-frills' voyage across the seven seas," Lauren said, "us young sailors probably woulda' taken 'em up on it. Think about it. A cruise ship… well, that's pretty much how *Arizona* was, at the time… but stripped down to no frills."

"Unless, of course, you were Captain Franklin Van Valkenburgh… or Rear Admiral Kidd. They had the life. "

"All the rest of us… hell of a lot less pampered."

"The biggest difference between *Arizona* and today's cruise ships? The three 'B's. No bars, no beer… and it could've meant the brig if you were caught bringing any flask aboard."

Not to say he wasn't tempted, but Lauren never tried. He knew better—having worked shore patrol.

"I've stood with sailors coming aboard late at night with a flask tucked inside their socks. We'd laugh like hell when a Marine or the Master of Arms patted the culprits down with their billy-stick."

"When the baton hit the glass flask… you'd hear a good thump. Then came broken glass, followed by a hell of a lot of cussing and laughing… depending on how drunk they were and how many friends stood with them."

Lauren found the best thing for those who got caught was to laugh it off and hope the Master of Arms would, too.

"If you didn't, and started to give 'im any shit, he'd have a Marine take you to the brig for two days of bread and water. And no pay, to boot."

Lauren and his gang—Billy, Casper, and Al—
spent most of their nights, "…hangin' around the stern, 'cause there was a lot more room out there. Guys'd be out there playin' cards or Acey-Deucey, which was kinda' like backgammon."

"We liked listening to Billy strum *Red Sails in the Sunset* on his ol' guitar. When his singing and strumming wafted out across the harbor, everything sorta' hushed up around the other ships, moored close by. Always believed they were listening, too."

"Same time… Casper would often work on one of his drawings… of life aboard ship. Damn he was good. Of average build, only about five-seven in height, he was a hell of an artist."

"One regret. As a young man, you often pass up opportunities that you shouldn't… then wish later in life you hadn't. That's how it was for me with Casper. In addition to his regular duties, he was *Arizona's* official artist for *At 'Em Arizona…* the ship's newspaper. As a Signalman, he had plenty of time to draw… stationed up near the main bridge."

"Turned out, one of his drawings of *Arizona* appeared as the masthead on each edition of the paper. I'll never forget how proud he was every time the paper came out. And we shared that pride because he was our friend."

"Casper got a lot of special privileges, too, because of his talent. But I sure do wish I'd taken one of his originals when he offered one to me."

A fortunate event happened to Lauren, as a result of their friendship. Casper's grandniece, Molly Baumann, began to correspond with Lauren. She had heard the story of their friendship and how much Lauren had admired her uncle's illustrations.

"Outta' the blue," said Lauren, "this wonderful young lady sent me copies of two pieces of Casper's artwork I swear I'd seen him working on."

"Among them was one of the drawings I watched him work on when we were all together. The first… a sketch of the ship's bell; the other, of *Arizona,* while out on maneuvers."

"Damn. I couldn't believe my old eyes when I opened up Molly's envelope… and discovered copies of those drawings."

"Swear to God. I can still see Casper working on the ship's bell, one day as we sat, sunbathing on our favorite part of the ship. Doesn't that beat hell! You never know what's coming down the road."

Lauren let out a hearty laugh.

"Sonovabitch… who says you can't step back in life."

In her letter, Molly wrote that each of these—and other drawings—were sent home to Casper's brother and his wife in Mequon, Wisconsin, along with his letters. In his last letter home, which he mailed on Friday, 5 December, he wrote:

U.S.S. *Arizona*
Pearl Harbor, T.H.
C.C. Ehlert (SM3c)
Dec. 2, 1941

> "Dear Anna & Alex, …my teeth finally went [*bad*] on me and… I went to [*a dentist*] on the beach and had all my teeth fixed, it cost me nearly $40.00, but it's worth it as I did have

> a heck of a toothache... As things are now I don't know when I will get out of the navy [*sic*] although my time is getting short.... We are at sea and I am standing plenty of watches [with] very little sleep. We expect to go in port this weekend, which should be something of a rest anyway.... Say hello to Ma and Pa and tell them everything is well with me. There is some talk of our being in Long Beach for Christmas.... I hope it's true, as many others do... There isn't much else to write at present, as all our orders are very confidential... will write you a long letter as soon as we go into port this weekend...
> Casper"

Lauren recalled how a week or so before, while out on maneuvers, Casper had "...moaned about a toothache. But our ship's dentist wasn't able to fit him in... what with fifteen hundred sailors on board."

"Anyway," Lauren said, "a copy of his artwork of the ship's bell now hangs on my living room wall. Right across from where I sit in my Lazy Boy. I look at it, re-imagine the good times... and smile at the memories."

Lauren's life on board often allowed him a chance to relax up on deck, after the sun went down. As a young man, he'd watch the stars and survey the thousands of ships' lights in the harbor. It was always aglow at night, especially after a rain.

"I'd look over the railing into the water and watch the ships' reflections. If I'd squint my eyes, it'd be like a million stars reflecting off the calm waters and the ships' decks."

"If I really let my imagination get carried away, it'd take me back to the blanket of stars that covered the forests of Washington, where I grew up."

Arizona's Ship's Bell
"Artwork by My Friend Casper Ehlert"

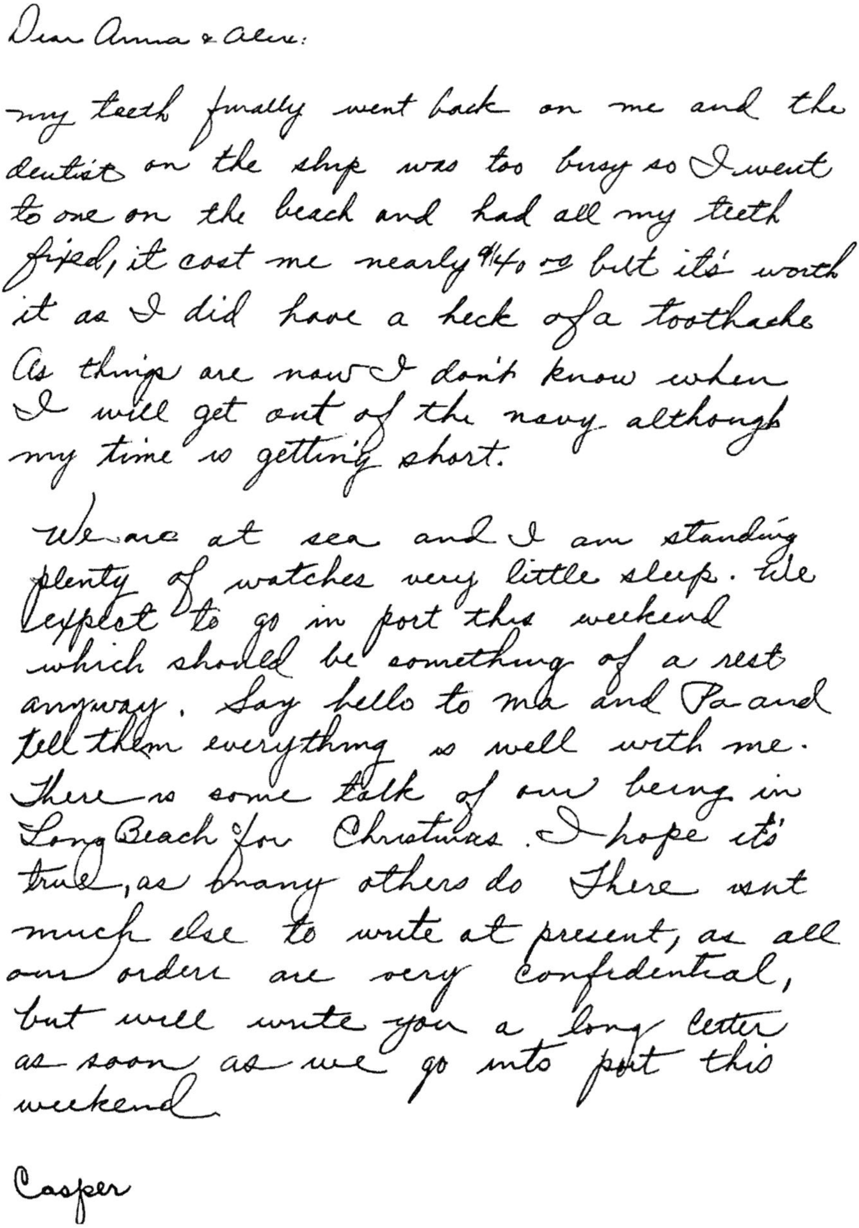

Dear Anna & Alice:

my teeth finally went back on me and the dentist on the ship was too busy so I went to one on the beach and had all my teeth fixed, it cost me nearly $40.00 but it's worth it as I did have a heck of a toothache As things are now I don't know when I will get out of the navy although my time is getting short.

We are at sea and I am standing plenty of watches very little sleep. We expect to go in port this weekend which should be something of a rest anyway. Say hello to Ma and Pa and tell them everything is well with me. There is some talk of our being in Long Beach for Christmas. I hope it's true, as many others do There isnt much else to write at present, as all our orders are very confidential, but will write you a long letter as soon as we go into port this weekend

Casper

Original Hand-Written Letter by Casper Ehlert
Mailed Home on Saturday, 6 December 1941

At night, Lauren could glance across Pearl Harbor's forest of ships' mastheads. In spite of the harbor's smells, the sight evoked the scent of Douglas fir and cedar—as though he were in his mother's backyard in McCleary, Washington.

He'd recall when, during track season for Elma High School, he and Billy jogged through the alders, maple, and poplar of the Capital State Forest.

And Lauren could still imagine the summer's airborne fluff off the cottonwood trees that floated like tiny clouds and resembled snow on the ground under the larger poplars.

"Some might've gotten homesick. But for me, I'd just think about how beautiful the harbor looked in the evening."

"Occasionally, on these casual nights, we'd all head down to the 'gedunk stand' and get an ice cream bar. Hell, they were only a nickel. So we'd bring them back to our spot, up on deck, while we just lay around."

On his blanket, eating ice cream, looking at the stars and lights, Lauren would remind himself how "damn lucky" he felt.

"...Uncle Sam paid me to be there with my pals, in paradise... while others in Europe were up to their asses in alligators."

"Looking back... we all felt a little overconfident. Money in our pockets. Three good meals a day. A place to lay our heads. Not much of a care in the world."

"They say being smug can make you complacent about the dangers around you... and you just might not see the enemy coming."

"We all knew the war raged on in Europe. But we figured it was a long way from Paradise. And we all felt pretty damn safe in Pearl... especially aboard *Arizona.*"

In Lauren's mind, he compared *Arizona* with modern day ocean liners. Both were equally as large, self-contained, could travel anywhere in the world, *and* take care of all their needs.

That was heady stuff for a young man who, for much of his early life, was passed around from family to family and didn't have much while growing up.

"It was especially heady to be called a Battleship Sailor," said Lauren.

His only concern on those nights, just laying around, was "...thinking what girl I might meet next, and where. At that time, my mind kept returning to a good-looking girl named June. I'd met her while on shore patrol, breaking up a fight at a local cathouse."

To Lauren, experiences living aboard *Arizona* "...could fill volumes."

But what brought a smile or made him laugh is symbolic of the good times, as defined by the Hawaiian principals of "Huna," the secret to life itself molded in the past and handed down by their Polynesian ancestors:

> A free, contented, and loving life of ease;
> living, in the present, linked to all that
> exists—as long as the work gets done.

The Navy, with all its history, knew that when a sailor wasn't on duty or on maneuvers, he was fantasizing about a pretty girl, thinking of getting a beer—or of his favorite watering hole where he could find one. Most of the time, all three.

"Think about it," said Lauren. "When thousands of men live on a Naval Base as large as Pearl Harbor... each being a family member of one ship or another, you need rules that need to be followed."

"That's why, on the bigger ships, they had shore patrol and the brig."

Besides rules the Navy developed to contain their energy while on board ship, it also developed a sophisticated athletic program between ships and their crews. Everyone was expected to participate, whether they wanted to or not.

"You might say, it was considered 'orders from headquarters.' "

"Because of this, we turned everything… and I mean everything, into a competition. You might say competition was in our DNA. From who had the best, or better, gun crews… to whose ship had the best boxer."

The men in Lauren's battle station, which was the ship's port-side Anti-Aircraft director, took these competitions seriously. They included rivalry contests to compare how sharp their anti-aircraft crew was at performing duties.

"Our battle stations were the tipping point where what we'd do would begin an entire chain of events. Eventually that chain directed all our projectiles to find their marks, or bullseyes."

"That's how our gun crews earned the large, white 'E' for excellence and battle efficiency that *Arizona* had always painted on both sides of her smoke stack."

Prior to War in the Pacific, gun crews who were determined to be best of the battle-ready won the right to have a large "E" painted on the ship's gun turret or smoke stack. It was a yearlong contest to determine which ships had the most efficient crews, and proved to have "the highest state of battle readiness."

An "E" painted on both sides of a ship's stack, gave the ship bragging rights.

"We all took that seriously, and worked like hell to win those rights. It gave us a sense of pride, signifying that *Arizona* crews were among the best in the fleet."

But what had given the sailors a sense of pride became a beacon for any enemy who might swoop down upon them once the war had started. Following 7 December 1941, the colored 'E's, 'F's, and other award letters were painted over "... faster than you could blink," said Lauren. "The Navy didn't want to invite enemy daredevil pilots to take a turn at ruining a sailor's day."

"In fact," he said, "it was the last time any letter was painted on a Navy ship's stack or bridge until well after the war had ended."

On days off, generally before sailors headed into town, many would spend part of the day at the Bosch Recreation Center on base. Most often, they'd drink nickel beer out of reusable tin cans, and play one sport or another against a competing ship. "The trick," said Lauren, "was to time our drinking between activities."

Turned out, the Bosch Center's bar was an enclosed area outside where sailors could retreat for their beer. The catch: beer could not be taken outside the designated drinking area. That meant no beer was allowed outside the grounds of the rec center, including on a basketball court or in the stands of a football or baseball field.

Lauren and his buddies would play hard on their days off. Often, they'd take multiple breaks from whatever competition they were involved in, head over to the rec center bar, drink up, head back to their activity, or, as was often the case, back to their ship to recover from a hot day's hangover.

Billy Mann loved playing baseball—whenever the ships could get enough sailors together, for a team. "And he was damned good. Everyone wanted Billy on their team."

"Al, Casper, and I often sat through Billy's games, up in the stands... and what else... drinking beer in the hot sun, over at the Bosch, then barely making it back to the ship."

"We'd pass out and spend the rest of the afternoon somewhere out on deck, in the shade... sleeping it off. Then, we'd wake up just in time to catch the old plantation train, the Pineapple Express, into town... and start drinking all over again. Makes you wonder how we ever got anything done. But we did... especially when it counted. Damn, those were good times!"

On some evenings, the four men would attend a "smoker," at the rec center. Today, that name might imply a sophisticated night out on the town.

"Back then, it was a rowdy boxing match, usually held at night, with a full roped ring, a bell, and even an announcer."

Navy smokers got their name because, in those days—before, during and after a fight— virtually everyone smoked cigarettes and cigars.

"Lookin' back, we musta' smelled like hell when we came outta' there."

Arizona had two skilled boxers. Casper was one of the two.

"And a pretty damned fine one, at that."

"I never bet on the fights much. But a couple of times, Billy, Al and I'd pool some money and bet it on Casper."

"More often, we'd do this when Casper knew who he was scheduled to fight. He'd tell us not to worry... that he could 'take the other boxer'. He'd even give us some of his own money to sweeten the pot... and to reassure us that we weren't throwing our money away."

"Once, Casper explained before his fight that night, that he was gonna' knock out his opponent from the *California*, by the fifth round.

"And, by God, he did it!"

"After that fight, we were so flush with dough, the four of us splurged and took a cab into town. Didn't want to waste a minute of celebrating."

"Now, Al… he was a pretty good shot at basketball. Just imagine the four of us, on Liberty, on a hot Hawaiian morning shooting baskets, playing games of horse… with the loser having to buy the next round of nickel beer. On those hot days, we were already drinking beer before 10 a.m."

"White shorts, black belt, black socks, black Navy work shoes, no shirt… sweating, cussing, and laughing like hell. Strange, but these are some of the good times I recall."

"Now, I have just two words," said Lauren. "Whaleboat racing and gambling. Of course, the first had much to do with the second."

Several times, Lauren was picked to fill in on a boat when one of the team members of *Arizona's* whaleboat crew was sick or on leave.

"The only reason they ever wanted me, I think, was because I was heavy muscled. And that's what you needed to pull on those oars in a race."

A whaleboat's length is between 20-25 feet. It seats 10 to 15 rowers and a helmsman, who'd call out strokes and steer the boat. All factors were important to win.

"We generally raced against three or four crews from other ships, right smack down the channel for a one mile race. Even though it was a hell of a lot of work and everyone was beat afterwards, it was also exciting as all get out."

As an oarsman, Lauren had a choice view when the whaleboats lined up for each race.

To his left was Battleship Row—ships' immense hulls rising up from the water. Entire crews from each ship stood on the rails. Others sat out on the ends of the big guns, or high above in the main masts.

On his starboard side, the scene was duplicated with hundreds more sailors—all up on their feet—aboard their cruisers moored along the docks.

"Everyone cheered their own boats on, and jeered, cussed and made fun of other crews as they passed by."

"The guys from *Arizona*... hell, they wanted us to know we'd better win, or else. They had money on us, and there'd be hell to pay if we lost."

"Usually, a ship's horn started the race. Once our crew heard the signal, we all pulled like our lives depended on it. Damned exciting to be up against other ships' teams, and to listen to all the racket as our whaleboat passed ships lined up down the channel."

The raucous sounds bounced off the steel hulls and echoed down Battleship Row. Taunting never stopped until a winner was declared.

"Even then," said Lauren, "the booing and cussing continued for the crews who lost... usually by the guys who'd bet money on 'em. Funny... because in my mind, I still hear their echoes float out across the channel. I'll tell you, it was a sight to behold."

"*Arizona* didn't win every time, but we'd always come in first or second. To us... second didn't count for much."

"Afterwards, of course, they presented some cockamamie trophy to the winning crew." When Lauren's crew won, it always ended up on the table of the Officer of the Deck.

"Ship's sailors couldn't miss it. The trophy was there when the OOD either checked them out for Liberty, or when they came back aboard ship."

"That damned trophy always brought a smile to my face," said Lauren. "When we'd win, it'd make up for the times when we'd lose... or for how sore you'd feel if you pulled a muscle."

"By 'Navy Rules,' sailors couldn't gamble aboard ship unless the officers wanted to participate. Then, it magically became all right to do so. In other words, 'follow the rules, and keep your mouth shut'... unless you were an officer making a bet. Then, it was 'follow my lead.' "

Nearly everyone on *Arizona,* or any other Navy ship, gambled as the occasion might allow "...even if they didn't consider themselves to be big-time gamblers."

One common "two sides of the mouth" wager occurred when the crew gambled on the exact time *Arizona* would tie-up after arriving at Pearl, or when it dropped anchor off some port.

True to form, the wager was called "Dropping the Anchor." Bet pools took several forms: one might be based on the exact time the first line was tied up at dock; another, the *precise* moment when the first of two anchors were dropped.

Bets on the anchor pool began the instant a ship's schedule was released.

"We all thought we knew our ship well enough," Lauren said. "We'd try to keep records of anchor drops and tie-downs, to narrow the potential times... given no delays."

"We'd then jump into any one of several types of pools."

Depending on how flush a sailor might be, and how long it had been since payday, a sailor could put in two or four bits—twenty-five or fifty cents. Separate pools existed for the big-time gamblers—most often the officers, who'd ante up two or three dollars.

"Me," said Lauren, "I never went for the big money. Always bet a quarter or fifty-cents. But you can imagine, when at least fifty-percent of the crew jumped in, it was big money to any sailor who won."

No matter what a sailor's assignment might be, as the moment approached to tie the line or drop the anchor, everyone searched around to compare what time they'd marked down—and how close they were to it, at any given point in time.

"If you had a watch, your eyes were constantly on it. If you didn't, you made damn sure you were standing next to someone who did."

"The funniest part," said Lauren, "You'd hear sailors cuss at the moment their bet times came and went. Then there'd be shouts of personal encouragement as your own time narrowed down."

"Eventually, an officer on the bridge would call out the official time, over the PA system. In concert, the moans, groans and cussing would crescendo on every deck."

"Soon, after it all died down, a sailor would yell out he'd won whatever pool he'd entered. That is, except for the officers or whoever won the larger dollar pool. They usually never said a word. They'd just won several hundred dollars, and didn't want to broadcast the fact to 1,500 other sailors."

"As you might think," said Lauren, "...all of a sudden everyone wanted to become the big winner's best friend. Especially when Cinderella Liberty rolled around."

"For me, it was more sheer luck than from any formula or from my meticulous record keeping. Just like the odds at Vegas... after countless times coming into port, I was pretty good at guessing and often came close. In Vegas, close isn't good enough. And in all the times I gambled on the anchor drop... I still only won once."

"Now don't get me wrong," Lauren laughed. "A win was a win. Gave me bragging rights for a week or so, and enough extra cash to buy beer for my buddies at Smith's Union for a couple of weeks."

— —

SECOND TO THE LAST TO LEAVE

Charles "Casper" Ehlert

Charles "Casper" Ehlert was born on 8 February 1919 in Sheboygan, Wisconsin to Jasper and Anna K. (Horst) Ehlert. He graduated from Sheboygan High School in 1937 and then joined the Civilian Conservation Corp (CCC).

Casper enlisted in the Navy on 9 March 1938 in Chicago, Illinois. At the time of his enlistment, he was 5'7", weighed 142 pounds, had blue eyes, medium brown hair, and a ruddy complexion.

He reported aboard USS *Arizona* on 9 July 1938, and *Arizona* was his first ship. **On 7 December 1941, Casper was 22 years, 9 months and 29 days old.**

"Casper Ehlert was a hell of a good guy, and I am proud that I got to know him. Casper and I first met through my best friend Billy Mann, and it wasn't long before he became a regular one of our gang.

Besides representing Arizona as one of the ship's two boxers, Casper was also the ship's official artist for its newspaper, 'At Em' and he was really good."

Casper Ehlert

Casper Ehlert, Sea 3/c

USS *Arizona*

KIA

Chapter 6
CINDERELLA LIBERTY

The fairy tale name "Cinderella" is a strange analogy to attach to a bunch of sailors heading out for liberty on a weekend or day pass. But there are more similarities than not, when details are compared.

After all, Cinderella spent much of her waking hours cleaning ashes, scrubbing floors, cleaning rooms and, in a sense, performing KP. Duties aboard *Arizona* included cleaning soot off the aft mast, holystoning the deck "…so white, you could eat off it," cleaning up personal quarters, in preparation for rigorous inspections—and KP.

On her one night out, Cinderella was given strict instructions to be back by midnight, or suffer the consequences. And that's where the analogy truly comes together. There were serious consequences for any sailor who abuses the privileges granted by their liberty pass.

The Navy couldn't allow sailors to carouse off base until 4:00 or 5:00 a.m., and then be expected to report for duty with only an hour or two of sleep.

"They'd never be ready for a full-days work," said Lauren. "Or battle-ready."

Hence, sailors regularly referred to their leave as "Cinderella Liberty." And it came, as everything does, at a price.

Every sailor at Pearl Harbor knew if they weren't back inside the base's main gate by midnight they'd have to deal with the nasty "stepmother,"AKA the Master at Arms, and his shadow Marine aboard each ship.

"If a sailor stayed out past midnight, all hell would break loose," Lauren said. "And it would mean the brig."

"It was a hell of a scene at the main gate as midnight approached. Sailors and Marines would arrive, in droves off buses and taxis. The docks were so crowded, the lines waiting for a motor launch to shuttle them back to ship were almost as long as lines to the brothels on Canal Street."

The larger battleships, like *Arizona,* would send out launches to ferry sailors back from the gates. To keep lines moving, shore patrol was in charge of calling in the launches. In between specifically assigned launches, they'd allocate another to water-taxi battleship sailors—whether standing or dead-drunk, back to their particular ships.

"You'd hear a shore patrolman yell out, 'All those for *Arizona,* drag your butts over here.' And we'd do everything we could to maneuver… stagger over to our launch, as quickly as we could. Now… if one or more of our gang were three-sheets-to-the-wind, we'd each try to support the other with our weight, just to keep 'em upright. The key was *not* to fall into the water while boarding a launch."

The main gate was an enormous area filled with sailors and Marines standing, some even lying on the ground. All were "safe" as long as they arrived inside the main gate by midnight.

"When the clock struck twelve," said Lauren, "the gates were locked down. At that point, once inside the gate, we really didn't give a damn what time we got back to the ship… as long as they were still runnin' launches."

"But any sailors caught outside could pretty well count on losing their next liberty pass if they couldn't get back to base on time. They'd usually end up heading to the brig or pulling double-duty. The choice often depended on your attitude."

"Craziness frequently occurred in between the launches taking off and new ones arriving. It got pretty rowdy. There'd be fights between battleship and cruiser sailors, and more fights between members of different battleships. There'd be one-on-ones or a whole bunch of sailors up against another."

"Many times, this happened aboard a launch while heading back to the ships."

"Across the water, you'd hear a coxswain yell out, 'We ain't goin' nowhere in this launch 'til ya' quit your brawlin'!' Sure enough, there'd be a big motor launch sittin' in the middle of the harbor... no wake behind it... dead in the water. It'd take about thirty seconds for the cussin' to stop... and to get quiet. Then, the coxswain would put 'er in gear, and the process would start all over."

There were procedures for liberty that everyone was expected to follow.

"To return to our ship at night," Lauren said, "it was always the same drill. Wait your turn to walk up the gangway from the ship's launch. Then, wait in line to be logged in."

Sailors would return to *Arizona* and report to the Officer of the Deck as they came aboard after saluting. The OOD would take each sailor's liberty card and on the next day, pass it back to the petty officer of the respective division.

The petty officer of each division—usually a first class boatswain's mate—would then hand out liberty cards to sailors who "...did their job and didn't screw up."

"Most of the time these petty officers were old-timers, who'd been in the Navy for twenty to thirty years. And you *never* wanted to piss them off... or you'd count on getting no liberty."

Occasionally, a sailor would screw up big time and cuss at an officer.

"He'd go a long stretch without seeing liberty... sometimes for weeks in a row."

Such was not was the case with Lauren.

"It didn't scare me none... I did my job, kept my mouth shut, and always got my liberty card."

Standing alongside the Officer of the Deck would be the Master of Arms and, always, a Marine to handle any problems or trouble.

"If necessary," said Lauren, "they'd help escort you to your bunk if you returned so drunk you couldn't make it to quarters on your own."

The Marine always carried a billy club, used to pat down legs of those he thought were too drunk or were trying to sneak a bottle of "hooch" back aboard the ship.

"Didn't happen very often," said Lauren, "but I can remember a number of times when he'd break a bottle, tucked into a sailor's sock, on the inside of his pant leg. When that happened, everyone got a good laugh. If the sailor just stood there and took it, he'd probably be escorted back to his bunk. Walking down to your bunk with glass in your sock was usually considered punishment enough."

"But watch out if the drunken sailor turned around and cussed at the Marine for breaking the bottle. He'd most likely be hauled off to the ship's brig to sleep off his drunk."

"Never happened to me," said Lauren, "but I can't say I didn't think about it, once or twice. We were always tryin' to second-guess what Marine'd be on duty."

Liberty began every time *Arizona* pulled into port as long as every sailor's work was done.

"I'll tell you... we all hauled ass to make sure whatever we were working on was finished in short order."

"Half the ship received liberty the first full day... usually Saturday and the other half the next. Most of the time, Billy and I were assigned the same liberty."

Having the day off didn't mean a sailor always spent the full day in the city or at Waikiki Beach.

"Hell, if you did you'd end up spending all your month's pay in a couple of days." For Lauren, he needed his twenty-one dollars a month to stretch as far as it could.

Pearl was a large base with an impressive array of recreational sites and events available to keep sailors occupied and maintain morale.

"There were many activities for us. Most often, Billy and I'd spend the day at the base recreation center, where we'd bowl, buy tin can 'nickel beer', and play baseball."

"This way," said Lauren, "we could drink five beers for the price of one that we'd pay in Honolulu. We'd drink to the point of feeling no pain, return to the ship to sleep it off… just in time to spend the rest of our liberty at night on Hotel Street."

"Some days we'd leave during the day to go to Waikiki Beach. Occasionally, we left base for Honolulu in late afternoon. Most of the time, with the nickel beer on base, we'd already approached a good buzz."

Often, Billy's friend, Casper Ehlert, along with Al Schreiner—from Fire Control School—would bum around with Lauren and Billy. They'd head into town after dinner, to avoid having to spend money on food.

"Most of the time, about six in the evening, our gang'd take a launch from the ship to the main gates in order to catch a small, narrow gauge train into town."

Before Lauren left ship, he'd make certain he had a handful of *Arizona* 'souvenir' matchbooks. Sailors from other ships did the same thing.

Immediately outside the main gates, they'd find a swarm of local kids waiting for a handout of matchbook covers that they could collect—or maybe sell in town.

Often, he'd have extra matchbooks to hand out from USS *Pennsylvania,* the *California,* the *Oklahoma,* the *West Virginia,* and the *Nevada.*

"After all," said Lauren, "a battleship housed fifteen hundred to three thousand sailors. The cigarette companies wanted all of them to smoke. So the matchbooks were free to us, and included bragging rights."

"And the kids loved to collect them. Without fail, they'd crowd around us for as many freebies as they could get. I doubt there are many battleship covers around today. They'd be worth a lot. Had a collection of my own Unfortunately, it was in my locker… and went down with the ship."

Once past the horde of kids and outside the base's main gate, the sailors would hitch a ride on the train called the Pineapple Express and head into Honolulu.

"It was both the cheapest *and* slowest way into town," said Lauren. "Don't know how the hell it ever got its name. There wasn't anything *express* about it. But that's what we all called it."

"From the train station, we'd walk the four blocks or so… mauka—mountainside—up to Hotel Street, which paralleled the Honolulu harbor."

"I swear to God," he said, "it was crowded as all get out, and sometimes difficult to maneuver anywhere while sailors made their way from one favorite bar to another."

On occasion, the guys would get their hair cut at a big barbershop by Aloha Tower.

"Not that we ever needed it," said Lauren. "Haircuts on the ship were free. But Honolulu was filled with female Japanese barbers. There were usually lines to get in… sort of like priming the pump, so to speak. The difference between 'free' and paying a woman to cut your hair? These were ladies you could actually talk with and flirt around. We were willing to pay for the privilege to talk about anything… *and* have our haircut."

"The gals knew it, too. And they'd flirt like hell to get a tip.

"Once finished, we'd walk up Nuuanu Street from Aloha Tower."

"The first place we'd hit was *Arizona* crew's favorite watering hole—Smith's Union Bar, 19 Hotel Street—right in the middle of all the action downtown."

Lauren's gang felt it was always a good idea to have their ship's boxer, Casper, with them. Like most young men, the more they drank, the easier it was to insult another sailor—or his ship—and end up in a bar room brawl.

"Not that having Casper alone would stop another ship's crew from picking a fight with us," said Lauren. "But it definitely made other sailors think twice before they did."

"I saw a number of brawls over the years. Been in a few, too. Last one I saw was only a couple of years ago at Smith's Union. Some things never change!"

"Trading insults usually brought on a fight. Especially when it was between sailors from two different ships. Mention how ugly your brother or sister was, how stupid your father was, or who might be sleeping with your mother or sister… and that's all they needed."

Lauren and Billy had two things going for them in that respect. Since Lauren pulled duty on Shore Patrol, he usually knew most everyone and "…. I could get away with almost anything. Not that I took advantage of my position too often. Didn't want to end up in the brig, myself."

Then there was our friend, Casper, *Arizona's* artist and boxer.

"Casper was best known for his appearances in fights at smokers both on and off base. The smokers brought Navy sailors and officers together in one place. They'd bet on the ship's fighters; who was going to get the knockout; and even on which sailors would win or lose their pay."

They'd smoke cigars and cigarettes so heavily, it'd look like a three-alarm fire—the smoke so thick, one could barely see across the room.

"Casper was a respected boxer. Most of those who attended the smokers either recognized him or knew his name. They'd almost always clear a path for him… and us. This, alone, helped keep me and Billy out of trouble."

Smith's Union didn't have pretty bartenders like I discovered at the Broadway Inn. Instead, it was, and still is, a typical and original Navy "dive bar."

"As you walked in," said Lauren, "it smelled like a combination of beer, sweat, smoke and piss, all of which are considered "Navy"… and smells a sailor can recognize in a second, after living and sleeping in close quarters.

"And there was always laughter," he said.

The front entrance wall was made of glass blocks. During the day it provides subdued sunlight. Walk through the beat-up front door, and a long wooden bar on the right stretches the length of the room all the way to the back wall.

About thirty stools lined the bar's edge. But when the bar was full of sailors, there were at least fifty bodies sitting or standing, while they swapped lies and sea stories.

Opposite the long, narrow bar, sitting up against the wall, were a set of small tables with high stool seats.

"My gang's table was always closest to the back of the room. Three or four of us would sit there drinking two-bit beer and dreaming about girls we were going to meet… usually more dream than reality."

When it came to women in Lauren's life, during liberty or while on shore patrol duty—unlike a lot of other guys—he didn't have to fantasize much about them.

Without bragging to his friends, Lauren first dated a good-looking, college-age hooker named June. After June left the Islands, he met a beautiful Japanese bartender named Nikki.

Lauren guarded both of these relationships and didn't mention them to anyone.

"Not even Billy," said Lauren, "because I didn't want to take any ribbing or bullshit from him, or from anyone else.

"I learned that early on. Women in my life were my business, and no one else's. There' s no way I'd introduce either girl to my friends… no matter how close we were."

Nice girls didn't go to Hotel Street. With few exceptions, there was little chance sailors would find the girl of their dreams downtown. Most barmaids and hookers didn't go on dates with customers. Lauren was an exception.

"As for Smith's Union Bar… not a place you'd take your mother, sister… or a date," said Lauren. "Just a Navy bar with a stale beer smell, a lotta' cussing, lying… and occasionally, fights."

Fights often broke out in the men's room. Considering the number of sailors who frequented Smith's at any one time, there wasn't a lot of space inside the can. Just a tin trough urinal and a toilet—with no separation between the two— same as it is today.

"No door… except on the women's," said Lauren. "Just a shower curtain hung from a pole for the men's. I'd say… one step up from an outhouse."

"A sailor'd get drunk, head for the john… then, in a drunken stupor with very bad aim… piss on the leg of the guy sittin' on the toilet, next to him."

"That's all it took to see two guys come tearing through the curtain, wailing on each other. One sailor's pants half down… the other with his pecker hangin' out… and no time to get it back in. Damn, it was funny as hell."

"Then, all the sailors circled around to see who'd win. Or some would join in… if one of 'em were a shipmate."

"Some wise guy'd usually pop up, taking money for bets on who'd win the fight. Or bet on if the sailor could get his pants up before the next sucker punch."

"More often, fights were broken up by Shore Patrol,before they went too far. I might have jumped in there, a couple of times, to break it up… if I wasn't too snockered, myself."

Hotel Street and Smith's Union bordered on Chinatown. Before the war started, it felt to Lauren and his buddies as if they'd walked Hotel Street from one end to the other "…a million or so times." They'd travel the streets and move from one bar to the next.

"But we'd almost always end up back at Smith's Union, with its gold, hand-lettered sign out front. It was either there or the Black Cat Café… down the street... Directly across from the YMCA."

All the good bars were located on Hotel Street, with Canal Street, which intersected Hotel, housing most of the cathouses. Some of the more popular bars gave you tickets with two drink maximums—not minimums— to keep the lines moving.

"Otherwise," said Lauren, "no one would ever get in."

Navy cathouses were easy to spot. They had the longest lines to get in. Even more so during Friday or Saturday afternoons and evenings—at the height of liberty. Often, their lines stretched down an entire block.

"Always way too long for me," said Lauren. That's where being on Shore Patrol paid off.

"Being a member of Shore Patrol had its advantages. I could enter any cathouse I wanted. By myself or with friends."

The bouncers knew they'd need Lauren's help sooner or later when trouble occurred. They were more than happy to let him into the bars and cathouses whenever he showed up.

"Not that I used them. June saved me from a lot of that."

"Believe it or not… a cathouse was the closest thing to being home for a sailor or Marine. In the bullpen—similar to a large living room—beautiful girls looked like maybe your sister's best friend… especially to a drunk sailor."

"Imagine..." said Lauren. "Cold beer, pretty women… a record player going, maybe some dancing. It was a welcome change from tight quarters aboard ship. The big difference… these *sisters' best friends* wore barely nothin.' "

A "working girls' hotel," which is what some called them, was usually on a second floor, with a "big bouncer" always stationed at the bottom step where the line began.

"A good romp in the hay would generally set a sailor back between two and three dollars. Believe me… there was an endless line to make payments."

Each house had an alarm system to call Shore Patrol if trouble occurred. And every room had an emergency button to ring a bell if a girl needed help.

"Occasionally," said Lauren, "a sailor would ask for his money back, due to… what do they call it today? Erectile dysfunction? Hell, we just knew he was just too drunk, couldn't get it up, and he'd want his money back."

"The girls would sometimes offer 'rain checks'. The catch was… rain checks were only good for weekdays, when they weren't as busy. Not weekends, when they made the most money."

Due to ongoing maneuvers, unless a ship was in port for repairs, liberty was rarely had on weekdays.

"Sailors would get pissed and start trouble. That's when the Madam would have to call Shore Patrol."

Every cathouse downtown was a clean establishment, checked by Navy doctors once every two weeks. The girls were all attractive. Mostly from the States. That made visiting a cathouse a little more like being home, despite being in the middle of the Pacific."

For added security, every cathouse had a bouncer. Usually Hawaiian. Always size Triple-X. Their main job, beside the one implied by their title, was to sit or stand by the door and let sailors and Marines in as others left.

"A couple of the bouncers, I recall, were both called 'Tiny'. They weren't. And then, there was a short but tough Hawaiian guy named Kalani."

"He was a good enough guy. Watched the door, at the Cottage Hotel, where my friend June worked."

This always helped make it worthwhile for Lauren. It was an added bonus to work Shore Patrol, as he knew most, if not all, the bouncers by name.

With influence and pressure from the Navy, the cathouses—with relatively pleasant surroundings—were hospitable places to visit. Each was usually run by an attractive Madam or Manager, "…many of whom I used to stop by and have coffee with," said Lauren. "Most of my shore patrol calls involved putting down an argument between a girl and her customer. Or I'd be called in to break up a fight between two sailors who happened to fall in love with the same girl."

"When Billy, Casper, my friend Al, and I looked for love in all the wrong places, I'd use my influence with Kalani or another bouncer who was working, to bypass the line. He'd allow us to go up the stairs into the bullpen, where the girls hung out to entertain guests before business.

"One thing," said Lauren, "You can bet there was plenty of cussing at us from sailors waiting to get in, when we bypassed the long line. Occasionally, I'd get some shit the next day, from another crew member who happened to be in line."

In the bullpen, music played on the radio or phonograph, couches and chairs were scattered around, and ice cold beer was 10¢ more than what it cost at Smith's.

"But at that point," said Lauren, "who the hell cared?

"There were two things any sailor who was stationed at Pearl could agree on: One, they never saw an ugly girl who worked at a cathouse on Canal Street; and two, every one of those ladies were all experts at making a sailor or Marine's life better. Anything else said, they were lying."

"Hotel Street and Chinatown was a hell of a place," said Lauren. "Let's face it.... There weren't a lot of places, in town, to entertain the troops like movie theaters and dance halls. The U.S.O. had just started up, in nineteen forty-one, and hadn't quite caught on, at the time."

"You could only go around the island once and then you'd seen it all. Or go to the beach so many times without getting your ass burnt to hell."

"For the sailors, going to Hotel Street was similar to visiting an amusement park. With so many rides, it was difficult to make up your mind which one to go to next."

Lauren felt that the merchants in Chinatown outsmarted most others, in the area. "They knew best how to part a sailor from his paycheck."

Apart from the bars and brothels, much of that was evident, due to the fact that Hotel Street and Chinatown were connected "...pretty much at the hip."

"What struck me most, when I first arrived in Hawaii, were the cultural differences between Hotel Street in Honolulu and Seattle, Washington, at the time. It took some getting use to. For example, we might run into a dragon dance, moving through the streets during Chinese New Year. Thousands of firecrackers goin' off everywhere.

"Then, there were the dead ducks hanging out in an open market. Every time I'd walk by and see that, I couldn't help but think what my mother would say. It always made me smile."

"When I arrived from stateside in what was then the Territory of Hawaii, I figured things would be pretty much the same. But they were so much different. Not better. Not worse. Just different. And for me… I liked everything about it."

Another "ride" in Lauren's new "amusement park" on Hotel Street was the abundance of Tattoo Parlors. On one particular night after drinking heavily, he nearly succumbed to getting a tattoo.

"Thank God… Billy kept reminding me that we wouldn't make it back to base in time to catch *Arizona's* last launch before midnight. Neither of us would. Kept sayin' that we'd both end up in the brig."

"We could have, if the artists needle had begun to etch into my skin.

"Truth be told," said Lauren, "I recall not getting the damned tattoo because I couldn't decide between a heart with a girl's name in the middle, or the Navy's anchors with *Arizona's* name running across it."

"Good thing I couldn't decide. Nearly got the heart."

The name Lauren felt deserved to be in the middle; the one he was drunk-in-love with—that particular night—was June, a banker's daughter from Chicago. Unbeknownst to her parents, she had left the University of Hawaii to do some moonlighting in a brothel on Canal Street.

"Damn… she was good looking and sexy. And at one point in my life… even if only for a brief time, I was certain I was falling in love with her."

Fortunately for Lauren, Billy's persistence won out. They made it back to base and aboard *Arizona* with only a hangover. No tattoo. His decision to forgo the artwork on his arm would later come with a smile—always, and only, to himself.

"I was pretty damned happy, later in life, when I didn't have to explain who June was to my mother or to either of my two wives down the road."

Lauren often thanks Billy for that nudge, "...sitting someplace in eternity waiting for me to join you," Lauren might say. "I've been grateful, many times over, that I listened to you instead of the devil inside me."

From time-to-time, Lauren and his friends would earn the right to put in for "Special Liberty." Granted—outside of normal liberty periods—for unusual reasons, they sometimes secured a 3-Day Special Liberty, as recognition for long hours worked or "as recognition for exceptional performance" of their duties.

Once obtained, Lauren and the guys would head up the coast on a Navy Bus, north from Pearl Harbor, to a small village called Nanakuli. It was a Navy recreation camp that provided pure R&R. " A chance to really let your hair down and relax," said Lauren.

They'd be put up in tent-like shacks with other sailors—usually six to a cottage. Located right smack on the beach, "...waves so close they'd nearly rock you to sleep. Perhaps, the best beach I ever visited in Hawaii or anywhere else."

"Couldn't have been more than a hundred sailors there, at any point in time."

"We'd swim and sunbathe during the day, drink nickel beer until we passed out, wake up to eat, then start drinking all over again. Same ol' regimen. To us, at the time, it was total relaxation. The camp was for us working sailors. Officers, well, they'd go to the Royal Hawaiian."

"No one else on the beach. Just an occasional local fishermen, on the best beach ever."

To Lauren, the village of Nanakuli was truly out in the country. Nothin' else there. Just Hawaiians resided in the area. "True Hawaiians," said Lauren. "Good people."

"At night, after dinner as the sun set and twilight crept into the sky, we "haoles"... as they called us white guys, could often hear locals down the beach, near water's edge, singing and playing their ukuleles into the night.

"On our second night, it was particularly beautiful as the sun set on the beach. Like no where else I'd ever been," said Lauren.

"From off in the dark, we heard voices singing and others playing ukuleles.

Billy wanted to check out what was going on. He grabbed his old guitar and asked Casper and Lauren to walk down the beach with him.

"Casper and I grabbed all the beer we could carry and headed toward the music. And I have to say... that night, I truthfully learned a lot about pure-blooded Hawaiians, and their ancestors... descended, they told us, from the original Polynesian explorers."

About a half mile down the beach from camp, Lauren and his friends met three "kanakas"—big, dark skinned native Hawaiians—sitting around their fire, with two women, who turned out to be sisters.

"But I swear to God, they were two of the most beautiful women I'd ever seen. We approached and one of them signaled for us to join them around the fire. Each kept strumming their ukuleles.

"They saw our beer, and one of the men said, "Hey brudda... come sit down."

"It was a moment in time I'll never forget. We walked over and just said, 'Howdy.' "

"At first, I couldn't understand anything they said. They spoke what they called "pidgin"—a mix between English and local. But we got the hint, and caught on. We were welcome to join them... in trade for beer."

"They were especially taken with two things: the beer and Billy's guitar… in that order. We discovered, quickly, that beer equaled "instant friends"… and it made for, what turned out to be, a once-in-a-lifetime evening."

"There we were" he said," sitting around a fire drinking beer, listening to the waves crash on the beach… so close, you could feel the mist in the breeze. And then, there was Billy, joining in with his guitar… trading songs with the locals.

"One thing that stands out… they sang 'Aloha 'Oe' together — a song written by Queen Lili'uokalani, the last queen of Hawaii. "

Billy's talent on the guitar intrigued their new Hawaiian friends. So, it didn't take long for them to hand over a ukulele, and attempt to teach him how to play it.

"Of course, the night went on and we'd run out of beer," Lauren laughed. "So Casper and I walked back to camp, a couple times that night, to get more. Don't think anyone wanted the night to end."

"For me," said Lauren, "apart from singing and strumming, the true experience happened every time one of the sisters got up to dance… what they called the Hula, around the fire."

"They were as graceful as palm trees swaying in a Hawaiian breeze, as their friends sang and played."

Lauren was only twenty, at the time. He had yet to grasp how special this opportunity was, for any group of non-Hawaiians to be invited into the inner circle of traditional island life. "Although I didn't have any idea as to what they were singing, I knew I'd never forget this night for the rest of my life."

Lauren was enchanted by these women, as they danced the hula 'auana, on the sand—between fire and water.

"These girls were easily two-hundred pounds. Dark brown skin, wild, dark black, crimped hair that moved with the ocean breeze. One sister's hair was shoulder length; the other… flowed down past her waist."

"They were as supple and nimble as any dancer on a stage. Yet, they performed with a spirit that transcended life."

"It was both graceful and sacred. This was where legend and tradition came together. The Hula, we were told, was how they expressed their stories, passed down over the ages."

Lauren and his friends had never seen anything like it.

"Sure," he said, "we knew of the hula dancers at the Moana Hotel at Waikiki.

"This, though, was a helluva' lot different."

"The sisters offered us smiles from time to time. But when they danced, they were focused solely on their Hula. It was only as years went by, I learned the importance of these traditions… their legends and history behind every movement."

"And I learned an expression that said it all, that night, 'Where the hands move, there let the eyes follow.' "

"Their faces radiated beauty the entire evening," he said. "It was as if a postcard had become 'the real deal' of days past."

"And I tasted it, just once. But enough to last my lifetime."

"Maybe it was all the beer. But I'll tell you straight… when they danced around that fire, in the moonlight... I thought they were the most beautiful women I'd ever seen."

"Over the years, I've never discussed this with anyone I knew. Just thought they'd never understand it… it was that special. I've always compared it to a shooting star. It was something unexpected that takes your breath away."

"Seventy-five years later, based on this special memory, the foundation that I created commissioned a special song and hula to help honor my ship and crew.

It is called the *Arizona* Hula and its song "Warriors of the Sea." On 3 December, 2016, this gift to my crew was first danced and sung in the shadows of the *Arizona* Memorial at sunset from Ford Island.

The fifth generation grandson of King Kamehameha The Great, Joe Recca, composed the song and his wife Shirley and daughter Delys choreographed and danced the *Arizona* Hula for the first time.

This was truly a special evening and three of the four remaining survivors of USS *Arizona* were in attendance, all with tears in our eyes as so great an honor was paid to our crew.

For me, it brought home that night on the beach so many years ago like nothing else could."

— —

William E. Mann

William Edward "Billy" Mann, was the eldest of twelve children, and was born on 20 April 1920 at Satsop, Grays Harbor County, Washington, to Arthur Carl and Charlotte E. I. (Borden) Mann.

Billy graduated from Elma High School in 1938 where he first met his best friend, Lauren F. Bruner. Billy, as he was nicknamed, joined the Navy on 10 January 1939 at Seattle, Washington, without knowing that Lauren had joined the Navy two months earlier. When inducted, he was 5′ 8″ tall, weighed 150 pounds, and had blue eyes, brown hair and a ruddy complexion.

Billy reported to *USS Arizona, which was his first ship,* on 29 April 1939 at San Pedro, California. **On 7 December 1941, William Edward Mann was 21 years, 7 months 17 days old.**

"Billy was my best friend on USS Arizona, as we went to high school together and ran track. He was good and lightning-fast, and I wasn't either, but we still had a lot of fun together.

On the morning of the attack and battle station sounded, Billy raced below deck while I climbed ladders five decks skyward. Less than fifteen minutes later, the enemy's high-altitude "Lucky Bomb" dropped, sending Arizona into her grave and literally dropped into Billy's lap.

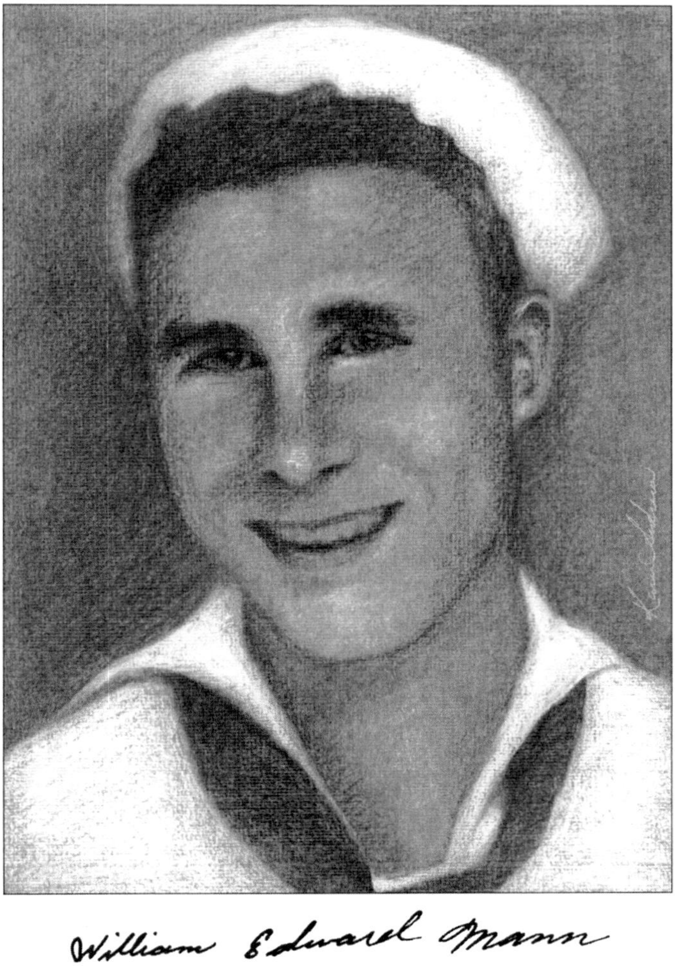

William Edward Mann, GM 3/c

USS *Arizona*

KIA

Chapter 7
"CODE RED, DO YOU READ?"

In Spring 1940, Lauren, then 19, and his friend Al Schreiner had graduated from the Vallejo, California Fire Control School.

"We didn't let any grass grow under our feet before we reported to be shipped out, as ordered. Eventually, we'd leave from what was the former Seventh Fleet's Headquarters in Long Beach."

"From there, we'd hitched a ride aboard a ship to meet up with *Arizona*... already in Pearl Harbor."

"Trouble was, by the time we arrived in Long Beach, the Fleet's offices were only a shell of what they use to be."

While Al and I were in training, the Seventh Fleet had pulled up anchor and moved to Pearl Harbor. Amid transfer, the Fleet's name was changed to The Pacific Fleet.

"And that's how, over time, the enemy would come to know us."

"For us few sailors left behind, taking training... we were in a big hurry to reach the land of hula girls and grass skirts."

"Still, we'd try to get off duty as early as possible, while waiting for our ride to paradise. That way, we could spend much of our time, still, with Marcella and Lillian... the girls Al and I had dated during our weekend drives from Northern California."

"During the few days we had left, Al tried like the dickens to sell his car. But he couldn't get his price. Didn't wanna' give it away for next to nothing, so instead, he left it with Lillian."

"She promised to get a drivers license and take good care of it for him. About that time, I figured things were getting pretty tight between 'em."

Lauren? He was off to meet hula girls.

"Don't get me wrong," he said, "Marcella Stapleton was a nice girl. Young and pretty; only a year younger than me. And that's the point. I still had some traveling and living to do… what I signed up for in the Navy. To see the world.

"I liked Marcella. And we had some fun. But Al somehow seemed older. He was ready to settle down. Not me!"

"Hell, I was on my way to Paradise. Far as I knew, every girl in the Territory of Hawaii wore a grass skirt and did the hula."

"Shows you what little I knew back then."

Although the wait seemed longer to the men, it was only a few days before they received orders for a "working ride" to Hawaii aboard a tanker—a new Navy Fleet Oiler, launched in January, 1939—USS *Cimarron*.

"By calling it a 'working ride', the term meant *no* ride in the Navy is free. During transport, we're expected to work our shifts like anyone else.

"In our case it was 'as you were'… chipping and painting, painting and chipping, halfway across the Pacific. No different than it was on our way up to Bremerton, Washington, aboard *Nitro*, when I caught *Arizona* and became a crew member for the first time. No use complaining."

"We *did*, of course… but only to each other."

"In spite of all the scrub work, I was damn confident, coming out of training. Thought I was doing all right, as I began to rise in the ranks of Fire Control."

"There's just one thing that upset me… even today. When civilians learn my Navy rank was 'Fire Control,' they immediately think of me as a fireman, who'd *put out* fires on the ship."

"Always have to explain the Navy term, Fire Control, means I was on a crew, as highly trained as a fireman... but with a different set of skills. In Fire Control, we helped manage the armament of the ship, by determining firing solutions to be used against the enemy."

Once in Hawaii, Lauren was transferred, from Deck Force Four to the more elite Fire Control Deck Force – referred to as 'F'. To accompany the upgrade, he was assigned new quarters, and moved from the ship's aft to housing adjacent to gun turret #2, just forward of the ship's main mast.

Bruner wasn't notified that he'd passed all his FC classes until after he reached Hawaii. "I felt confidant, though, after all the studying and help I got from my math tutor, who was Principal Charles Shank from Elma High.

"Although I made it through, Al wasn't as lucky. Not that he didn't do all right on his FC written tests. He did fine, there."

"But one night, at Smith's Union bar, he was crying in his beer. He had learned, according to his paperwork, his damn eyes were too close together to use the optics on a rangefinder."

"I didn't have that physical problem. My eyes were wider... set apart, more... easier to fit against the double lens eyepiece."

"You'd think the Navy would've checked his eyes before they put him through training."

Al still remained in the Fire Control Division but never moved up in rank. He told Lauren, that night, his plans had changed, and that when his enlistment was up, he was going to leave the Navy, "...a couple years, down the road." He added, "Then I'll move back to L.A. and ask Lillian to marry me."

Bruner always thought Al was similar to his own age. But until that night, "…I didn't know he was almost fourteen years older than I was."

For the next year or so, prior to Al's mustering out, the two men became even closer friends.

"Turns out, in October of forty-one, Al was one of the last to be released from the Navy, just before war broke out. He and another friend of mine… name of Chick Sackman, became my only close friends from *Arizona's* crew, once the war ended. "

The three would remain close friends throughout the rest of their lives.

Once settled, back aboard USS *Arizona,* Bruner found his work load more complicated than he originally thought it might be. "Turns out I had to wait until I was rotated in, to take someone's place in the division. That is, until someone moved on, kicked the bucket, retired, or was transferred."

"The key here was the same as when we hitched a ride aboard another ship. No one sits around on his ass, waiting for anything."

During this period of limbo, Bruner was assigned to work in the main battery plotting room, "…learning all I could.

"I was told it'd help me advance faster."

"The plotting room was located four decks below my Fire Control crew quarters, where our sleeping and dining area hugged the giant barbette housing for gun turret two."

To reach the plotting room from the main deck, Bruner would head below to the second deck; climb down past the third and splinter decks; take another ladder beyond the first platform deck; and eventually reach the second platform deck. Once there, he'd move through hallways, nearly two hundred feet aft of fore, to reach the watertight hatchway that led inside the computing room.

"Any farther, below," said Lauren, "and you'd be in the ship's hold. Beyond that was *Arizona's* double bottom."

There were several strategic—some might argue logical—rationales that led to the plotting room's placement so far below decks. First, it was four levels below multiple "armored decks" to protect the sophisticated equipment from potential enemy fire.

Second, the plotting room's intricate, electromechanical computer/rangekeeper, stable vertical, and banks of electrical switches and telephony weighed the same as a couple of small cars.

Third, the room was required to be as watertight as possible to remove it from the effects of humidity or a possibility of storm water damage to the electronics.

Finally, the equipment needed to be in close proximity to the ship's power sources. Therefore, the room was adjacent to the forward dynamo room, and the storage batteries/charging panel rooms for backup purposes.

"Still, there was a couple of things that bothered me," said Lauren. "Nearly adjoining the plot room, on the port side, was the five inch gun powder hoist. Directly above… the fourteen inch and five inch gun powder magazines."

More often than not, the plotting room's hatchway was kept open, to keep air circulating throughout. "With air blowers going, but no air-conditioning, imagine what it was like for a complement of thirty to forty sailors working in that long narrow room. It'd get hot and stuffy.

"Damned uncomfortable, most of the time… especially if we had beans the meal before."

"Hell, it was no picnic, working in the plotting room with all those guys. Some took daily showers. Some didn't. Then there were those who always farted… while the rest of us had to grin and bear it."

"Not that I didn't contribute my fair share of methane. But at least I showered regularly."

"Didn't help matters that the M-4 computer ran hot as hell. It was always on. And it hummed, constantly, especially when out on maneuvers."

"Doesn't take much to imagine the other stinking smells that fought for our attention, down below… particularly at the second platform level."

"There was the constant odor of forged steel, throughout. Add to that, a pungent sniff of ozone, and what was explained to me as nitric oxide, emitted from all the electrical equipment and miles of wiring… in continuous use."

"From beyond the plotting room came odors from the boiler rooms; the center, port, and starboard engine rooms; and from the tons of fuel oil that filled just about every cavity surrounding the hull, from the first platform deck, right down to *Arizona's* double bottom."

"It's been said that your nostrils adjust to work environment smells, like the ones we had to deal with daily. That you don't notice them, after a time. But I can still recall many of those odors… over seventy-five years later. They still cling to my brain like a hotdog on a stick."

The plotting room's watertight hatchway had to be screwed down tight during maneuvers, mainly while operating in heavy seas. Even when the door was open, the crew would have to step over its entry lip.

"If you weren't careful, a stumble over the lip could earn you some hefty laughter from the crew inside. At one time or another, everyone earns their laugh-stripes."

"Even by today's standards in a modern Navy, with all its digital electronics… back then, once you entered the plotting room, it was one damn impressive sight."

"The room was about twenty-four feet wide by thirty, long. The first thing you'd see was the M-4 computer, or what we'd call the Fire Control Brain. It was always busy humming. Sorta' like a Queen Bee in her hive, with all kinds of worker bees scurrying around feeding it."

Set in an extreme watertight section of the ship, the plotting room's analog computer and rangekeeper—staffed, at times, by up to 40 men—was, without question, the brainpower that computed complicated firing solutions for the ships armament.

"Sailors constantly fed the computer data, received by phone lines, from all parts of the ship."

After the data was analyzed, switches would be thrown and armament aboard *Arizona* would begin to track targets and guns would switch to automatic control—taking command of the 'trigger' away from gunners, above decks, if necessary.

"The ships fourteen inch guns were so accurate," said Lauren, "they could hit a bulls-eye twenty or more miles away."

"Whoever said that computers weren't around in the mid-to-late twentieth century hadn't been aboard *Arizona*."

"As younger people say today… that was pretty damn awesome to see. Even as a young sailor, then, I knew this was going to be my path in the Navy. Although I had no idea, at the time, it'd also be my pathway to survival."

The plotting room's computer, the M-4, had another given nickname—"Bertha".

"According to *Arizona*'s legend, Bertha was named years before, after an officer's grandmother. The name stuck with the plotting room sailors."

"She was a little over five feet long, about chest high and forty inches wide. Near the end was a flat top table, used only by chiefs and officers for charts and paperwork …and *not* by anyone else, or for any other purpose… unless you wanted to get your ass chewed."

"Bertha was painted a slightly darker shade of gray than the rest of the room; a standard-issue battleship gray, I'd say."

One couldn't help but notice, all the sailors. Each man was responsible for, and controlled, a bank of switches that lined freestanding and bulkhead walls.

Some wore telephone headsets, usually affixed over their heads, and hung down, while covering their ears. Others had chest sets hanging around their necks—each plugged into a socket, tethered close to their workstation.

"None of this new wireless stuff that allows people to talk through the air with no connections," said Lauren. "You could only move as far as your tether allowed. As a worker bee, there was no movin' around from a workstation, once plugged in."

In charge of these banks of men were others, higher in rank, who oversaw certain groups of guns. They'd read the computer findings, then report to a chief who, in turn, reported to Lt. Kleber Masterson. A tall, skinny officer, Masterson wasn't always around. Frequently, he remained in his office, a few hatchways down the corridor.

"Turns out," said Bruner, "Masterson ultimately was promoted to Vice Admiral. Over the years, especially after the war, he'd been heavily involved in missiles and nuclear weapons research."

"Depending on the chief on duty, though," said Bruner, "and what shit flowed down hill, most of the chiefs I remember were decent guys. I learned a lot from 'em. And that helped me later… down the road, during my Navy career.

"So, there I was on my first full day back, from California, standing just inside the plotting room… having managed to cross the hatchway door without tripping."

"Thought I knew what to expect. Felt confident…and maybe a little cocky, knowing that I'd passed both the written tests and physical requirements. What else could they demand of me?"

Bruner was in for a rude awakening.

"Turns out, I was way in over my head… with the room full of men, equipment, and switches. Lots of switches."

To Bruner, each man appeared to efficiently pull his weight, all in a hail of activity.

"Sailors crammed throughout the room… involved in one training activity or another. Each of 'em serious as hell."

"Here were all these men, standing at four banks of wall switches—monitoring up to 50 switches per wall."

Coordinates were shouted from various sailors while other men confirmed and passed them down the line.

"Though I observed them pulling switches down to the right, as they locked them in place… truth be told, I had no idea what they were doing. It was as if I'd forgotten all my training."

A couple of khaki-dressed officers, surrounded the rangekeeper. They fed information into the computer, as dials and knobs were adjusted to initiate final test firing solutions.

"And there I was… suddenly scared shitless."

The rangekeeper/computer managed firing solutions for armaments such as the 14" Big Guns—on down to the 5" AA gun batteries. In the process, it computed target range; ship's speed; wind and direction; pitch and roll of the ship; it's exact position; compass bearing; and up to two dozen other computations.

One look at it all, and Lauren thought there was no way he could fit in. "Suddenly felt it'd be impossible to learn all I had to know, in order to work in such a god-awful mess."

What in hell did I get myself into?

"For more than just a moment, I felt I'd be made a fool, as soon as these guys found out how bad I was at math.

"Then, it hit me."

I'd made it through all the training. So, what's the problem?

Just as Bruner was about to cave, on his first day in Fire Control, up stepped Fire Controlman, Chief Earle Melvin.

"He greeted me with what I'd later come to recognize as his dogged spirit and earnest smile."

"Welcome to the plotting room, sailor. I'm FCC Melvin. You Bruner?"

"Yes, sir." Lauren, attempted not to show panic. He glanced around the room and realized nearly every sailor was older, at least from his perspective as a kid of nineteen."

"The chief had been in his position, years before, and understood how nervous Bruner might have been. Melvin led him to a bank of switches and assigned him a sailor to shadow."

"You'll learn from this specialist, for now," said Melvin. He nodded to the sailor, "Bruner's all yours. See that he gets schooled properly."

"Can't remember the guy's name," said Lauren, "but I'll always be appreciative of the first thing out of his mouth."

"Don't worry kid," the specialist said. "In a month or so you'll be doing fine… and remember everything you'll need to know."

The specialist showed Lauren around, and began to coach him on the equipment and its functions. "It was then I recalled several instructional films, we'd watched while at FC school. Much of the same equipment was featured."

"And my nerves began to settle down… making my first day in Fire Control not so bad, after all."

"Even today, I believe that's when fate tapped me on the shoulder, to let me know I'd better learn as much as possible about the ships armaments as quick as my wits allowed."

"Boy, did I dig in, paying close attention to the details."

"Eventually, what I'd learn would save my life... many times over, in the years that followed."

An outside observer might believe that with a computer the size of an M-4, little could go wrong. "Back then, just as it is today, a computer is only as good as the personnel running it. Today they call it GIGO... garbage in, garbage out. It was no different in the plotting room."

Each switch, of which there were a hundred or more, was attached to the room's four full banks of equipment, situated on the forward bulkhead; another two-sided bank, about 6 feet out from the bulkhead; and a smaller bank of switches, at the end wall, closest to the computer. On each switch, a flashlight-size light bulb let sailors, in charge of each switch, know it was working.

"Trouble was," said Lauren, "all sorts of things went wrong and it was our 'mother hen', the Chief, who on occasion helped solve the problems. More often, it was up to an individual sailor to fix anything wrong, knowing he was being watched and evaluated, at how quickly he could fix the snag... whatever it might be."

That could scare the hell out of Bruner. When the FCC yelled out an order, where a gun crew had indicated something wasn't working—for example, if the ammunition lift, from below decks, had stopped transporting shells, "...it was our job to find out why and fix the problem, in short order."

"We were constantly watched, and judged, by how well we did. If our reaction wasn't fast enough, or we couldn't make heads or tails of a complication, we'd be issued 'demerits.' Reminded me of being a kid back in school."

"Only the chief kept these records. And nobody ever questioned his authority... or gave him any lip."

If, at the end of a shift or a work week, a sailor had too many "demerits" after his name, he could lose his next liberty pass, receive extra duty, or both.

"Nobody wanted that," said Lauren. "Get on that list *too* many times… and your ass was kicked up to the Captain's Mast."

"Fortunately, for me, fixing a problem was often as easy as checking the small light bulb above a switch. Other times, it might be that I didn't throw the switch hard enough for it to engage and lock."

"Each hand-thrown switch was so large, I had to use a full hand to throw it, and lock it in place. If a click-sound didn't immediately follow, it hadn't engaged, and I'd have to repeat the procedure."

"With all the chatter going on between battle stations and plotting room crew, it was easy to miss hearing the click if your mind wasn't focused directly on the gun switch."

"There were several things to check-off if a problem occurred. But this was always my first 'go to fix' when inspecting a gun switch."

Even if a switch was in place, it may have come loose from its socket on the main battery switchboard.

"If I couldn't determine the problem at once, then my life and job could become more difficult. It required that I begin to trace back circuitry, from the wall switch, all the way to the gun crew captain."

"Last thing you'd ever want to do was to admit to the chief that you just couldn't figure out the problem."

"Sounds easy… just being responsible for controlling your switches, until you consider how stressful it could be. Especially since we knew we were being watched and judged. The FCC was always looking over our shoulder."

"Funny now but not so much, back then."

"Hell, the sonovabitch had a master control. He could override everything in the room, including individual gun control switches… just to shake us up and keep us on our toes.

"Occasionally, when the Chief wanted to test a particular sailor, or give a slacker a wake up call, he had the ability to turn off any switch, then watch to see how long it took a sailor to figure out what went wrong."

"Fortunately, that was one of the first secrets shared with me by the sailor who trained me. He explained that if I first went back and followed the circuit, and examined everything… including the fuses, I was most likely being tested and observed. It always paid to resolve a challenge quickly."

"After once solving one of those challenges, straight away, I just happened to glance over to the FCC's station and caught him with a wry smile on his face. I could swear he winked back 'good job' to me."

"At least, that's my story… and I'm sticking to it.'

"Though I may not have been the smartest turnip on the truck, I can't recall a time I wasn't able to solve a problem in the plotting room. Credit goes to the sailor who trained me for that."

"Hell, I was determined to make Fire Control my Navy career, and worked my ass off to that end."

"To this day, I can still hear the Chief's primary threat, he'd yell out to anyone screwing up or screwing around. 'Straighten up, fly right, or ship out.' If we didn't follow his orders, he'd transfer our asses, quick and fast, to the lowest division with an opening."

At this time, around nineteen forty, radar aboard *Arizona* was just be introduced, and the ship was being retrofitted to include two bridge wings that would support twin anti-aircraft directors, above the captain's bridge.

Bruner would eventually be assigned to one of them, to assist in optically measuring target range, bearing and elevation, with his fellow crew mates, for transmission of coordinates down to the plotting room's rangekeeper.

Lauren's AA director would sit port-side, with its sister director situated on the starboard bridge wing.

"But that was still far down the road."

As a result, Bruner ended up spending a considerable amount of time in the plotting room.

"I was determined to learn as much as I could. And it seemed to pay off. My officers kept throwing new challenges at me. To test my mettle, as they said."

Bruner grew accustomed to procedures critical to obtain firing solutions for the ship's guns.

The men on headsets would receive essential information sent down from various FC personnel, above decks and, in particular, from the bridge. Sailors, at their battle stations—within a big-guns director, for example—would calculate target range and bearing, then send it by chest mic or phone to the staff in the plotting room.

"Think about it," said Lauren. "Today's computers are digital. But there we were, in nineteen thirty-nine, essentially using analog machinery that had metal gears, shafts, cams, and beveled gear differentials… almost like a car."

The difference was that a car would get you from point A to point B. The plotting room's rangekeeper, however, had to simultaneously send hundreds of shells—of various sizes—through the air, with pinpoint accuracy toward targets, while taking into its calculations multiple values sent throughout the computer.

The rangekeeper computed time of flight, changing wind direction and speed, gun elevation, initial shell velocity—while still calculating the ship's movement, roll of the ship, range changes, and about two dozen other elements, in order to arrive at ultimate firing solutions.

Contingent upon quality of data, fed to the computer—based on the skill sets of the men sending information to the plotting room—it could hit or miss targets as close as a mile or less, and as far away as twenty miles or more, contingent on weather conditions.

"During maneuver exercises," said Lauren, "underway at any particular time, there could be a full complement of men assigned to various positions."

"If you consider four banks of electrical switches that stretched nearly the length of the room, the large computer itself, various support instruments, and the chiefs plotting table, there was little space left for moving about during high-level activities."

"Truth be told", said Lauren, "I was in awe of its capabilities, and of the men who ran the computer."

"No one sat on the job. They couldn't. There were no chairs, anywhere. It was serious business… no room for error."

"A demerit system took care of that. Sailors caught goofing off, slacking, or unaware of their job requirements could end up at the Captain's Mast. And believe me… you didn't want to go there."

Any Navy man—enlisted or officer—sent to a Captain's Mast, often held on the ship's forecastle "…was in deep trouble."

Not as hard on a sailor as court-martial, but it could be serious enough to get up to 30 days in the galley, confinement to quarters, loss of pay, extra duties, reduction of grade/rank, or other punishments handed out by the CO or XO.

"If there were any regulations designed to keep us in line," said Lauren, "it was the threat of demerits… and Captain's Mast."

"One of my first assignments beyond the plotting room was Rangefinder Operator in the big fourteen inch guns director, located just above, and behind Gun Turret Two."

"The exterior-based stereoscopic rangefinder always reminded me of a pair of giant rabbit ears."

What Bruner referred to as "rabbit ears" were ultra-high-powered optics that allowed him to sight forward, and to each side of the ship, across Gun Turret One and Gun Turret Two. The big-gun director controlled all three guns on Turret Two.

Compared to the port-side anti-aircraft director, scheduled to be added during a retrofit, in the summer of 1941, the Number #2 Gun director was small and cramped.

"Only fit two men at a time."

"To enter the damned thing you had to grab hold of the hatch at the top, put your legs in first, then wiggle down inside. Kinda' like climbing through a Jalopy racing car's window with the doors welded shut. Or as our astronauts did when they climbed through a small raised hatchway on an Apollo command module."

"It was a hell of a view, though, whether I looked through the rangefinder, or out through the hatch above."

"It was mesmerizing up there, as we sat on that perch. Imagine how we felt with the ship, right there in front of us, just plowing through the waves… especially in high seas. What a thrill.

"Took some getting used to, but didn't take long to fall in with the rocking and rhythm of the ship. Sorta' like being rocked as a kid."

"The experience was soothing. And because of that, I never minded the duty."

Over the next couple of years and through the summer of 1941, Bruner occupied himself with assigned duties of Fire Control FC, taking turns in the rabbit ears, then spending the remainder of his shifts absorbing processes and procedures, to learn how to function in *Arizona's* plotting room.

"During this time of limbo, I was assigned to a continuing stint there."

Bruner was instructed to master the skills associated with his assignment.

"I wanted to pick up all I could. And this, as it turned out, would help me advance faster."

"I was confident I could handle just about anything at my battle station, once the new port anti-aircraft guns director was in place, and within the confines of the plotting room, itself. My training would serve me well… but at that moment, a lot of it was intimidating."

"This was considered one of the most sophisticated areas of the ship. Looking back, for my superiors to trust me to perform duties there… out of a crew of over fifteen hundred men, it was pretty much an honor."

However, *Arizona* had not yet been retrofitted to include the two new bridge wings and directors, planned for the main mast. So, Bruner would have to wait for his ultimate assignment, high atop the Admiral's Bridge.

The bridge wings would ultimately house the twin anti-aircraft directors as part of the ship's superstructure. It would allow each director's crew to have a view, as distant as possible, of *Arizona's* horizon. Lauren's director would be set at Port-side; the other would mirror it, to assist in obtaining firing solutions for the Starboard AA-guns. But retrofit would not be calendared for another year—six months prior to the Attack.

As a result, from the moment Bruner arrived back aboard *Arizona,* he would spend a substantial amount of time in the plotting room—learning as much as he could.

In spite of working a heavy schedule in Fire Control, there were still activities that fit in with being a young man.

"Our pastime pursuits included chasing girls, drinking beer, and trying to stay out of trouble… basically in that order."

It wasn't out of the norm for Lauren's group of friends to catch a launch to the main gate, grab a seat on the Pineapple Express, into town, then take a trolley car to Waikiki Beach, "…especially if we could begin Liberty early."

"One day, near the end of summer in forty-one, Billy raced over to me, right after morning mess. Some DJ on the radio had spilled the beans about the movie star Lana Turner. Said she was staying in Waikiki at the Moana Hotel."

"Now, this was a big deal for young sailors, like us. Everything we'd seen in the paper was about this new, young actress known as 'The Sweater Girl'… for wearing tight, low cut, form fitting sweaters."

"And she was an eyeful. Didn't take me but a second to decide… when Billy suggested we spend the day in Waikiki, to see if we could spot her. I was all in."

Lauren and Billy spread the word among close friends. And soon, four of the guys headed out on their quest, in search of the sweater girl.

That morning, they had nothing more than hope—and their swim trunks—of ever being able to get a look at her.

"That's when my friend, fate, again intervened in my life. Billy and I, Al, and Casper, had just come out of the surf at Waikiki that afternoon."

"We plopped ourselves down on the sand, when Billy literally let out a breathless shout."

"Guys… there she *is*… the sweater girl… Lana. Just down the beach." He pointed in the direction of Diamond Head.

"Look, down there… sitting under that umbrella."

"We strained to pinpoint our quarry," said Lauren. "But didn't take long. You just couldn't miss that beauty… that figure, anywhere."

"Our gift from God had been placed at our feet… well, about fifty yards away."

"Funny thing was… you'd think we would have flown down there to meet her. But it took at least a half hour to pump up our nerves as to *how* we'd make our approach… and decide *who'd* talk to her first."

Lauren and his pals decided the four should first return to the surf. They'd get the sand off and nonchalantly walk down the beach—closer to the Moana Hotel—as if they didn't know Lana Turner was near.

"We were gonna' see us a real goddamned movie star. Of course, it was difficult to pretend not to notice Lana Turner. There was already a small, but growing, crowd beginning to gather around her umbrella. "

They walked further down the beach, carrying their towels, decided on a spot, and set up as close as they could.

"Since Billy, by far, was the best looking of our group… or so he kept telling us, we convinced him to go over first to talk to Miss Turner. From what I'd heard from Billy, who was the real film buff in our group, MGM had recently finished shooting her film, called 'Honky Tonk' with a lucky guy named Clark Gable."

"Hell, she was only twenty at the time. Once we saw her in real life, we all agreed that this Gable guy was a lucky son of a bitch."

"There weren't any men accompanying the movie star. So we thought it was a good thing, in our favor. Instead, there were only a couple of girlfriends. And the gals seemed to relish all the attention they were getting, from Lana's fans."

Billy rose from the sand and proceeded to head toward Lana Turner's umbrella. The line that had formed was getting longer as time passed. He took his turn, standing in line, after we reminded him not to forget us.

"True to his word," said Lauren, "it wasn't but a few minutes after he moved up the line, of mostly military gawkers that Billy waved for us to join him. And as usual, he ended up doing most of the talking when we reached the front of the line."

"He introduced us, one by one," said Lauren. "But as Billy mentioned my name, time seemed to stand still. Miss Turner looked over to me, and it no longer mattered who she was. I couldn't take my eyes off her chest. I'll tell you true, she filled out her swimsuit like a glove."

"Can't even remember if we shook hands. Hah! Didn't matter. She was a true beauty. And real nice to us."

"Gave each of us a black and white pin-up photo that magically filled her hands. Hell, she had a pile of 'em on her blanket. One of the girls who was with her would hand another photo as the next guy in line moved forward. Lana's other friend helped to keep the line moving."

"Lana signed a photo for each of us, and made small talk while she did so. Asked about our ship… and mentioned how lucky we were to be stationed in Hawaii."

"As if we didn't already know."

"We were all damned proud of those autographed photos. And real careful with them all the way back to our ship."

"Hell, I was almost giddy with excitement. And with the new bragging rights I had, there was an awful lot of bullshit I threw around, when I returned to quarters… about how Lana Turner was my new best friend."

"Truth be told, with or without the lies… once back aboard *Arizona,* our photos of the Sweater Girl were in high demand to be seen."

Each time Lauren showed off Lana Turner's eight by ten photo, his little lies grew into bigger ones.

"But who the hell cared."

About a week later, one of the plotting room chiefs asked Bruner to bring in that "special photo you've been hiding".

"Matter of fact," said Lauren, "I brought it in on my next shift."

The chief was so taken by Turner's photo, he suggested that Bruner share it.

"He handed me a roll of black electrical tape, and told me to hang it near the hatchway door."

"Understand… it was the chief's suggestion. Not mine. I wasn't too keen on the idea… afraid something could happen to it, or that some asshole might fleece it."

"Wasn't long after I hung it, every sailor who entered or left the plotting room would stop and take a gander at Lana Turner… and her chest."

"There were times her photo would cause a backup, at the hatchway."

"Soon, it became a ritual. The men couldn't just *look* at Lana Turner. They had to touch and rub her breasts, each time, to the laughter of anyone near… other than myself."

"Me? I was scared to death. All I could envision was my prized photo getting soiled or, worse yet, ripped."

Much to Bruner's relief, on a subsequent shift, another chief approached and handed back the photo. In a voice, loud enough to be heard by just about anyone in the room, the chief said, "Take your photo, sailor. Something like this has no place here."

As he handed it back, in more of a whisper he said, "Wasn't my idea to take it down. Orders came from Lieutenant Masterson."

"The skinny officer," Bruner duly noted to himself.

"Of course, I didn't mind. I prized that photo and the bragging rights it gave me. So I lifted a roll of electrician's tape and, that night before mess, I secured it to the inside of my locker door. And Lana would safely remain there, guarding my small metal drawer filled with loose change."

"Even after all these years, I can still remember everyone waiting for calls that came down to the plotting room, from sailors who worked up in the starboard anti-aircraft director."

Consider the seriousness of tasks in the plotting room, the constant threat of demerits, or being called to Captain's Mast if caught violating Navy regulations aboard ship or on shore. With all that, there were times when the men still had to let off steam without somehow "breaking regs."

"One of the sailors, stationed in the starboard director would send coded messages down to the plotting room,about an activity that took place, weekly, over on Ford Island."

"We referred to that activity as 'Code Red.' "

"And when those words were sent down the line, anyone aware of its meaning could barely wait for noon mess."

"It was a secret code name, coined by some smart-ass in the Starboard Director. Though I had my suspicions, we never did find out his name. But we all appreciated the time he took to let us know whenever operation 'Code Red' was in effect."

"This so-called operation began to occur during the summer of forty-one."

"I had recently met a pretty Japanese bartender in town at the Broadway Inn. And her beauty was enough to set my mind thinking about more lighthearted activities, as well."

By this time Bruner had graduated from the big gun's "rabbit ears" director, to the recently installed port-side anti-aircraft director, located at the same level, high up, on the sky control platform.

Its twin starboard director rested at the opposite end of the sky control platform, nearest Ford Island. From its surrounding cat walk, the director's crew could easily look out over the eastern banks of Ford Island and observe many activities.

"Because we were so high," said Lauren, "we could look out over the trees and bushes that lined the shore, and into the officers' housing area. The homes were clustered together around a large grassy setting.

Each week, beginning in late summer 1941, up through the first week of December, a group of officers' wives who lived in Navy housing on Ford Island, enrolled in a series of hula classes. The lessons were organized by a local Hawaiian lady. Held outdoors in the neighborhood, the wives were able to participate while their children played.

For Bruner, it often worked out if he and his friends had an alternating shift in the plotting room. Someone from the starboard director would call down "Code Red" over his headset. That was their indication the officers' wives had gathered and were ready to begin shaking it up.

It was also a signal that "Clutch Butt", a leggy, long haired blonde, was there as well.

"There must've been at least a dozen women, of all sizes and shapes. But one woman stood out in particular."

"That lady took to the hula like a duck to water," said Lauren. "She knew how to shake it. So, the men nicknamed her 'Clutch Butt.' "

"Of course, she got the title from her ability to rev up her engines. She was particularly good at holding the muscles in her derrière tightly together… to control the shakes and shimmies."

According to Bruner, "The women had to have known a gaggle of young sailors watched their every move as they swayed their hips around during classes."

"They seemed to enjoy the attention as much as we enjoyed watching. We'd see them eyeing us back, through our binoculars… and pointing us out to other dancers."

"Some would even wave back, laughing among themselves. And an extra smile or two got broadcast our way, from time-to-time."

"The ladies knew they were safe… and we knew our place. But it was a sure way to relieve the boredom, once a week."

"Ya' know… when we were stuck on our ship, twenty-four hours a day… with little recreation, we'd seek just about anything within regs that'd bring a smile to our face. It was pretty harmless, at the time… and I think the ladies got a kick out of it."

"Don't think any sailor ever knew Clutch Butt's name, or to what ship's officer she was married. But I still think about the woman, occasionally, and the laughter and antics us fella's shared over some innocent ogling."

"And my hope has always been… that she and her family were able to lead a long and happy life if they made it through the attack."

— —

SECOND TO THE LAST TO LEAVE

Earl W. Riner

Earl Riner was born on 5 December 1921 to Thomas Eldin and Estelle (Barrett) Riner in Atoka County, Oklahoma.

He joined the Navy on 26 February 1940. At the time, he was six feet tall, weighed 148 pounds, had light brown hair, brown eyes and a ruddy complexion.

He reported aboard USS *Arizona,* which was his first ship, on 24 August 1940. **On 7 December 1941, Earl was 20 years, and 2 days old.** He was one of six USS *Arizona* sailors to escape the ship in what Military historians call *Arizona's* Greatest Escape.

"Earl Riner stood with my crew and escaped with us from USS Arizona. I didn't know him well, but he was a crew member of my friend Larry Farquhar, whose battle station was the starboard anti-aircraft director opposite from us on the ship. Earl ended up with us after the explosion aboard Arizona killed the others in his crew. I was proud to know him."

Earl William Riner, GM 3/c

USS *Arizona*

Survivor

Chapter 8
NIKKI & THE BROADWAY INN

August 1941

Lauren was a ruggedly built young man, approaching twenty-one in the fall of '41. He had spent his last two years before high school graduation working his own business—cutting and selling firewood to villages that surrounded Elma, Washington.

As a strapping teen, Lauren would approach landowners with timber on their properties, and strike a deal. He'd thin out trees the property owners designated, trade back half of what he cut to each owner, keeping the other half for himself to sell on his own.

All this resulted—to his benefit—in building a strong physique at 5'11" and 153 pounds. That alone made him a candidate for Shore Patrol duty in Honolulu.

Shore Patrol allowed him a lot of advantages—especially since his duty downtown involved patrolling Hotel and Canal Streets, "...right in the middle of the action, so-to-speak."

If there was ever a Navy town, in the truest sense of the word, it was Honolulu, before *and* after the war. And Hotel Street was the epicenter.

Large numbers of liberty-bound sailors were emptied into the streets by private taxis and Honolulu's big silver buses. As they arrived from the base, sailors were dropped off at a giant roundabout directly in front of the YMCA—just across the street from the King's Palace. They'd walk across a small park—"the green" as it was referred to—and race for one of their favorite watering holes, the Black Cat Café. It was the very first bar they could get drinks at, on their circuit. The line to get in was always down the street.

From there, they'd head up Hotel Street toward Chinatown, hitting every bar they could along the way. The ultimate goal for many was to meet and have an encounter with one of the girls in the district. These were not girls like your sister's best friends or the girl next door. In fact, the parents of those girls would *never* let their daughters stay out late at night, or get caught anywhere near Hotel Street or Canal Street.

"Bus fare into town wasn't too bad," Lauren recalled, "…about ten cents, or three tokens for two bits. Taxis were more expensive, but were usually covered when several men jumped in and shared the fare. Often, the taxis appeared to be more like circus clown cars… with so many sailors crammed inside. "

"Occasionally, I'd share a taxi with a bunch of the guys. But, personally, I preferred the bus or the free train."

A few blocks away, a slow-moving, narrow gauge train known by everyone as "Pineapple Express," dropped off sailors and Marines who didn't want to spring for the cost of a bus or taxi. Jumping on the train was often their excuse to save Liberty money for drinks, girls, and gambling.

"…. Not necessarily in that order," added Lauren.

Lauren's memory kicked in and he laughed as he told of the Pineapple Express.

"The prime reason sailors rode the slow train… they figured, 'If I go slow, and go free, I got that much more to spend on in town'."

"The sailors would hitch a ride and hop on board any one of a number of open-air flatcars fitted with beat-up wooden benches. So many asses sat on 'em, over time, the seats had become smooth as glass."

"Some flatcars had no benches, and were used to haul everything from pineapple to timber," he said.

"If the bench seats were taken, soldiers'd jump atop the timber-laden flatcars hoping, through the rough ride, they wouldn't pick up too many splinters in their butts before Honolulu."

"Sailors," he said, "also nicknamed the train the 'Hinky Dink,' 'cause of its stubby, crotchety old steam engine… and the less-than-comfortable ride. The train's whistle was so shrill, it'd test the strength of anyone's eardrums. Especially if you sat closer to the engine.

"Some said the nickname actually came from the WWI doughboy song, 'Mademoiselle from Armentieres', that referenced an odd lady with questionable talents. The last line of each verse always ended with 'Hinky Dinky Parlez-Vous.' "

"The crazy part," he said, "and this is where the nickname 'Pineapple Express' came from… was when sailors jumped off the slow-moving train as it rode through the miles of pineapple fields. Their challenge was to hop off the moving train, quickly harvest a pineapple with a knife, then jump back on before they'd lose their seat."

The sailors either ate it on the way into town, or saved it to give to a girl they'd hope to meet… in order to strike up a conversation.

"Usually it was a barmaid or a gal who worked in a cathouse," said Lauren. "Regardless, we never got any discounts… although we never gave up trying."

"Our friend Casper always carried a pocket knife… rolled up in his scarf. This made him the lucky one to cut open a poached pineapple and share it whenever we were in the mood. Trouble was, it was a messy business, but always tasty and sweet."

"Occasionally, a sailor'd get greedy for more than one pineapple or wait too long in the field… and miss his flatcar. It was always accompanied by lots of laughs, cheers, and jeers from fellow shipmates. It'd be a long walk into Honolulu, if the Pineapple Express passed them by."

Once in town, the sidewalks, bars, cathouses, and tattoo parlors were often jammed with lines down the block. Thousands of sailors' hats bobbed up and down as Sailors, Marines and occasional soldiers from the other side of the Island, scrambled from one watering hole to another. All were ready with pockets full of cash to spend—on anything.

".... Good times for young men that have never been forgotten," said Lauren.

He was no exception. By working shore patrol, he could occasionally mix work with the diversions that came with his assignments. Such was the case when he met an engaging Japanese bartender at Broadway Inn, while on duty.

The bar was just a block "mauka"—mountainside of Hotel Street—still considered, at the time, to be among the heart of downtown. It was just two blocks up from the YMCA and the Black Cat.

It was only by chance, one afternoon while working shore patrol that Lauren walked up Fort Street and decided to pass through a bar where he'd never been before. His shore patrol patch was his free ticket to pass the long lines that always waited outside Honolulu's bars.

"Once in," said Lauren, "you'd instantly hear tall tales told between ordering drinks."

The place was nothing fancy, most easily recognized by a large front window covered in big black and gold lettering that read, BROADWAY INN.

Unlike the open-fronted Black Cat, on Hotel Street, "... to enter the Broadway, you passed through an always-wide-open door. Once inside, its big window provided plenty of light. At night, it was dark and smoky."

Lauren first noticed two Japanese bartenders serving sailors from behind the bar. It was a constant battle to gain attention of any bartender or waitress downtown, let alone the three other barmaids who waited tables at the Broadway. But immediately, he was drawn to the bartender who yelled, "Hey, sailor. Come sit with me and have a beer."

Was she calling to someone else? He glanced around the crowded tavern. *I'll bet she says that to every guy who comes in,* he laughed to himself.

On the spur of the moment, but mostly due to her smile, Lauren grabbed his Shore Patrol arm patch, pulled it off, and cupped it in his hands. Quickly, before any other sailor mistook her invitation, "…. I secured my rear in the last empty seat at the bar, and ordered a twenty-five cent beer."

He turned around to survey the lounge and its mostly youthful patrons—many not much older than himself. To Lauren, it was pretty much like all the other bars in the area. Each competed to take a month's pay away, as quickly as possible, from any sailor who walked through the door.

Directly in front of the window, Lauren noticed an electric bowling machine. "The kind," he said, "which scored on metal pucks rather than rolling balls." A short Japanese man took bets from sailors and played the game, against them. Over time, Lauren would learn this man was Harry Shigeo Yamada, the bar's owner.

"Here you go, sailor," said a melodic voice.

Lauren turned back to the counter. The bartender wiped it off and set down his beer.

Her beauty instantly struck Lauren.

"What's your name?" he asked.

"Michiko."

Lauren liked the rhythmic sound of it. "Mi-chi-ko…. What's it mean?"

"No one's ever asked me that."

"I'm sorry…" answered Lauren.

"No, it's okay," she said. "My parents taught me, when I was young… each syllable has a different meaning." She blushed slightly. 'Mi' means… beautiful." The word was accompanied by a slight, almost flirtatious, curtsy.

"Oh," Lauren said.

She stood taller to define the second syllable.

" 'Chi' means one who shares wisdom."

"And 'ko.' What does that mean?"

"Child," she laughed.

"So, you are then a beautiful, smart woman child. Is that right?" Lauren smiled widely.

Michiko laughed. "Just call me Nikki. Like my friends do. You'll never remember my Japanese name."

Lauren recalled, "Seventy-odd years later, I remember thinking, at the time, that I'd always remember her name. She was that attractive and different. Truth be told, I never did forget Nikki, *or* her real name… Michiko."

Lauren finished his beer that first afternoon, laid down a quarter, put his arm patch back on, and turned on the stool to return to duty. To his surprise, Nikki reached out and touched his sleeve.

"Come back after your shift, sailor."

"You'll still be here?"

"Sure. Got no place to go and no one to go with."

Lauren decided then and there to come back.

So began his love affair with the Broadway Inn, and a beautiful young lady named Nikki.

"I'd truly grown to like her. She was so damned easy to talk with."

Nikki stood about 5′ 5," shiny black hair hung almost to her shoulders and she wore little makeup.

"Didn't need to… not that it mattered," he said. "But I'll tell you, Nikki had the most captivating smile. Made *me* wanna smile back, every time."

Lauren was drawn to her "bedroom eyes," as he referred to them.

"Eyes that pulled me in… at least that's what I thought, as a young man. From our first meeting, I had every intention of getting to know her better. "

"Then, there were her beautifully formed breasts. I just couldn't take my eyes away. She tried like hell to hide them… well, they were much more ample than the other girls who worked there."

Behind the bar, Nikki would wear an apron over her buttoned blouse and skirt. "Not that she was prudish," Lauren added. "No way. Just self-conscious she looked that way, though every other girl there would've gladly traded places with her."

"The waitresses and other bartender didn't wear aprons. Only Nikki. I think it made me like her even more."

Over the weeks that followed, Lauren became friends with the bar's owner, "Harry" Shigeo Yamada, who ran front-of-the-house activities. His wife, Kinuyo, a sharp businesswoman, managed the financial end. Kinuyo shrewdly had pots of chili cooking in the kitchen—served free to all customers. Nikki confided to Lauren, "The chili was intentionally spicy and hot to make sailors drink more." She explained that Hawaiians called the ritual "pupus"— the Hawaiian word for appetizers. In reality, for the Yamadas, the chili was a tremendous boost to drink sales.

"Kinuyo was altogether different than Nikki," said Lauren. A tiny lady with short, jet-black hair, she stood about three inches shorter.

According to Nikki, Kinuyo's hair was "permed"—filled with curls. "She consistently wore a gray or black, silk dress," said Lauren. "Never any bright colors."

"Aside from being the boss's wife, she ran staff and managed the money side of the business." There was no nonsense with Kinuyo. Most of the time, Lauren never saw her; she was generally out of sight in one of two places: either in the kitchen, cooking up a pot of spicy chili, or in her small, behind-the-bar office, counting money.

"I was always nice to her," said Lauren. "And she was at least civil to me. Of course, she was polite with the hundreds of sailors who came through the front door."

For nearly three months, Lauren dropped by, either while on Shore Patrol, or when on leave. He'd always duck in to see if Nikki was working, which, fortunately for him, was most of the time.

On slow afternoons or above the din of a packed bar, they'd just talk. "Really, that's all we did."

"And I was struck when I realized I never got butterflies in my stomach when we were together. She put me at ease. Whether across the bar, from one another, or when I secretly held her hand in the dark... I realized I'd developed a longing to be with her."

On liberty, or on shore patrol, Lauren had met other girls while in the bars, clubs, or while patrolling brothels on Canal Street. Nikki was a "local" girl, too. But unlike the others, "Michiko was so much more," he said. "Bright, quick-witted and sensible. And, boy... was she a looker."

"Until I met her, I'd never known a Japanese woman, or thought about what they were like, up close and personal. There was a mystery about her. She just radiated warmth from inside. And with every conversation we had, her passion for life became more and more contagious."

"And then there were her eyes..."

4 November 1941

When Nikki tended bar, Lauren would wait for an open stool at her side of the bar. On his twenty-first birthday, Lauren spent most of the afternoon at Nikki's station. From that day on, as if by magic, free rum and cokes would appear in front of him—always accompanied by one of Nikki's endearing smile.

Kinuyo was all business, and kept a close watch on her girls.

"Often, I'd get more than a little nervous with Nikki's free rum and cokes. There was no way I wanted to piss Kinuyo off, or get Nikki in trouble."

"Sometimes I'd share my concerns with her. But she'd only smile at me with those eyes of hers, and tell me not to worry."

Lauren often tried to play against Shigeo at the bowling machine. Each time, he'd lose. And every time after he swore he'd never try to beat Shigeo again.

"After all, I figured if I were going to lose a quarter, I'd just as soon leave it for Nikki, as a tip."

Shigeo Yamada's personality was everything his wife was not. He served as the bar's talent, talking with, and making comfortable anyone who entered his establishment. He, too, was all business.

"This guy was a hustler." Lauren laughed. "And he was handsome… around five-seven in height. His black hair was combed in a slicked-back style, gangster like. I'm certain he would've been a movie star in Japan, if he'd been raised there."

According to Nikki, Shigeo hired the girls. "He made sure they were pretty and spoke good English," Nikki had said. "Not too much pidgin."

Shigeo was always at-the-ready to meet new customers, as they came through the door. Street-smart and "akamai," he could become a father confessor to the sailors. "He could talk about anything with them," said Lauren. "Families and girlfriends longed-for, life at home, the hard work aboard ship, adventures at sea, hopes for returning to school after their service, and occasionally, politics."

His talent was to make them feel like long-lost friends, rather than customers.

"But let's face it," said Lauren, "truth be told… he was an incredible bullshit artist, with a great gift of gab. And that's why he'd take in fists full of quarters at the electronic bowling game. Especially after the sailors had downed more than a few beers."

Many a time, Shigeo would sit with Lauren at the bar. They'd talk about the Navy and Lauren's stories of Washington state.

Always well-dressed, Shigeo appeared the way a sailor wished he could dress—sharp and in fashion "…if he could afford it, and didn't have to wear a uniform."

The Yamadas had two children—a boy and a girl.

"Sometimes I'd see them, late at night," Lauren said, "curled up in the back of Shigeo's big black Dodge… forever parked right in front of the bar. Not something parents could do today."

"But their towering Hawaiian bouncer, Alika, with shoulders wide as an aircraft carrier, kept an eye on that car, the kids—*and* the block-long line to get in."

"I always thought Alika had to have the eyes of an iguana… in order to see everything."

Next door was the Yamadas' pool hall—Harry's Billiards—where Lauren would often wait for a seat to clear at the bar.

"On a couple of occasions while killing time, I'd play pool with Shigeo. Now, this guy was both athletic and damn lucky. And I learned, early on, not to bet with him on bowling or pool."

Shigeo had shared how, in his youth, he'd grown up on a pig farm up Palolo Valley, on the island of Oahu.

His parents were "Issei"—first generation Japanese immigrants.

"Once, he told me that on Sundays in the late twenties and early thirties, he'd played in a city-wide Barefoot Football League, on an entirely Japanese team called the Moiliili Blues."

"Said he played the positions of end and quarterback. Some of his friends I met at the pool hall told me he ran like a bat outta' hell on the field, and caught the quarterback's passes as well as he could throw them."

"The local papers gave him the nickname, 'Speedy Yamada'. In fact," Lauren said, "I recall hearing how they called him a… what was it? Oh yeah… an 'uncanny ball toter'… usually getting it to the goal line."

"These guys would play barefoot," said Lauren, "mostly because their parents—many plantation laborers or cannery workers couldn't spare enough from their meager earnings to pay for shoes."

" But truth-be-told," he said, "the kids preferred not to wear shoes, even to school."

The leagues recruited players based on weight, rather than age. Shigeo's league was made up of teams of young Japanese men and boys from other working-class towns on Oahu—often from plantation towns or the rougher neighborhoods. His squad fell in the 135-pound limit, and was considered the leading Honolulu team in their weight class.

"There were also leagues made up of teams of beefier Hawaiian players… who had more meat on them. We didn't play against those teams," Shigeo had told Lauren. "They would've crushed us."

"Back in nineteen twenty-eight," Shigeo had explained, "plantations and canneries provided the flimsy uniforms that consisted of loose-fitting t-shirts, open-faced helmets and cheap shoulder pads."

"Sometimes, the poorer teams would pad their shoulders with huge, split grapefruit peels. Occasionally, peels would fall out on the field and players'd have to scrounge around in the mud to find them."

"We used to carry our folded-up helmets in our pockets," Shigeo had said. "So you can imagine how ineffective they were when you were hit hard by another player. There were a lot of injuries."

Lauren added, "He told me his parents and others would provide the teams with rice balls, called 'musubi,' for the players to eat during a game for energy."

"Funny…" said Lauren, "I'll always remember that story, even when so many other things have been lost to memory."

It was in Harry's Billiards that Lauren discovered how much access Shigeo had to the business bosses and politically connected "locals" of the territory—many of whom would hang out in the back room of the popular pool hall, telling stories, drinking, and gambling.

Though he was anything but quiet, in the bar or with his friends, Shigeo was known as the "quiet power-broker of downtown." He had friends in both high and low places, but always knew how to use his influence to bring them together, behind closed doors most often in the back room of the pool hall when something needed to be carried out in the Legislature, or between various interests in Honolulu.

It was said that Shigeo was a friend to the common man. He could use subtle persuasion to get things done in the city, "…when politicians couldn't or wouldn't."

"I was once told that Shigeo could get a vote changed in the Territorial Legislature," said Lauren "and that he held sway with many of the business owners… especially if a new law seemed to be moving against the little guys… you know, the workers or union members fighting to get fair wages."

"Some of his friends once told me that local gangsters hung out there, too. But, as a member of shore patrol, I never saw any evidence of it, on or off duty."

Apart from being a great BS artist, pool player, and gambler, in Lauren's eyes, Shigeo was likable and appeared to him to be a good guy.

"I was glad to have met him. He was someone who had not just passed through my life, but who had stuck in my mind, with fond memories, all these years later."

And that made it easier for Lauren to open up the next chapter in his life: getting up enough courage, after nearly three months, to ask Nikki out on a real first date.

— —

Harry S. Yamada

"Harry Shigeo Yamada owned and operated the Broadway Inn in downtown Honolulu located at 1248 Fort Street, just three blocks mauka (mountain side) from Smith's Union Bar on Hotel Street.

It joined other bars, tattoo parlors, clubs, and cathouses, all trying to part sailors with their money. Broadway Inn like most other bars prior to and during the war, had long lines of Military standing out in front waiting to get in. Business was so good for Harry that he opened up a pool hall next door to the bar, which is where I would spend time waiting for Nikki to get off work.

I learned that Harry was born on 19 March 1910 in Honolulu, and was a nisei (second-generation) Japanese American. Nikki worked for Harry as one of his bartenders, which is how I came to know her."

On the day of the attack on Pearl Harbor, Harry Yamada was 31 years, 8 months, and 18 days old. He was short in height, had black hair slicked back Hollywood-style, and always dressed well. Harry was a hard worker, and was usually always at the bar.

Harry Shigeo Yamada

Proprietor

The Broadway Inn

Chapter 9
WARRIOR OF THE SEA

6 December 1941

Lauren spent as much time as he could visiting Nikki at Broadway Inn. After nearly three months, he'd finally found the courage to ask her out on a "real date."

By 6:02, the sun had set in downtown Honolulu; it was a perfect, warm evening for any sailor out on a date. Lauren had arrived early, as a golden-hour twilight painted soft, red hues of light across the sky.

Nikki was due off work at 6:30. Lauren waited for her outside the bar.

It wasn't easy killing time before the end of her shift, but he could talk with Alika, the Inn's bouncer, who handed out entrance numbers to sailors and Marines as they waited in line to get inside.

"Have to admit, though," said Lauren, "I was more than a little nervous. There I was, in my dress whites, waiting for Nikki. I felt like a school kid, wishing I'd asked her out sooner. At least I could 'shoot the breeze' with Alika, to calm the butterflies. He could talk Pidgin English with anyone, so long as you could understand him, and still maintain control at the door.

"Despite that, six-thirty couldn't have come any slower."

After what seemed an eternity, Nikki appeared at the door.

"Ready to go?"

Lauren turned, in surprise, and couldn't take his eyes off her.

"Between my being scared stiff that night… and the fact she emerged looking even more alluring than I'd imagined… I was close to speechless."

"Ready to go?," she repeated.

"Yeah… sure," he stumbled.

They began to walk into the early evening air. Nikki leaned into Lauren.

"Are you hungry? Feel like trying something special?"

Lauren found himself staring into her eyes. He nodded quietly.

A few sailors standing in line yelled out good-natured taunts. Others, catcalls. Many of the sailors knew her by name.

"Even though I shouldn't have been," said Lauren, "I was a little jealous."

Nikki sensed it. Immediately, she looped her arm through his, flipped her hair—to shake off the dust of the sailors' comments—and kept walking as they started down Fort Street. Down the block, she gently pulled him to a stop and looked directly into his eyes.

"Lauren… I want you to know I've never gone out with anyone who's *ever* come into the bar. I hope that tells you something."

Immediately, Lauren's entire body relaxed.

"Anyone looking could've seen my smile a block away. I asked where we were going."

"It's a surprise," she said. "But I've never been there, either."

"How do you know its any good?" asked Lauren.

"Don't exactly. All I know… my roommate, Yaeko, suggested it when I told her we were finally going out. She teased me about dating a *haole*."

"She said it's dark and romantic… and even a little scary."

Lauren felt on top of the world, walking with Nikki's arm in his. Most of the shops in the area had already put up holiday decorations. They approached Woolworth's

Five-and-Dime window display, decorated for Christmas, and peered through the window. Several customers sat at the soda fountain, some with packages at the base of their stool pedestals. Lauren turned to Nikki.

"Reminds me… gotta' get some Christmas shopping done in time to mail a present home to my little sister, Mary-Lu."

As they rounded the corner to Hotel Street, Nikki squeezed his hand. "Maybe I can help you find something."

"My heart jumped when she said that. Didn't think I could be any luckier. And I felt, at the time, my life was only going to get better."

They reached Nuuanu Avenue and, after waiting nearly ten minutes, caught a city bus. Lauren missed the destination sign in the window that read "Pali Lookout."

He reached for bus token money, but Nikki placed her hand over his.

"Put your money away, sailor," she smiled. "Tonight's my treat. My belated birthday present, to you"

Lauren didn't want her to pay. "But this woman… with such beautiful eyes…. I just couldn't argue with her."

He glanced toward the back of the bus.

"It wasn't packed. Maybe three-quarters full… a lot of military. Mostly sailors. A few guys had dates, and the rest rode stag… just takin' in the sites."

The ride took about twenty minutes to travel five miles, through city traffic, out of the lights and up into the Pali Highway, toward the Ko'olau Mountains.

"I recall, though I didn't know where we were heading, how much I'd wished it were farther away. I just enjoyed sitting next to Nikki, on that bus. And it felt so easy to talk with her."

Off the main highway, it was just a two-lane country road with few, if any, headlights approaching, in the growing dark.

The bus slowed, and pulled into the parking lot. Then the driver yelled, "End of the line, Nuʻuanu Pali Lookout."

"As we stepped from the bus, from where we stood, I noticed a moderate breeze, just shy of being windy. It gently blew colorful Japanese lanterns whose candles flickered above picnic tables and benches… each clustered around several food stands. With no power at the Lookout, the lanterns provided the only source for light.

"Touching my arm, again, Nikki commented on how beautiful it was, and how she'd always wanted to come visit the Pali."

"There's a lot of local history, here," she said.

Hand-in-hand, Lauren and Nikki followed others who meandered from the bus, past the food stands, out into the dark night. The view, once they reached the end of a path, looked over the northeastern "country side" of O'ahu.

They approached a concrete wall, and ledge, that served as a guardrail at the edge of a sheer cliff. The closer they came to the wall, the more a heavier, constant wind blew. Seeing other sailors leaning into the wind, they decided to try it, as well—laughing alongside everyone else.

"It was like a natural wind tunnel," Lauren said.

The mountain pass—combined with strong trade winds that blew toward wide-open cliffs—overlooked the landscape nearly twelve hundred feet below. Even in the dark you could look out over the island and see sporadic lights in the distance.

"It was a spectacular, panoramic view," said Lauren. "But was windy as hell. Some sailor said it must be gusting over thirty-five miles an hour. By my calculations, that's over thirty knots… considered near gale force winds."

"Now… I'm a fairly big guy. But these winds were as fierce as some we've encountered at sea. So much so… you could lean heavily into the wind, without falling over. Lean back and… well, you'd probably have a hard landing, flat on your ass… it was blowin' that hard."

Nikki clung tightly around Lauren's waist, his arm girding her against the wind.

"This must be the scary part my roommate mentioned."

She looked lovingly into his eyes and pulled tighter to his body.

"The wind," Lauren recalled, "was the fun part of the trip. For me? It was a great excuse to hold Nikki."

"I'm sure most of the sailors were itching for the wind to catch any girl's skirts. Smart dates knew what they were getting into. Nikki was one of them. She had changed into a longer silk dress that night."

"At first, when we looked out over the wall, it was pitch-black. Then our eyes focused 'makai'—to the distant sea."

"A hint of a moonrise was beginning to show, on the horizon."

"It was a new moon… or so I thought. "

Thin cirrus clouds formed, high in the atmosphere, and diffused light from the moon—surrounding it with a slight circular haze—more like a halo.

Nikki laughed, slightly. "Ring around the moon, means rain soon. That's a blessing, in Hawaii."

Lauren nodded. He'd heard that saying before. But somewhere, in the back of his mind, laid another memory—a recollection—something unsettling.

He forced the thought from his mind, turned to Nikki, and laughed. "Yes," he said, my grandmother Bruner told me the same thing."

Lauren and Nikki watched the moon climb higher into the sky. It brightened the surrounding cliffs, and its light sent a glow off far-away waves that crashed on shore, several miles away.

Nikki turned back toward the valley, below.

"Isn't this beautiful?"

"Of course, I answered 'yes'. But I'm sure I was more distracted by her, than by the distant waves we could sometimes hear, between wind gusts. Truly? Both were magical."

As they stood in the moonlight, Nikki explained, what they saw in the distance was the other side of the island. Two areas, named Kailua and Kaneohe.

She pointed out over the cliff.

"It's more country on the windward," she said. "No city lights... just local people. Hawaiian, Japanese, Chinese, and Portagee... most of them living off the land. Usually on small farms of their own."

"There're two bays... and lots of beautiful beaches."

"If I ever settled down, on Oahu, this is where I'd want to live. It's almost like Maui," she said, "...where I grew up."

Lauren had some knowledge about the island of Maui. "The fleet used to moor off of what they called Lahaina Road, when out on maneuvers. We'd pick up a fine sand, from the island... to holystone the ship's teak decks."

Lauren commented on the height of the cliffs, and Nikki recalled what she learned, in school.

"They taught us about the Battle of Nuuanu Pali, and about the most famous of the old kings of Hawaii.

"King Kamehameha the Great," said Lauren.

"Yes... how'd you know?"

"Some local guys I met, on the beach up in Nanakuli, told me about him. He was a heck of a warrior, they said. They called him a warrior of the sea."

Nikki was impressed. "Sort of like you, Lauren, and your ship."

He felt proud she thought of him that way.

"Kamehameha," she went on, "was from the Big Island. Over a hundred years ago, he invaded O'ahu, after defeating the armies on the island of Maui."

"In his fight to become king of all the islands, nearly a thousand war canoes, and over ten thousand warriors landed on Waikiki beach. Then, Kamehameha chased the local warriors, up the Valley, then over these cliffs, to their death."

"How can you remember all this?" said Lauren.

"It's the most famous battle in Hawaii," said Nikki.

"When I was in school, they taught us, a long time ago, that they found over eight hundred bones and even skulls, at the bottom of these cliffs. Hawaiians believe that's why there're so many spirits and ghosts, who live up here."

Then, Nikki took his hand.

"Listen Lauren."

"If you listen closely, they say you can still hear the cries of the warriors… as they jumped over the cliff."

They stood, silent in the dark, holding hands. Lauren listened, but could only hear the wind as it howled past them. Occasionally, a faint crash of waves, slipped through.

"Then" recalled Lauren, "looking out into the valley… I swear I heard a distant cry."

Lauren turned to Nikki. "Did you hear that?"

Nikki, still listening for any sign, shook her head.

"Must've been my imagination." Squeezing her hand, he looked directly into her eyes.

"Do you believe in ghosts and spirits?"

"I think if you have a good heart, Pali spirits are good… and not to fear."

The moment was charged around them.

He wanted to kiss her, but feared it wasn't the right time.

"But damn, I sure wanted to."

Suddenly, a shyness overtook him that had rarely been present before. Kicking himself, inside, he pulled back slightly.

Hand-in-hand, they turned and walked toward the dimly lit tables near the food stands.

"When I was a little girl, on Maui, I always feared Obake, a Japanese ghost who prowled around at night. He wasn't a good ghost. And I knew he was real. Because my grandmother told me stories… they made me afraid."

"As a little girl, I was terrified by stories about him… especially when I sat on the steps of my parent's home, in the plantation's village."

The food stands were over the base of the hill, from the disintegrating Old Pali Road. At the tables, there was more of a gentle breeze. Oddly, they saw feral chickens wandering around the tables, picking at food scraps left behind.

"All right," said Nikki. What should we have for dinner to celebrate your birthday and our first date?"

"Came very close to saying I'd have a hotdog. But instead, asked Nikki what she'd recommend."

Heck I can get a hotdog anytime, anywhere at Pearl.

Nikki suggested a Hawaiian plate lunch, and Lauren agreed. She asked the lady, scooping out their plates, for two 'hashi'—Japanese for chopsticks.

"I ordered Coke. Nikki, green tea. We found an empty picnic table made of roughly hewn planks, and benches slick from so many butts sliding across them."

"Reminded me of sittin' on the old Pineapple Express benches."

"Ya' know how certain things stick in your mind… no matter how long it's been. Hanging above us were colorful Japanese lanterns. They swayed back and fourth, in the breeze, and provided just the amount of light needed, to make our first dinner romantic as hell."

"I could've stayed there with Nikki for the rest of my life. So easy to be with. She seemed to enjoy everything we did that night."

Once seated, Lauren received another lesson in eating with chopsticks. Nikki began by breaking them apart.

"….Then you rub the two wooden sticks together…."

"To make a wish?" Lauren interrupted.

"No… to get any slivers off the wood."

Nikki and Lauren's dinner included teriyaki chicken, rice with gravy, boiled cabbage, and macaroni salad.

"Although I'd been schooled to use chopsticks at Broadway Inn, whenever Nikki served me pupus, this was my first real lesson in how to hold them."

During dinner, and between their laughing at Lauren's fumbling with his chopsticks, Nikki shared how it was to grow up on Maui.

"In Japan, my mother and father were hired to work on the Island of Maui at the Pu'unene Sugar Mill. So they immigrated, as a young married couple, and immediately went to work in the cane fields. That's where I lived and grew up… in the plantation workers camp. I've always thought my parents were brave, coming to a new life, on Maui… having never been there before."

"Wouldn't you say you kinda did the same thing," said Lauren, "…leaving your parents and coming to O'ahu, on your own, to make a living and a new life? I'd say that's pretty brave."

In the dark, Lauren couldn't see Nikki blush. He asked if her parents were still living.

"Yes," she said. "We have a big family. Four brothers, two sisters… all live on Maui. And my brothers still work the fields, alongside my father. My mother takes in laundry, now… from the field workers, who live in the plantation village."

Lauren was captivated by her stories, and wanted to hear more.

"But it was right then," he said, "…and I'll never forget the feeling… knowing I felt so comfortable with her… when I interrupted her story."

"Nikki," I said, "are you working tomorrow? Sunday?"

"No," she happily replied. "Have something in mind? I've got the day off."

"Me too," he answered back. How 'bout we continue our date, and go to the beach?"

Nikki quickly nodded. "Yes. I'd love that."

Lauren's heart beat so hard, he could barely catch his breath. In a split second, both looked forward to more time together.

"Right down there," Nikki pointed past the food stands, "is the Old Pali Road. Let's walk down there."

Lauren was happy to agree. She grabbed his hand and pulled him alongside. They strolled down the path and came to the decaying remains of the first road—cut alongside the cliffs, and used for carriage traffic in the late eighteen-hundreds.

The moon was partially hidden by old trees that hung, like large hands, and stretched out over them from the mountainside. It was much darker and more difficult to see near the steep cliff, on their left.

The wind picked up and whistled eerily across the road, long ago closed to traffic. Hoping not to fall in the dark, Nikki clung to Lauren as they stepped on the old dilapidated, macadam road. It didn't take long for her to have second thoughts.

"Let's do this another time," she said, "...during the day, when we can see better." Lauren agreed and they turned back toward the Pali Lookout, where the moon, and lanterns from the food stands, guided their way.

They approached an older section of the lookout, and a slight glint caught Nikki's eye. In the darkness, alongside the protective railing, she saw a commemorative plaque.

"Look, here," she said.

Curious, Nikki bent close in to read from the old tablet. "I can barely see the words, but..."

Lauren pulled out a Ronson cigarette lighter from his change pocket. He flipped open the cover and snapped down on the thumb-lever, and then held his hand around the flame to protect it from the wind.

"Wait a minute," said Nikki. "There's something, here, that's..." She began to read from the plaque:

> "Pali Road...Constructed in 1897 and opened for public traffic in 1898.... original survey was made by John H. Wilson... W.W. Bruner, Highway Engineer..."

Lauren perked up. "A Bruner's listed there? Let me see."

"Yeah! It says, 'W.W. Bruner, Highway Engineer'. Maybe he's related to you."

Lauren moved closer.

"Don't know... don't remember anyone mentioning him, at home."

"A distant relative," said Nikki, "...maybe he lived here most of his life. Could still be Bruners, somewhere in the islands."

"That'd be somethin', wouldn't it..."

Just then, they heard a bus driver yell out, over the wind, "Last bus to Honolulu. Last bus back to the city."

Lauren glanced at his watch. "Holy cow! It's almost nine-thirty. We'd better catch that bus. I'll end up in the brig if we have to walk."

Nikki grabbed his hand and pulled ahead of him. "Come on. Don't want you to be late."

It didn't take any more convincing to get Lauren going. He couldn't wait for Sunday.

The bus pulled out. Loaded mostly with couples that had come to the lookout, during the evening, they had lingered as long as they could. Nearly every seat was taken.

Lauren managed to convince a single rider to move to another seat, so that he and Nikki could sit together.

They held hands all the way back to town. The light fragrance of her perfume was intoxicating.

With so many couples caught up in their reverie, the ride was considerably more quiet, heading back.

"Secretly, I wished the night would never end," said Lauren. "Funny how long it seemed… getting up to the Pali, from the city. But how all too quickly it went, on the return trip."

The bus dropped its riders off at the same corner where they had earlier come aboard.

Lauren and Nikki walked a short distance to escape the bus fumes, and stopped to linger under a dim street lamp. Neither wanted to speak, for fear the night would end too soon. Finally, Lauren broke the silence.

"I'll walk you to your bus stop."

Nikki told Lauren her apartment was in McCully, and that it bordered on Waikiki. She smiled, as they headed down the block, toward King Street.

"I secretly… or so I thought, kept an eye on my watch, to make certain I'd get back to base on time."

They arrived at Nikki's stop, and waited together for her bus.

"Lauren, you don't have to wait with me. You'd better get back before you get into trouble. I'll be fine," she said. "Really."

Lauren began to protest. No sooner had the words come out of his mouth than headlights from her bus approached.

"I stayed with her until the doors swung open. We said good night and agreed to meet in front of the Broadway Inn, the following morning."

"I'll see you at ten, sharp" he said. She nodded reassurance and stepped onto the bus.

At the first step she turned, leaned down, and kissed him softly on the cheek.

"I had a really good time," she whispered.

The door closed and the bus pulled away. While it disappeared down King Street, the roar of the bus engine, and black smoke from its exhaust, made him feel unsettled.

He dismissed any negative thoughts. She was gone and Lauren missed her, already. It had been a great first date. He couldn't wait for the next morning to arrive.

Lauren glanced at his watch, again. Time had slipped away. "I had only slightly more than an hour to get back to Pearl."

He took off at a good jog—glad for the exercise he got aboard ship. The thought didn't occur to him that he hadn't had a drink, the entire evening, after he met Nikki at the bar.

" I ran at a good pace back down Nuuanu toward Hotel, still dodging foot traffic towards the YMCA… to catch one of the last buses back to base. Reminded me of running track, with Billy, back at Elma High."

"As I ran to beat hell, I noticed a lot fewer sailors on the street."

Not a good sign.

In Lauren's mind, it signaled how close he was to being one of the last left in town.

Another ship's sailor was down on the sidewalk, out cold. Two friends, "…pretty drunk themselves, tried unsuccessfully to get him back on his feet. As much as I wanted to help the poor bastard… and would have if it'd been earlier, I ran into the street to dodge the drunks."

It wasn't a night for Lauren to miss getting back through the main gates before midnight, and have his shore leave taken away, the next day.

He was determined to be with Nikki. "Just the thought of being with her at the beach made me run like a bat outta' hell."

Lauren approached the bus turn-around at the "Y." One packed bus after another began pulling away, before he could get there. Then he noticed a few sailors still sitting across the street, at The Black Cat.

That's a good thing.

Instantly, he relaxed. "They were still tossing down their last beers. And that's when I knew I'd make it back to Pearl in time."

Lines, to get aboard the final buses were long. It was a crapshoot to see which one might still have room.

"I wasn't certain which one I'd take until a familiar voice called out. It was my crewmate, Alvin Dvorak."

"Hey, Bruner! Over here" he yelled, leaning out a window of the third bus in line. "I gotta' seat for ya'."

"Funny… his words were unclear, but I was damned happy he called out."

Once on the bus, he moved to an empty seat next to Dvorak. Lauren nudged him on the shoulder.

"Thanks, Alvin. You saved my butt," he said.

"Hey… *Arizona* sticks together," he slurred. Then, he leaned against the window and closed his eyes.

Just as Lauren sat down, the driver turned off the lights and the bus jerked forward. It followed a line of buses and taxis as each vehicle jockeyed out onto the Honolulu/Pearl Harbor Road.

A bus ride back to base was always an adventure.

"That night, I had a totally different buzz on than most of my traveling companions. My senses were much more heightened and alert than most guys heading back to base."

As they rode in the dark, all manners of sound effects emitted.

"Snoring, retching, farting, laughing, cussing, and everything in between. A couple sailors still drank in the back. And once I heard the sound of a bottle break against the floor."

Thinking Dvorak was asleep, Lauren didn't want to wake him. But nearly five minutes into the trip, Alvin spoke up.

"Where ya' been? Didn't see ya' at Smiths." He didn't wait for an answer.

"Bet ya' been out again with that good lookin' workin' girl I seen you with, at Wo Fats a few weeks back? The one in those sexy dresses and black nylons?"

It took Lauren a moment to figure out who Alvin was talking about.

It sure as hell wasn't Nikki.

Then it occurred to him. Alvin was talking about his friend, June, who'd left the islands a couple of months before—well before he began to think about Nikki.

June must already be back home in Chicago. No one there would ever know her like the sailors and Marines did... on Canal Street.

"No," Lauren answered. "You're thinking of June. We were just friends. She's already left for the mainland."

"Her father and his banker friends told her war's on the way and demanded she come home from… what he *thought* was 'college' at the University of Hawaii. Put her on the Lurline, myself."

As quickly as Lauren had answered Alvin's question, he was snoring again.

Two Marines sat behind them. One tapped Lauren's shoulder.

"Hey Bruner," he said, "how in hell did you ever end up with a babe like that? My friends and me hated your ass, whenever we saw you and that beautiful lady at Forbidden City."

"Yeah, I remember you assholes," Lauren answered.

"Shit Bruner," said the Marine, "Don't know what ya' did. Or what you're made of… but every time June, was with us, and you walked through the door… she'd *always* get up and leave our table… just to be with you. You som'bitch."

"Shut the hell up," Dvorak suddenly piped in, "and stop listening to our conversation."

"We all broke out laughing," said Lauren. "Figured Alvin was asleep. I knew, then, he was just playing possum but listening to every word."

Alvin told Lauren he'd been in town with his friend, Ed Bodey, Boatswain's Mate Second Class. Bodey shared the same crew quarters as Alvin, and was staying at the Y, with an overnight pass. He explained they'd been out drinking and carousing—making their way between the Black Cat and Smith's Union, then back to the Black Cat, in order for Dvorak to catch one of the last buses.

Lauren asked Dvorak if he'd heard of the Pali Look Out.

"I was surprised by his answer," said Lauren. "He'd heard of it, all right. Said it was supposed to be haunted by spirits, from long ago."

"No one'll ever get me up there," Dvorak had said. "My grandfather, back in Minnesota, told me stories about the dead… and how they'd hang around places where they died… 'specially when their deaths were in battle."

"You know me pretty good, Lauren," said Dvorak. "Not much scares me. But ghosts? Shit! Ain't gonna' mess with 'em."

Instantly, Lauren recalled Nikki's conversation about the Warriors, chased over the cliffs by King Kamehameha. And how their spirits still hung around.

At that moment, a cold chill hit him.

"Though a warm night… with my undershirt soaked with sweat, from my run back to the bus… I still got goose bumps."

Then it dawned on Lauren. The image, in his mind—of the moon rising over the Pali—took him back, as a young boy, when he'd visit his grandmother Bruner, in Sundance, Wyoming.

One night, he'd sat with her in a yard swing while she told him of an old Indian legend about the moon.

"The way my grandmother explained it… a certain kind of moon rising… kinda' like the moon, at the Pali… would bring on death."

"Her story was different, of course, from the evening I spent with Nikki. Even if we *were* surrounded by spirits."

Dvorak was, again, leaning against the window—snoring. "This time," said Lauren, "it was for real… and loud."

Looking out, past Alvin, Lauren watched the moon's glow cast light and shadows on the streets and buildings of Honolulu.

"Though it was a different time and a different moon," he said. "…to me they looked pretty much the same." It was then, his grandmother's words came flooding back.

"She had said that, when a moon rose in the sky… and was full… with a halo around its edges, the Indians believed some tragic event was sure to follow."

She told me it was nothing to take lightly. "The Indians of Wyoming," she had said, "called that type of moon a 'death moon'."

According to Lauren's grandmother, "a death moon" meant tragedy was sure to follow. "Death was on its way to visit," she had said.

Lauren hadn't thought much more about her story. After all, he was only a kid at the time.

"There was nothing that could derail my thoughts of Nikki and I at the Pali. I was flying pretty high. I even decided I wouldn't wash the cheek that Nikki kissed.

"Her kiss would be my good luck charm. Even if there was some truth to the Indian legend, I was sure it wouldn't visit me. I had destiny on my side."

"Little could I have imagined how wrong I'd be."

— —

11:54 pm

The bus approached Pearl Harbor's main gates. Each time the driver took his turn to pull forward, toward the front of the line, the bus jerked a little, with each release of the clutch.

Lauren hated to wake Dvorak. But he gave him a good nudge and glanced down at his watch.

"Six minutes to spare, Alvin."

Lauren couldn't be more content. Not only had his first date with Nikki gone well, but he 'd make it back to base before lockdown.

"All in all," he said, "it was a hell of an evening. I figured, though, as excited as I was to meet Nikki in the morning… I wouldn't get much sleep that night."

As was the case, the last launch out to *Arizona* always transported a sad group back to the ship. Some were "knock-down-drunk"—held upright by their friends. A couple, out cold—lying amongst the dirt and water spray, on the launches deck.

"You can imagine," said Lauren, "…for some, they were dirty as hell… and had screwed up their dress whites big time."

"Alvin, of course, had really tied one on. Amazingly, he was able to function. I just knew… his head was gonna' hurt like hell in the morning."

Lauren hadn't had a drink since having a beer at Smith's Union while waiting for Nikki, early in the evening.

"I was one of the first off the ship's launch, and up the gangway in a flash. Alvin took my lead and followed, close behind."

Lauren handed the Officer of the Deck his liberty card and signed aboard.

"You not feeling well, Bruner?" said the Marine on deck. "I don't smell a thing on ya' and you're standin' straight up."

"Never felt better," answered Lauren. He saluted the OOD and acknowledged the Marine.

He walked the deck, toward aft; stood on the rail with a smoke; and gazed out at thousands of lights, on the ships. Their reflections, throughout the harbor, accompanied a new mood.

Though a beautiful sight, for a moment his thoughts turned to those caught up in the war in Europe. And "… that little guy with the mustache who believed everyone with blond hair and blue eyes was better than everyone else."

"I figured this guy was crazier than hell, 'cause he'd never seen my girl."

Turning away from the railing, Lauren nearly flicked his cigarette butt over the side. But he caught himself, in time—realizing he'd be in a world of trouble if he'd let that butt fly. Quickly, he pulled out his snuffbox, rubbed the butt out, closed its top, and returned it to his waistband.

Lauren glanced once again at the moon, thinking of his grandmother, and of the old Indian's legend.

— —

Once inside crew quarters, next to gun turret two, Lauren got out his cot and undressed in the dim light. He sat on the cot's edge and, as his eyes adjusted, stared at cold, hard, steel walls.

Surprisingly, there was comforting warmth, inside, he'd never felt before.

"I thought how much I'd really grown to like Nikki, more than anyone else I'd ever met. She was a woman who could change a man's life."

What would it be like, to spend the rest of my life in Hawaii… living out in the country… raising a brood of kids… with Nikki?

The idea began to grow on him.

"So what if I'm only twenty-one? Hell, my father married mother when she was seventeen."

His thoughts turned to Nikki, again.

No matter what else happens, I'll never forget tonight.

Silently, the memory of Nikki's kiss on his cheek, would stalk him through the night. And for years to come.

With his thoughts of an evening, like no other, he finally lay down, and closed his eyes—with a sense that, somehow, his and Nikki's lives were about to change forever.

— —

SECOND TO THE LAST TO LEAVE

USS *Arizona* Entering Pearl Harbor 5 December 1941

"This artwork depicts USS Arizona entering Pearl Harbor on the afternoon of 5 December 1941, returning from a week of maneuvers. I was on the ship as it passed these sailors shown standing at the channel's edge near the Naval Hospital at Hospital Point. Like the rest of the crew, I was looking forward to a cold beer and Cinderella Liberty.

As compared to the artwork showing USS Arizona At Full Dress in Chapter 2, this artwork illustrates how Arizona looked after its last retrofitting. One noticable difference is that at the time of this drawing we carried three single-wing Vought Kingfisher planes, rather than the old double-winged Curtiss Seagulls which are shown in the earlier artwork.

My friend Lou Conter was the Helmsman bringing Arizona into the harbor channel that early afternoon and heard the conversation between Admiral Kidd and Captain Van Valkenburgh, who were standing alongside in the wheelhouse.

According to Lou, Admiral Kidd told the captain that he felt something was wrong, as this was the first time that he had ever seen all the battle wagons in port at the same time, and he didn't like it one bit. Sure makes you wonder."

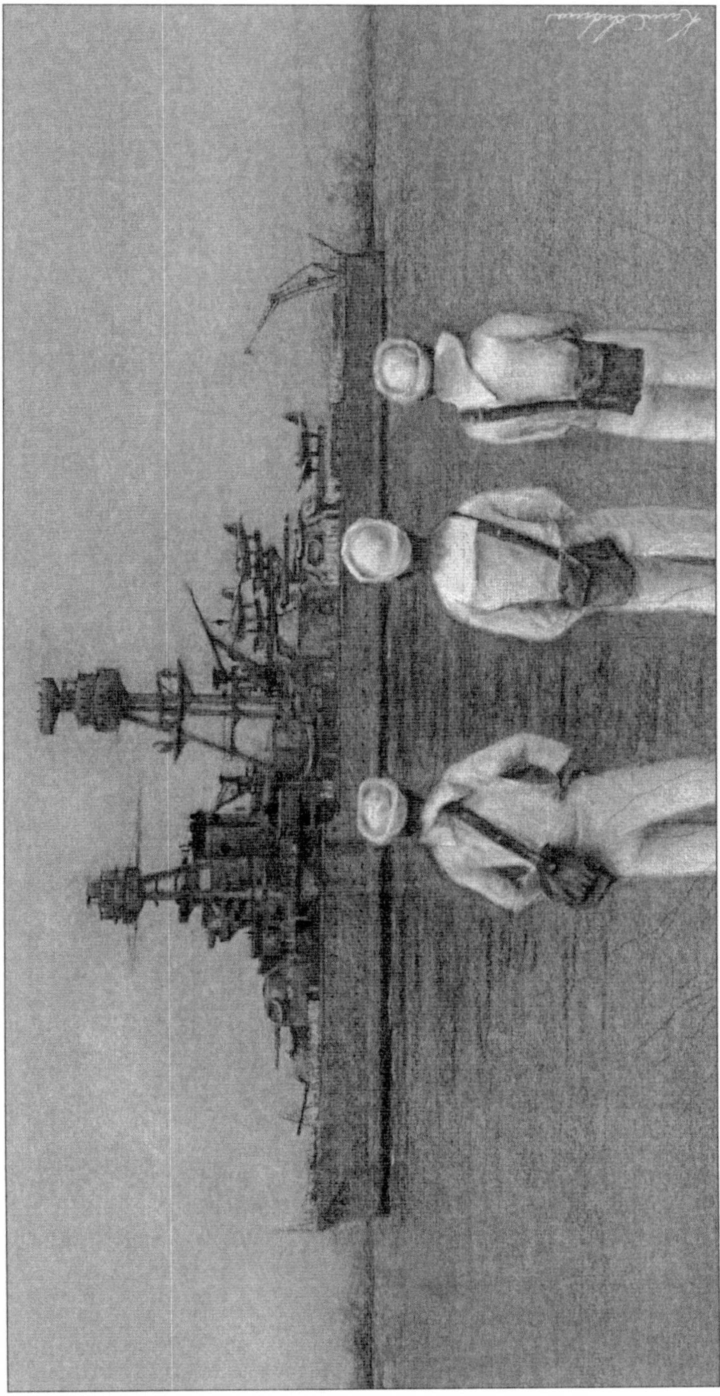

USS *Arizona* Passing Hospital Point While Entering Pearl Harbor
Just After Noon, Two Days Before the Attack

Michiko "Nikki" Takahashi

"**Michiko Takahashi** *was a bartender at the Broadway Inn when we first met. I was working shore patrol and was walking through the bar when she called out to me and asked if I wanted a beer.*

'Nikki', as I remember her, was small in height, and I would guess about 5'4". She had black, shiny hair that hung down to her shoulders, copper-colored skin, and brown, beautiful eyes. Although I never knew her exact age, I learned later in the War from Harry Yamada, who owned the bar, that she was older than I was by at least a couple of years, but she sure didn't look it.

To me, she was always just Nikki, and on the night before the attack I thought I was falling in love. I never thought of Nikki as being Japanese, but instead only a beautiful young woman who was easy to talk to, and boy was I ever looking forward to spending Sunday, 7 December with her at Waikiki Beach.

This portrait of Nikki was created from my memory, working with the artist Karin Andrino, and turned out exactly as I remember her. Life is funny sometimes, as depending on the road you are forced to take, it can change everything including dreams of what might have been."

Michiko Takahashi Nikki

Michiko "Nikki" Takahashi

Bartender

The Broadway Inn

Chapter 10
7 DECEMBER 1941

0450

"This was one morning I didn't need reveille," said Lauren. "My mind was already up and at 'em. In spite of my lack of sleep, I wasn't one bit tired."

Eyes wide open, they automatically adjusted to the dim light in Lauren's crew quarters. It felt as if only moments had passed since he'd shut them.

The fragrance of Nikki's perfume, overrode Lauren's senses—even in the hull of *Arizona,* despite persistent smells of the harbor—and an aroma given off by twenty or more crew members, all of whom had baked beans and cornbread for breakfast the day before, as they did every Saturday morning.

A cool breeze slipped through the doors and portholes—always hatched down and watertight when battle stations sounded, but wide open while in port. "They helped create a cross-breeze through crew compartments, from one side of the ship to the other."

In close quarters, surrounding the base of Gun Turret Two, little escaped Lauren's mind, from the night before.

He recalled the brief moment Nikki had fallen asleep during the bus ride back from the Pali—her head on his shoulder—after a long day's shift at Broadway Inn. Then, an embarrassed look on her face when she realized what had happened. Japanese women were brought up to exhibit modesty and decorum. Even working as a bartender at Broadway Inn hadn't changed that.

But Nikki had been comfortable in his presence. And he could recall the electric touch of her hand in his, as the bus bent around the winding curves of the old road, before it reached the Pali highway that headed back into Honolulu.

A fart from Zimmerman interrupted his thoughts. To Lauren, these things never seemed to change. He'd heard them everyday since joining *Arizona*.

Heavy breathing a variety of melodies from snoring an occasional shout from a sailor's dream or a woman's name called out—a girlfriend or a favorite working girl.

"Of course," Lauren said, "it didn't stop there. More than occasional creeks and groans accompanied sounds from men moving around on their cots. Tall, short… men of all sizes… feet hangin' over the edge. All trying to sleep on too small a Navy-issue bed… if you could call a cot a bed."

"Wasn't one to complain, though. Cots were a hellava' lot better than the hammocks we once called home. Thank God they replaced them, earlier in the year."

"Ever live under the landing pattern for an airport, or next to a railroad track? Eventually, the sounds disappear… unless you can't sleep. Anyone kept awake by night sounds, surrounding Gun Turret Two, generally handed out a few taunts to the perpetrators, at breakfast, the next morning."

Lauren's mind switched to fast track—and plans for the day. In his mind, it would be the first full day with the only woman with whom he'd ever developed the feeling of a true relationship.

Time couldn't pass quick enough. He shut his eyes, once more, and thoughts turned to how Nikki might look in a swimsuit. He fantasized about the day ahead, and wondered what it might be like lying next to her.

"What'd they say? Something I remember from high school... 'We are such stuff as dreams are made of?' From the moment Nikki first greeted me, with her bedroom eyes, I sure as hell wanted to get her into bed, someday."

"Just not in the way others might think. She was different... she was smart and exotic. But I was a little worried about what she might think of my haole ass."

"Suppose you might say... Nikki was the first and only local girl I ever dated. For a hundred or more reasons, I was hooked."

0530

Lauren had remained on his cot for a good forty minutes, daydreaming typical fantasies of most young men. Then, reveille blared over the P.A. System. It was followed by the typical moans and groans, from the men.

"Especially," said Lauren, "from those with hangovers. Reveille came much too soon for them."

Regardless of the rude awakening, in Lauren's mind, nothing would keep this day from being as special, or more so, than the night before.

He was convinced it'd be a day to remember. But with reality setting it, time slowed to a crawl. "My second date with Nikki... and I was rarin' to go. But it was a case of 'hurry up and wait.' "

One of the first out of bed, it would still be four and a half hours before he'd see her, again.

For several moments, Lauren stood in Navy-issued boxer shorts and t-shirt, looking around their quarters. Nearly everyone's eyes remained closed. "In retrospect" he'd later say, "near where I stood in my underwear, would turn out to be historic, in relation to events that followed."

"Normally, I'd still be snoring like the others. On Sundays, even after reveille sounded, we'd usually catch a few extra minutes of shuteye. Eventually... the Master of Arms would patrol through quarters, swinging his nightstick against any sleeping sailor's cot. Our daily reminder we were still in the Navy."

Twenty men or more, from Fire Control, considered their quarters at Gun Turret Two to be home. Spread around nearly a third of the distance, attached to the outer walls of the turret, their personal lockers—and bins, for stowing cots and bedding—were fastened to its base.

Lauren's eyes adjusted to the brighter light, turned up after reveille. With a mental list of things to accomplish, prior to leaving the ship, he immediately rolled mattress and blanket, together, with his Navy-issue pillow "…if you can call it that," then folded, wrapped, and stowed the entire rack in the bed bin, for the day.

Upon enlistment, to prevent mix-ups, the Navy issued a stencil to every sailor. They were expected to use a small paintbrush to apply their names and serial numbers in black, indelible ink on all personal items—from bedding to clothing.

"If we didn't properly mark and stow our personal articles, or an item was left around quarters, it was considered 'gear adrift'… especially if it was left unmarked. As the saying went, 'Gear adrift is a gift'. You might never see that item again."

Lauren made certain his name and serial number was stenciled on everything, including the inside of his cap.

"Our caps had to be worn just right... straight across and just above the eyes. But most sailors only wore it regulation-style while aboard ship… or to get permission for liberty. Once off... they wore it all different ways. Pushed back... or tilted to the side…. anyway they could to make themselves look 'slangish'. Mostly to stand out more to any girls they met."

"A few early risers were up, besides myself… mostly those who, for whatever reason, didn't take liberty the night before."

In t-shirt, shorts, and old flip-flops, Lauren grabbed his shaving kit and a towel "…and headed for the head."

He was one of the first to shower; then moved across the hall to grab a sink. There, in the polished steel mirror, he remembered the kiss. The one by Nikki, the night before. A wide grin crossed his face. He recalled the promise to himself, not to wash that cheek, again. Still, he had to shave—and did so—figuring there'd be plenty more kisses to come.

Afterwards, he patted on Old Spice aftershave "…and added a little extra for good luck."

Lauren stowed his shaving gear and towel, and pulled out a clean change of clothes—uniform of the day being white shorts and a clean t-shirt.

He glanced back inside his locker.

"Funny what goes through your mind, when you've got an agenda for the day. Not much special to note…. Some letters from home, and a few from Marcella Stapleton, the girl I'd dated in Los Angeles. She kept writing… though I didn't know why. Here I was, in Hawaii… twenty-five hundred miles away."

"Marcella was nice, and I appreciated her letters, especially when I hadn't heard from home. But hell… it wasn't like I'd planned to marry her. My new life was in Hawaii, maybe even livin' in the country.

"After meeting Nikki, I was reminded, again, why they called the islands 'paradise.' "

Lauren rolled up his swimsuit and a clean towel, for the beach, and tossed them into a small canvas duffle.

When ready to go ashore after church services, I'll just grab the bag and head out.

He checked his billfold, to make certain he had enough cash for the day. It was tossed into the bag, along with a handful of coins he'd kept in a metal box.

Lauren reached for his Elgin watch and buckled the leather band around his left wrist. "A graduation present from mother and John," he said. "Must've cost thirty-seven bucks, at the time. Even Clarence chipped in with money earned from driving a road-paving truck.

"That ol' watch saved my ass a hundred times before. Don't know how often I mighta' lost my next liberty, if I hadn't paid attention to the time."

Lauren shut the locker, and was about to turn the combination dial, when he realized he'd forgotten his smokes. Quickly, he grabbed a pack of Camels, a couple of *Arizona* matchbooks, and his snuffbox, for stowing butts.

As was his habit, he rolled the small snuffbox into his t-shirt's left sleeve, and the Camels into the right sleeve.

By this time, only half of Fire Control Division had started to move around quarters. "The other half," said Lauren, "well… they weren't much trying. So, I headed up to the main deck, for a smoke."

On the way out, he passed by Zeke Zimmerman's cot. A member of Lauren's battle station, in the port-side anti-aircraft director, Zeke was still asleep.

'Zeke," Lauren shouted, "rise and shine. Gonna be a beautiful day." And he kept walking.

"Hell of a good guy, that Zeke… though I'd never met *anyone* who took more showers, in a day, than him. Before breakfast, after lunch, before dinner and again, before bed… musta' been some habit he developed from growin' up in the Midwest. We'd constantly kid 'im about it… suspecting he'd do anything to get out of work."

0620

Lauren's thoughts returned to Nikki, as he headed out through the hatch door. "In fact," he said, "she's *all* I could think about. That... and the fact I just knew I'd remember our second date, forever.

"Little could I have imagined... it'd be for all the wrong reasons."

Lauren walked out onto the deck. Having been cooped up in close quarters, all night, he took in a good breath of fresh air.

"Well... as fresh as it could be for a naval harbor."

It had rained during the night, after he'd returned to ship.

Nothing new for the islands.

The decks were shiny-wet and reflected the ship's lights in the still darkened shadows of *Arizona's* bulkheads.

As he walked aft, Lauren was certain it'd be a beautiful day for the beach. He approached the aft deck.

Not many people up and about.

"But that's when I saw the old man. Admiral Kidd, himself... out for his morning exercise, walking the deck at a pretty good clip."

"Two details gave him away," said Lauren. "His big hat and his Shadow Marine, following beside."

Shit!

For a moment Lauren looked for a means to avoid the Admiral. But no easy way existed to dodge a possible confrontation.

The Admiral's uniform was soaked with some sweat. This was the first time Lauren had seen him this early.

"Although it had rained and the morning was already warm, I couldn't tell if the heat was getting to him, or if the old man had really hauled ass around that deck."

Admiral Kidd and Bruner continued to approach each other, "...like two freight trains about to crash," said Lauren.

We had no choice.

"Immediately I stopped, stood at attention... as Kidd began to pass, and gave him my best salute."

The Admiral returned it.

"Figured I'd narrowly avoided danger... and was just about to drop my salute and resume walking, when Kidd came to a dead halt and turned to me."

"At ease, sailor."

Lauren observed his Shadow Marine was in full uniform "...sweating like a stuffed pig."

"Then," said Lauren, "I detected a slight smile from the Admiral."

"Aren't you Bruner, from Fire Control?"

"Yes, sir," Lauren replied.

The Admiral's smile grew, slightly.

"Is *Arizona's* name on the aft hull clean this morning?"

"Yes, sir," Lauren repeated. "I'm sure it is, Admiral."

In an instant, Lauren flashed-back to when he'd been "dogged" for over-the-side duty to polish and keep clean the ship's name—often reserved as a punishment for hijinks performed on board.

He realized the Marine wasn't carrying his rifle. "Even when the Admiral dressed me down, the son of a bitch's right hand still rested on top of his leather holster... and his forty-five sidearm. It both pissed me off and scared me a little."

"What the hell! Did he really think anyone would attack and do bodily harm to the old man?"

"No one was so stupid that they'd attack a Rear Admiral. But that's the Navy for ya'. Always prepared, with nothing left to chance..."

Then Admiral Kidd turned and resumed walking. His bodyguard couldn't resist giving Lauren one more "stink-eye."

"Little did either of us think that'd be the final encounter between me and the Admiral… or his body guard."

Lauren continued his walk aft. He smiled at the Admiral's joke, and how months before, his hi-jinks had got him in trouble and left an impression. "… a deep enough opinion," said Lauren, "that the Admiral remembered my name outta' the ship's crew of fifteen hundred."

He'd heard scuttlebutt about Admiral Kidd's morning walks, two or three times around the ships deck, for exercise. "Never thought it important enough," he said, "to get outta' the sack, as early as the admiral, to confirm any truth to the rumors. "They were obviously true."

There was more activity, as Lauren approached the ship's stern. Members of the Fourth Division Deck Force were already unfurling the canvas for church services, while others were beginning to place chairs in rows.

Lauren asked a chief in charge for permission to borrow a chair, to sit for a smoke.

"Sure kid," said a chief. "Just put it back in line when you're finished."

Funny, I can still remember that chief's name… Barth. DeWayne Barth. I ran into him once at a Survivor's reunion, and we remembered each other… "Just before the world went to hell," I remember him saying.

Lauren grabbed a chair and moved to the farthest end of the ship. He settled it close to the chain railing, and sat—one foot resting on the lowest chain.

Fully relaxed, and with time to kill, he knocked out a cigarette and lit up—making certain that even the dead match was stowed.

Though it had been dark, when he'd come out on deck, the morning sky was slowly turning blue-gray. Looking down the ship's side, the suns rays barely popped up over the distant mountains. "As the sky began to brighten, I could see clouds and a rain shower on the horizon."

A damned pretty sight.

And to think... Uncle Sam pays me to be here. Hell... not much could be better. Pretty much exactly what the recruiter had promised.

With time on his hands, he reviewed the coming day in his mind. First, he'd relax with a cigarette, followed by breakfast, then he'd bide his time attending church services.

Afterwards he'd retrieve the canvas bag, loaded with his suit and towel, from his locker. Later, he'd catch a launch, and a bus into Honolulu from the Main Gate. He planned to be early, so Nikki wouldn't have to wait.

Lauren was confident the day would be special.

After all, with a good-looking lady—that I was falling for—how can anything go wrong?

"Didn't know much about hormones, in those days," said Lauren. "But in hindsight, I guarantee mine were running at a pretty good clip, that morning."

Lauren glanced right, down battleship row, then back again at USS *Nevada,* behind him.

Life can't get much sweeter than this.

He inhaled a final drag off his Camel, crushed out the butt, and joined it with the match. A gentle breeze carried his last trail of smoke out across the water. He picked up the chair, turned to leave and, on the spur of the moment, leaned out over the side to check *Arizona's* name—painted on the ship's hull.

Yep... it's clean, all right.

He recalled a much earlier chance meeting with the Admiral, and laughed out loud. "It sure as hell wasn't our first encounter."

The thought touched off memories of how he'd been assigned to clean the ship's name, as punishment for screwing around with the Admiral while cleaning the yardarms—the two long poles jutting out from the main mast that rose high over Admiral's Kidd's deck, and Lauren's Director.

"In the early days aboard *Arizona*," said Lauren, "when we'd pull into port, I'd have to shimmy out to the tip's end of the yardarm… hangin' out there with my skinny ass and a bucket of soap and water… about sixty feet above the Admiral's bridge… tied only by a rope around my waist."

"Imagine what it was like, first headin' out to the far end, over dirt, sea salt, bird shit… and crap tossed up by the ship's smoke stack. Then, I'd have to shimmy backwards, over the same crap, as I cleaned each yardarm with a huge sponge.

"By the time I finished, I was covered head-to-toe in all that smelly shit."

"One day, just for the hell of it, I dropped a wet, soapy sponge from high above the Admiral's deck. Just missed 'im… but splashed his Marine."

"At that point, I yelled down, 'Sorry, sir, it slipped.' They both looked up. If looks could kill, I'd been dead. I got away with that shenanigan the first time."

"The second time… not so much. All hell broke loose and I ended up hanging from a boatswain's chair over the ship's side, cleaning her name…"

"Five days a week, for a month."

"Can laugh at it now," he said. "But it probably wasn't my finest hour. Such is youth… tempting the fates to find out what you can or can't get away with."

0647

Lauren returned the chair to the line, and glanced at his watch.

Breakfast on the table in ten minutes. Then… only a couple more hours' wait.

Back in crew quarters, everything would be changed from when he'd left. All cots would be stowed; he'd find part of his division seated at the mess tables, pulled down from the ceiling. Several men would be reading the morning paper; at least one writing a letter home."

"The thought reminded me... I'd better write to Mother, to avoid any further shit. Didn't want her complaining to the captain, again, that her son never sent letters home.

"She did that, once," he said. "And I took a good dressing down for it."

"Why the hell she thought to write that letter, I'll never know."

"After my father died and Mother gave me away… around age five… she never bothered to write… for almost ten years. Not one single line."

"Anyway… didn't need that shit coming down around me again, so I tucked it in the back of my mind, and was determined, that night or the next morning, to write her a short note."

"Hell… I guess, at the time, I loved her. But I felt that's all she deserved, after farming me out as a kid."

Then, the devil in him took over, for a brief moment. What if he wrote to let his mother know he was dating a Japanese girl?

That would certainly stir up the pot, and sure as hell give the family something to talk about.

"In those days… in our small lumber town, it would've definitely rocked the boat." Fortunately, Lauren thought better of the idea. *No sense to cause grief within the family… or give Mother a heart attack.*

"What she didn't know wouldn't hurt either of us."

0655

By now, all three tables were nearly filled—waiting for breakfast. Lauren took his regular place, with sailors of a higher rank. One table was reserved just for "lowly seamen."

"In the pecking order, you won't sit with a Seaman First Class… a member of the deck force. Been there, done that, back in thirty-nine."

"Ya' have to understand… when you've taken meals with the same group of guys, three times a day a couple of years… it's nothing special. Hell, there's almost no talkin' other than maybe sports, or just shootin' the breeze."
"Like the night before, in Honolulu, there was a big local football playoff between two stateside college teams. I recall talkin' about that game. But other than being in the same division, we had little in common. We usually just ate and got outta' there.

"With the exception of 'Zeke' Zimmerman, most of the other guys worked in the starboard director or on gun crews. So the two of us felt closer with our own port-side fire control crew… what with six of us being crammed into that small workspace, day-after day, while on duty."

"Zeke was the only one I was near, at breakfast."

I recall looking across the table at him, a couple of times, and saying one thing or another. Not much else.

"He was a good looking fella. But I couldn't understand why the guy always bitched and moaned about not being able to meet a girl. Shit… ten thousand sailors and Marines were all thinking the same thing. You had to *do* something about it."

"Easier said than done. So I was happy for shore patrol duty, and the opportunity to meet the women I did."

"For the life of me, though, I couldn't figure how come… a country boy like me, from the backwoods of Washington, didn't have the same problem. 'Course, I was pretty full of myself… especially that morning. Hell, I had a date with a local girl who kissed me goodnight, just hours before."

"Looking back, the furthest thing from my mind was any thought my world could possibly change… in less than an hour."

"There I was… finishing up my second cup of java. No idea of how the day would eventually go… and oblivious to the fact that I'd be caught at its epicenter, mere feet from where I sat."

Just then, visitors interrupted the crew's banter.

"Now… few people know," said Lauren, "on the evening of December sixth, *Arizona's* crew was temporarily expanded by a dozen unknown Marines… 'boots,' they called them… who'd just come aboard from sea school. This occurred from time-to-time, with young recruits."

"On this particular Sunday morning… a Marine showed up outside our crew quarter's door, with about four or five guys from that group. The Marine let us know that the boots had come aboard Saturday night. "*Arizona* has the room and extra bunks," he said. "So they're bunking with us until tomorrow morning."

"Seeing space where he could squeeze a couple more men in, at the table," said Lauren, "the Marine told us to 'make room'. And two bushy-tailed young Marines sat down and shared what would be our only breakfast, together."

"Some of the guys felt obliged to haze the recruits a bit. Being a little green around the edges, it wasn't difficult to poke fun at 'em while waiting out official assignments to their first ships. If it hadn't been breakfast, one of the sailors mighta' pranked the new recruits by tasking 'em to go find a chief on deck, and ask for an Eye-Dee-Ten-Tango Form… "

" 'And step on it', they'd say."

"Kind of a cheap in-joke, for more hardened sailors to have fun at the expense of inexperienced recruits," said Lauren. "If you write out the abbreviation, 'I-D-10-T', it spells 'Idiot.' Fortunately, for these kids, no one brought it up."

Rising from the table, Lauren glanced at one of the unassigned recruits. It occurred to him, *how the hell young the kid look*ed.

But on board any ship, age and maturity levels are separated only by degrees.

Just then, the young man looked up. Lauren nodded to the recruit, and gave a smile of reassurance.

"I was certain my three years on him, at age twenty-one, made me a hell of a lot more seasoned."

0747

Lauren left crew quarters, again. This time, for Protestant church services, back on the ship's fantail. Out on deck, he was greeted with the sound of *Arizona's* band practicing for Morning Colors. It would mark the official beginning of our day. The bugler's Church Call would sound shortly after.

Most of the teak deck was still damp from overnight showers. The morning sun had begun to dry out the wood, as Lauren watched steam rise from its surface. The resulting mist seemed to cleanse his soul. As he had earlier, he paused to take in another deep breath of fresh air, and then found a dry spot to sit and tighten his right shoelace.

Leaning against a bulkhead, he looked out across the harbor. The sun lit up the surrounding mountains, behind, and reflected off the water—a golden color that had inspired young sailors for thousands of years.

For the first time, since joining the Navy, he was relaxed and at-ease about himself; his determination strengthened by his surroundings.

Unaware it was the last moment in his life he'd have that feeling, for a long time, Lauren felt on top of the world.

Nothing could go wrong.

— —

SECOND TO THE LAST TO LEAVE

Rear Admiral Isaac C. Kidd

Isaac Campbell Kidd was born to Isaac and Inez Nellie (Campbell) Kidd on 26 March 1884 in Cleveland, Cuyahoga County, Ohio. He graduated from high school and was appointed a Midshipman on 23 September 1902, and then went on to graduate from the U.S. Naval Academy in Annapolis, Maryland in 1906 as an Ensign.

Isaac Kidd reported to USS *Arizona* on 17 September 1938, and was the ship's captain when Lauren Bruner joined the crew. Captain Kidd was promoted to Rear Admiral on 7 January 1940. **On 7 December 1941, Rear Admiral Isaac Campbell Kidd was 57 years, 8 months and 11 days old.**

"Rear Admiral Kidd was all Navy and most of the crew was scared to death of him, myself included. Less than three hours before the attack, he and I had our last conversation together on deck, just as the sun was coming up. Thinking back on it now I guess it was less of a conversation on my part, as the Admiral did all the talking, with me just standing at attention, saluting, and answering 'Yes, sir.' "

Rear Admiral Isaac C. Kidd

USS *Arizona*

KIA

Chapter 11
99 MINUTES OF HELL

The day was typical of most Hawaiian mornings Lauren could recall, since arriving in Pearl Harbor nearly two years prior. Except for his thoughts about Nikki, and their day ahead, it was shaping up to be a pretty routine morning.

The sun was up... already a balmy 74 degrees... expected to climb to around 84, by afternoon.

Perfect weather for me and Nikki to spend at beach, he thought.

The surrounding mountain's beauty was distracting, for the moment. He took it all in, as he had most mornings, while in port.

Lauren had learned to appreciate the difference between the natural splendor found in the islands of Hawaii, and the beauty of his youth-filled surroundings, back in Washington—now world's away from his boyhood days.

Thoughts momentarily turned to his best friend, Billy Mann, and their endless hours spent hanging out and running track together, in high school.

Not to mention hanging around *Arizona* on days off, or double dating, on leave. He made a mental note to spend some time with Billy… *when we return to Long Beach next week.*

Compared to the last few months of rigorous battle readiness drills, this Sunday would be a walk in the park for Lauren. Since returning, following refitting and overhaul, in Bremerton, Washington in early July, "…our crew had been involved in intensive training."

"Scuttlebutt was heavy about the growing tensions in the Pacific, and we participated in heavy drilling. Often, we had mock air attacks that originated off the carrier, *Enterprise*. And our director's crew felt we were pretty much battle-ready for anything that might come our way."

But for now, Lauren could relax and take in the cool morning prior to heading for shore.

Dissonant musical notes floated out over the water, while *Arizona's* individual band members warmed up for morning colors.

Sitting against the bulkhead, he reflected on his early days in the Navy. Endless mornings after exercises, bleaching the teak decks—almost pure white from constant holystoning of the surface. In the rising sun, the deck's displayed a special shine that came from using salt water to wash away the fine sand used for scrubbing.

These days, he could sit back and watch the new scrubs as they scoured away. And he quietly appreciated how far he'd come since graduating Fire Control School.

Lauren figured he'd lucked out after high school. He had struggled with math. And he needed help to get through his Navy exams.

It was his principal, Mr. Shank at Elma High in Washington, who came to the rescue. Lauren recalled the tutoring he received by mail, after requesting his help. "Will always appreciate what that man did for me while in training, and movin' up the ladder."

Lauren sat on the main deck's port side that looked south and east, along Battleship Row. Clouds remained over the distant mountains. And he recalled Hawaiian lore, telling of rain showers that always brought blessings.

"If that were the case", said Lauren, "and I had no reason to doubt it, at the time… I could look forward to my own personal blessing, that day."

"For me, it included the anticipation of seeing Nikki in a swimsuit."

Just imagining her figure at the beach in a swimsuit brought on a grin. The realization hit him—he was looking forward to their day together, and he could feel his own smile. Lauren glanced around to see if anyone was looking. He was alone in his reflections.

Bruner checked his watch.

Time to head aft.

His thoughts turned back to meeting Nikki in front of Broadway Inn. *This day could begin the next chapter of my life.*

"Truth be told", said Lauren, "the only reason I was heading to church services… I couldn't meet Nikki 'til ten. Still a couple hours away, at the time. Figured church services would take a good hour, following morning colors."

For the first time since joining the Navy, Lauren felt charged with a new energy he'd never felt before. Even a distant hum in the air couldn't distract him. Romantic memories would linger for decades.

"But it was at that moment," he said, "a stranger named 'Fate'… who I'd come to know, stepped back into my life."

Whomp! A vague sound cluttered his mind.

"It sounded like thunder. And I thought it must've been the thunderclouds I'd seen earlier against the mountains."

Might end up with more of a thunderstorm rather than a Hawaiian blessing.

From where he sat, Lauren couldn't see pillars of smoke that began to rise over the palm trees and housing units on Ford Island—on the starboard side of the ship.

Whomp! Whomp!

The teak-laden steel deck, beneath Lauren, shuddered slightly. Throughout the harbor, seawater rippled between hulls, as if stones had been skipped from one ship to another.

Lauren's heart beat hard, just thinking about the day, with a woman he'd come to care about, over the past three months. It was typical, during liberty, to plan out the day, in his mind.

We'll take a trolley car to Waikiki beach. The surf'll feel great on a hot day. And afterwards we'll…

Distracted from retying his shoe, Bruner heard the shrill whining of a low flying aircraft. He continued to sit, as the engine's howl grew louder.

It had come in from the southwest, over Ford Island and then *Arizona,* heading out into the east channel. Other sailors on deck scanned the sky, to locate the plane.

"Didn't know what it was, at first. Thought it maybe was some dumb bastard, probably a fool pilot from Ford Island on a Sunday joyride."

Some stupid flyboy's gonna get his ass kicked.

Whomp! Whomp! Whomp!

0756

Bruner was mesmerized by what was happening. Another sound joined the engine's whine... the staccato pummeling of machine gun rounds.

Men scattered in all directions.

Within seconds, other engines screamed as they flew directly over him.

"So close to the ship… So close above me, I swear, I could've thrown a baseball and it would've bounced off a wing."

"Scared the shit outta' me… still does today."

"I could see rounds popping off the ship's deck and

bulkheads… all around… like someone had thrown thousands of marbles at our ship."

Bruner followed the ricocheting sounds of bullets as they created divots in *Arizona's* thick, painted surfaces.

Still transfixed, and looking skyward, Bruner's eyes followed plane after plane out into the channel. Though he'd already spotted the Japanese rising sun painted on its wingtips, his heart and mind didn't comprehend what his eyes and ears were witnessing.

"Holy shit!" a crewman yelled. He sucked in a hard breath and shouted another warning. "We're being attacked by the Japs!"

Sailors below began pouring topside, and raced to battle stations.

Heels of their shoes slammed down so hard on deck, the sounds were only matched by machine gun clatter.

Simultaneously, the bugle's *Prep Signal* for morning colors was interrupted by more distant explosions. And wild cries erupted throughout the ship.

"Japs! Japs!"

Wide-eyed, Lauren regrouped his mind. For one stunned moment, he tried to comprehend what he'd heard.

It couldn't be…

"Honest to God… I still didn't understand we'd just come under an actual attack."

"My brain was slow to react… mixed with fear and a growing feeling of being pissed off. Not because those machine gun rounds had almost taken me out, but because of what the bastards were doing to *Arizona's* teak deck."

"In the first moments of the attack… that really ticked me off. I just wanted to beat the shit out of the lousy bastards who were disrespecting *Arizona.*"

"I'd spent my first couple of years as a crew member of Deck Force Four… every day, keeping it immaculate. And it was now being torn to shit."

Slivers and chunks of wood flew far and wide.

"Thank God the rounds were moving forward, with the plane's thrust, sending the slivers forward and sideways… none back towards where I still sat, stunned as hell."

Bruner looked up from the ruined deck and, this time, noticed more of the red suns—or as some referred to them, meatballs—painted on the wings and sides of each plane.

"One plane after another flew over… some with their bombs still strapped to their undercarriage."

Inside a small compartment on the bridge, a Marine grabbed a handle on the red contact-maker, for General Alarm. The klaxon sounded as the ship's speaker's blared into action—first with the general quarters alarm bell, set to ring 100 times. Over that came a continuous blast of the whining air-raid siren, followed by the air defense call, played by a Marine over the loudspeaker. And all sailors heard:

"Set condition Zed. Set condition Zed."

The harsh siren tore into the morning air, and jarred Bruner's senses.

Whoop! Whoop! Whoop! Whoop!

That got his attention.

"It was at that point my brain caught up with what was happening. And I bolted upward, turned left, and stepped out onto the shredded deck."

Across the harbor, a hundred or more ear-splitting alarms echoed the warnings that raced throughout the channel.

"Set condition Zed. Set condition Zed. This is not a drill. Man your battle stations. This is not a drill."

Training and reflex propelled Lauren across the main deck for his battle post.

He sprinted through scattered clumps of puzzled sailors, and headed for the series of vertical ladders to propel him up to his battle station.

The port-side director, for anti-aircraft fire control, was one of two revolving, steel-clad cabins perched high on the sky-control platform, above Admiral Kidd's flag bridge.

First he'd have to reach a ladder off the main deck, then one from the superstructure deck, a ladder to the radio shack, another to the admiral's bridge, and a fifth to his station—over 70 feet above waterline.

The speakers continued to roar: *"Battle stations! Battle stations! All hands man your battle stations! This is no drill! Repeat, this is no drill."*

Realization had set in, and sailors moved with purpose. Officers appeared, from aft in all sorts of dress—all heading for their posts.

The first wave of Japanese Zeke fighter planes, Kate torpedo-bombers, and barely visible high-level Kate bombers occupied the sky.

In what would be the first wave attack, over 180 aircraft had swarmed in from the northwest near the Waianae Mountains and spread out, toward Ford Island, Hickam, and Wheeler Fields—then, onto Battleship Row.

On Ford Island, bombs whistled—one after another—that devastated most of the US Naval Air Station hangars, the field, and aircraft that had been parked, wingtip-to-wingtip.

Lauren raced for the first set of ladders, keeping one eye on another approaching enemy plane.

He ran across the deck, reacting to the surrounding action. Machine gun rounds popped and ricocheted nearby "…even after the plane was several hundred yards past the ship."

How in the hell are rounds still pinging off the bulkhead I just passed.

"Now, ya' gotta' understand… we'd never been in an actual battle, before."

"Hell, *I'd* never been in battle before, period. And I'm thinking'… How is this possible? The machine guns, intent on killing me, were located on the plane's front. And it had already flown over."

"Then I noticed… one plane flew over and banked up the channel, its machine gun barrel stuck out of the plane's canopy at its rear, and sighted our ship, long after it had flown over."

"The barrel continued to jerk and spit flames, followed on deck by pings that ricocheted rounds of death… and hit all around us."

Bombs splashed in the east channel; constant strafing to hit anything in the water—moving or not—followed close behind.

Bruner picked up his run, again, and almost tripped over the shoelace he'd forgotten to retie.

"I'd been looking at the deck, so as not to trip over debris or bodies, still with an eye on that last plane as I moved toward the first ladder."

"It's difficult to imagine," said Lauren. "…but it all appeared to happen in milliseconds. It was as if I'd been sprinting in slow motion. And then I'd hear the whine of approaching aircraft… then another, and another."

"In the confusion, sailors yelled, cussed, and raced across decks, same as I was… all of us heading for battle stations."

"Hadn't taken but a few long strides, across the deck, when I first saw the horrors of what was to come."

"Machine gun rounds stopped many sailors in their tracks, right in front of me. And off to my right… laying on the deck, near the ship's rail, was a downed sailor."

"He moaned… and groaned in agony. Hundreds of hard teak slivers had stuck through his t-shirt and shorts… some piercing him clean through his arms...and well into his face."

Bruner's mind flashed back on running into a mad-as-hell porcupine in the woods where he grew up. "Fortunately, that kid was already being attended to."

"Then, as I dodged more potholes in the deck, I came across another sailor bending over a fallen buddy. His white t-shirt stained red, where large slivers pierced through it."

"The downed sailor still had his hat on," Lauren recalled," and the slivers of death stopped just after his face… a bloody, pulpy mess."

Continuing full out, Lauren heard and felt aircraft vibrations, overhead, as they repeated the same hellish dance.

It was then that Bruner heard rounds emanating from *Arizona's* crow's nest, and then from *Nevada,* behind them.

"Made me happy as hell to hear we were finally taking the fight to those dirty bastards, 'cause I was even more pissed. They'd screwed up my date with Nikki."

"We hadn't gotten any big guns goin' yet. Just the Marines', with their hand-held machine guns up in the crow's nest. Better than nothin'. At least we were answering back."

"Don't think I was ever more proud of calling a Marine my shipmate."

Bruner reached the first ladder, heading up the superstructure, off the main deck.

"But I ran smack into a traffic jam. Others, starting up the same ladder held me up. We were all in line yelling for the ones ahead of us to get their asses moving."

Some sailor up the line yelled out, "We're being attacked by the damned Japs."

The thought occurred to Bruner, *Where the hell has this guy been?*

"Of course, I couldn't talk... considering how long it took for me to catch on."

"Just as I started up the ladder...following the butt of a sailor above me, I heard loud explosions from somewhere up Battleship Row... then another, across the channel, and another, even closer. They just kept comin'."

"It became apparent the Japanese had finished up with Ford Island with the first wave "... bombing the shit outta' Officers' quarters, hangars, landing strips, and planes... shit... everything.

"Then, they'd turned their attention to the new quarry, tied up like sitting ducks, on Battleship Row."

Torpedoes or bombs. He couldn't tell which.

"Each one made my heart skip beats, as I raced for my battle station."

Lauren could feel them. With each explosion, *Arizona* shook like a dog shedding water. And they'd reverberate throughout the hull, the bulkheads, then through his entire body. He found it difficult to breathe.

"Felt I was gonna' get sick... but just kept movin' with the ladder-line in front of me."

Through the din—with Battleship Row vessels berthed so close together—yelling and cussing echoed off all ships in the harbor. Lauren could hear the cries repeat from one ship to another.

"Som'bitch comin' in at three o'clock."

"Another bastard at eight o'clock."

Lauren watched sailors, clinging to the ladder rungs, duck "...as if they could avoid being hit, while moving up the line. Hell... short of jumping off a ladder, there was no way to avoid the rounds and heavy bomb shrapnel flying at us from all directions. Guys were droppin' off the ladders like flies. And we'd just keep movin'. "

"How I made it up five ladders, without getting hit, I still don't know."

All crew trained to take two to three rungs at a time. Even then, each guy behind someone else could be heard yelling, "Come on! Get movin'!"

Bruner started up the second set of ladders. He spotted Don Stratton, a crew member of his battle station, about a dozen or so behind him.

"Our eyes caught each other for only a second. Don looked just as glum as I'm sure I did. And I'm guessing as scared and ashen-faced a sailor as I was."

"You gotta' understand… there we were, climbing' those ladders… no way to move up or down any faster than the line allowed. And those sons-a-bitches, devils in the air, were comin' at us with everything they had. Machine gun rounds hittin' and ricocheting off bulkheads… takin' out sailors left and right, death all over."

"Neither of us knew if we'd make it through the day… let alone that morning."

Lauren's eyes moved off Stratton and he looked below. He caught his first sight of the growing graveyard of *Arizona* bodies—lying on the decks, "…damn machine gun rounds were cutting 'em down."

The scene was indelibly etched into Lauren's mind. It would lurk there, forever.

"But, I realized I couldn't let that picture affect my mind that day. It had to be put outta' my head, or I'd never be able to deal with what was happening around me."

"We kept moving up the ladders, as fast as possible… all of us shaking like leaves."

"You might call it 'ordered chaos.' Sailors and Marines trying not to be targets, while they headed for battle stations."

"But if anyone who lived through the attack on Pearl Harbor described themselves, afterwards, as *not* being scared… I'd bet a dime to a donut, and win, no matter who was doing the talking, they were lying through their teeth."

"That isn't to say they didn't do their jobs, or hadn't become heroes in some way. But truth be told, we were all, deep down in our hearts, and throughout the fibers of our souls… scared shitless."

"Amazing what your mind takes in… in the height of battle. You have two choices to survive, I'd learn, later. They called it 'fight or flight.' "

"But, on that morning, my mind became an instant photographic warehouse for scenes I'd never forget, but always wanted to."

"Scenes that played out in seconds, but slowed down in our minds to allow us to respond."

As Bruner climbed higher, the disastrous attack continued to unfold before him. He watched two low-flying Kates head, in succession, right over Battleship Row. "They let loose their machine guns, shooting at anything that moved… and anything that didn't."

Black shadows beneath their wings morphed into bombs or torpedoes, as they released toward their targets.

Just then, machine gun rounds hit one of the platform searchlights above, and thick shards of glass rained down on the men.

"Heads and eyes down," someone had the sense to yell, above us.

"Shit!" Lauren covered his head with one arm as he and others felt glass fragments nick at their skin.

"A coupla' guys above me got hit, pretty good," said Lauren. "Sonovabitch… one of the poor bastards lost his footing, and dropped to the deck below… screamin' as he fell."

Glancing out toward the channel Bruner realized he had a view of the repair ship, *Vestal*—tied up alongside.

"Its decks were in full pandemonium, with sailors sprinting in all directions… dodging bullets, bombs and explosions, just like us."

At that moment, three deafening explosions burst, just up Battleship Row. All heads turned, so quick, toward the noise "…they coulda' twisted off."

Lauren searched for the root of the noise. He caught remnants of water geysers, south of *Arizona.*

Three, eighteen-foot long torpedoes, carrying 452 pounds of explosives, had found their target. Columns of water, taller than a battleship's masts, had shot into the air, next to *Oklahoma*.

Then, screams emanated from their battleship, just two ships ahead, outboard of USS *Maryland* berthed at Foxtrot 5.

"We all watched this giant battleship shake like a rag doll." Six more torpedoes would hit the ship, as sailors attempted to escape.

Tennessee would be next.

Shit! *What the hell's happening*?

At that point, one thought was set in Lauren's mind, *I'm gonna' die.*

0757

"I turned back to the ladder, and my face ran smack into the forward sailor's ass. The line had come to a dead stop."

"Holy shit", someone up the line exclaimed. "We got a dead Marine on the next landing… at the foot o' the ladder."

"Step around 'im," someone else yelled, "…or we'll all die right here."

The line started moving again. But within seconds Bruner found himself stepping around the downed marine.

Two other Marines—one of them Lauren knew, Jim Cory—kneeled close to their fallen comrade, Second Lieutenant Carleton Simensen.

Bruner approached, stepped around the Marines, and turned to move up the next set of ladders. Cory was bent over the dying Marine, who lay face down in a fast-spreading pool of blood. The other Marine rolled him to his back. It was then they discovered the man's chest and stomach was shredded.

"Jim was doing his best to search out the worst wounds, but there were so many holes in his chest. The poor bastard was staring up at his friends with a look I'll never forget... as if he couldn't understand what had just happened. He just... stared straight up."

"I'd known Jim Cory for a year or so. Shared beers with 'im at Smith's Union, a coupla' times. As he turned his head... our eyes met. They were filled with tears."

Cory turned back and placed his ear close to the fallen Marine's lips. "I'd find out, years later, the poor fella' was saying his last words."

"Wouldn't see Jim Cory until after the war. We sat together at an *Arizona* reunion. Both of us were, I'd guess, on our third beer, when we touched on this story.

"Jim shared that the downed Marine was well liked by the ship's company. As I had passed by on the landing, that morning... and our eyes had met, Simensen had just told Cory and the other Marine to leave him be... and to take care of themselves."

Jim said Simensen died "...right then and there."

He recalled how, just after, he put the Lieutenant's hat under his head, to cushion it, another Japanese Kate approached, 'with a vengeance' and they scrambled to take cover. And that opened up a floodgate of memories.

"The attack came on so damned fast. My mind was only intent on reaching my battle station... whatever I could do to help stop the attack, and just stay alive."

"The dead Marine seemed to infuse even more adrenaline into my shaking body."

"The line in front of me had thinned out as sailors moved off onto other levels of the main mast... wherever their battle stations happened to be."

Bruner was able to move faster and higher into the ship's mast—his legs stretched to the limits, taking ladder rungs three at a time.

"I was moving fast when I passed the navigation bridge."

"Captain Van Valkenburgh could be seen there, any time, day *or* night. Apparently he hadn't yet reached his post, as I never saw him... or *any* activity, for that matter. Sorta surprised me... and scared me a little."

The next, and last set of ladders, took Bruner past Admiral Kidd's bridge.

"It, too, looked like a ghost town."

"But as I passed the bridge, I saw machine gun rounds had just torn his surrounding deck to smithereens... including his old leather chair, on the outside... or what was left of it."

"I continued to climb past this mess, and it occurred to me... whoever the son of a bitch was who fired on the bridge, must've known what his target was. It wasn't a passing round either. That rear gunner had to take aim, and lock on that chair as he flew by. It was shredded to bits."

"Funny what you think about, in times like that. But I knew the old man was gonna' be *pissed* when he saw one of his favorite chairs shot to shit."

The base of Lauren's director sat on a bridge wing, attached to what was called the sky control platform. The platform stretched the width of the ship—port-side to starboard—with each of two directors sitting on their own circular bridge wings.

The platform's starboard, held an exact duplicate of the port-side director—used to sight targets for the starboard's other four 5"/25 caliber anti-aircraft guns. Each director's specific purpose was to track the current location for any target, by determining range, elevation, and bearing.

"A director didn't have guns, inside. But it did have a funny-looking set of scopes sticking out each side that resembled big ears."

By the time Bruner reached the sky control platform, he was breathing pretty hard.

"Don't remember Don Stratton coming up from behind and moving past me, but he must've. I could see, before I entered, he'd already climbed up into the director through his left-side hatchway. Alvin Dvorak and Ensign Lomax were inside, as well."

He raced to the port-side director's rear hatchway jumped up on the short ladder to his door, and rode it around 20 degrees, as Dvorak turned the small cabin on its turret, in order to sight clusters of incoming planes.

Lauren's peripheral vision caught sight of a Kate bomber that was coming down the channel, after it had dropped its payload. With its load lightened, the plane banked over the West Channel, circled back, entered

Battleship Row, and then appeared to head in a direct line for *Arizona*.

"In my mind", said Lauren, "he was the grim reaper, come to visit."

Still standing on his hatchway ladder—ready to enter the director's rear door, Bruner was transfixed—mesmerized by how low the Kate flew over the channel.

0758

"Funny," he said, "but the fear that I'd felt in the beginning had left my body. And for a brief time, as I approached relative safety of the director's metal bulkhead… I just couldn't go in. I was just like a deer caught in the headlights."

Bruner stood, holding onto an outside handgrip at his hatchway, as he watched the enemy pilot and crew "… come right at me and the ship."

"Sure as hell, I thought he was gonna smash into *Arizona's* side, on purpose. Figured it had to be his plan, because that sonovabitch… I swear, was flying no more than twenty feet above waterline, heading straight for us."

For whatever reason, Lauren's shoes felt glued to the step. With one hand resting on the left side of his hatch door, time slowed, segmented, and froze in place.

"Should've entered my post, but didn't. It was like watching' one of those frame-by-frame, slow motion films. Just couldn't take my eyes off that bastard pilot and his plane comin' at us and into view."

0759

In the back of Lauren's mind, he heard the ongoing attack—as explosions and gunfire pummeled the harbor. Torpedo bombers and fighter planes continued their runs.

But Lauren's entire focus remained on that one particular Kate.

Back in dry dock, at Bremerton, Washington, Lauren had learned how thick *Arizona's* metal hull was, after first joining the crew. "I wasn't too concerned that the plane could sink our ship by a direct crash. But I feared he might have another bomb, tied to his undercarriage.

He instinctively braced for impact.

"My head must've flipped side to side, as I gauged and took in all that surrounded me."

About this time, Ronnie Lott, who was Bruner's and the gun captain's telephone talker to the plotting room, had arrived on deck and climbed up into the director's port-side hatch.

Lott spotted Lauren, still standing outside.

"Bruner!" he shouted, "Get up in here. You're gonna' get killed."

Lauren ignored the warning—still transfixed on the scene unfolding before him.

His eyes passed over the big, white 'E', awarded for fire-control efficiency—painted on the director, just outside his hatch door.

A lot of good that'll do us, stuck in the harbor.

He focused back on Battleship Row.

What had begun as a large green dot, over the channel, had grown larger with each second—still flying just above the waterline.

"Truth be told… I hated that pilot's guts, but I had to admit the sonuvabitch sure knew how to fly."

Then Lauren heard gunfire emanate out of the crow's nest, above.

"Music to my ears. It reassured me… someone else was watching the same event unfold."

"Our machine gun kept up a continuous chatter, but I never saw one of its rounds hit the oncoming plane. And it occurred to me… our shooter had to be as scared as me, up there."

"Understand… all these hidden memories I've dredged up, happened in half seconds. For me, it appeared in slow motion."

As the enemy approached, 50 yards out, his machine guns opened up. Bruner saw repeated puffs of smoke and flames shoot from both ends of the plane.

Yet, he still couldn't move.

Then, as if the pilot had planned his next move—machine guns still smoking, "He pulled up just before impact… but kept coming directly at me. Or that's what I thought."

"With guns blazing, the bastard kept his approach… so close, I could've hit 'im with a baseball bat. Machine gun rounds ricocheted all around me, off the metal bulkheads."

"Shoulda' been more scared, but for that split second, it was like I was in a fool's trance… not afraid of anything."

"I should've been."

No one else was close to Lauren, outside. For the briefest of moments, his eyes met the pilot's, and they locked on. For him, it recorded an ongoing chapter that would appear in nightmares for years to come.

The plane's color was best described as dirty green, "… with a big red sun staring down at me… like one 'a those glowing neon signs you used to see along Route 66."

As the Japanese pilot and Bruner assumed their fighting stance, they both squared-off with their eyes, "One hell of a lot about the gangster, whoever he was, transferred to my mind… as he flew by. We stared, eyeball to eyeball. And he never took his finger off the trigger."

"As he passed by, his machine guns were still smokin'."

The Kate's canopy was pulled back open—like his gunner's, two seats behind. The pilot had a small pencil mustache, and wore a leather helmet. A pair of "cat's eye" aviation goggles rested on his helmet, out of the way.

"The bastard added insult to injury, smiling from ear to ear as he flew past. And sonuvabitch, I swear to God, I could see his gold teeth."

Lauren wanted to give him the finger. But he was gone in an instant. "Unfortunately, my slower thinking was no match for his speed."

The pilot pulled the plane's nose up, tilting slightly sideways as he flew past Bruner, and soared right through the ship's superstructure.

The empty undercarriage confirmed it had already dropped its torpedo.

"Prior to that moment, I felt little fear. Following the encounter, however… it frightened the piss outta' me."

"Still does, all these years later."

"Can't recall if I pissed my pants or not."

The incident was almost over. Except that Bruner's eyes—once unlocked from the pilot's—followed his canopy back to the rear gunner. Sticking out of the interior "…was a damned big barrel of a machine gun pointing upward, toward the sky, still smokin'."

"The second gunner could've easily killed me, and finished the job that his pilot didn't."

"Right then and there, though… I figured this guy would re-aim and mow me down. He could've cut me in half with his rounds."

"But the gunner's barrel never shifted. Instead, like his pilot, he looked over at me. Only, this guy wore goggles."

"Then, the damndest thing happened, as he passed. I swear to God… in place of cutting me in half, he held up a small Japanese flag and grinned a full-toothed smile."

"In a split second, he and that daredevil pilot… soared off to their next target."

The intense incident happened with such speed, that all noise, including the plane's engines, was blocked from Lauren's mind.

Then something else broke his mind-filled silence. Lott cried out, "We're gonna' die. We're all gonna' die."

The thought occurred to Lauren, *What the hell was Lott yellin' about?*

"Shit! He didn't even come down to dance with the enemy."

— —

Lieutenant Zenji Abe

Lieutenant Zenji Abe was born on 18 August 1916 in Kano, Japan. **On the day his squadron Attacked Pearl Harbor on the morning of 7 December 1941, Lt. Abe was 25 years, 3 months, and 19 days old.** He was one of hundreds of enemy pilots who descended on Pearl Harbor, flying his Kate bomber off the aircraft carrier "Akagi."

Abe was a short man with light olive skin, cropped short black hair and dark brown eyes. For most of his life after taking part in the attack, Lt. Abe believed that he was the pilot whose plane dropped the high-altitude bomb that sent USS *Arizona* and her crew to their deaths.

History has proven that he was not, and for that assurance throughout the rest of his life he was grateful often saying in interviews how very sorry he was.

"I will always remember how the enemy pilots looked as they attacked amd flew by. Each wore leather flying helmets and goggles, some with silk scarves wrapped around their necks. Hell, we were so close to each other as they would fly by that I could see them smiling, even some with gold teeth. Like everyone else I was scared to death and I'll tell you, it was the worst day of my life and no fun."

阿部善次

Zenji Abe

Lieutenant Zenji Abe

Attacking Enemy Pilot

Chapter 12
CHAOS & CONFUSION

0800

At the rear hatchway entrance, Lauren turned on the small ladder, grabbed two side grips, and began to pull himself inside the director. He almost tripped and fell back.

"Thank God for those hatch handles. I might've gone straight over the bridge-wing's railing, a helluva long way down."

His mind chalked up his near-fall to being clumsy… or that he'd tripped on his shoelace. He'd been distracted while retying it, as the attack began.

He glanced down to avoid tripping, again.

Sonuvabitch! he whispered, under the din of battle.

Just below the knee, his left leg bled "…like a stuck pig… blood already flowing into my sock, and down into my shoe."

"My right shoelace was still untied… but hell, the other shoe had filled with blood."

"At first, it hurt like all get out."

Thinking back to what his mind wouldn't allow him to feel—during the Japanese pilot's face-off —Bruner sifted through memories of the flyby attack.

His subconscious mind raced, as he recalled machine gun rounds that hit him "…like two red hot pokers, the width of a nickel… being poked real quick like, right through my left leg, then out the other side."

"Figured I'd better stop the blood, somehow… but didn't have time."

He turned, and with both hands on the side grips, "… again pulled myself up and through the opening."

A bright Hawaiian morning altered into subdued darkness.

"The director wasn't pitch black", said Lauren, "and you wouldn't call it well lit. Somewhere in between, as daylight streamed into what might become our metal coffin through its hatchways, hatches, and observation windows. That is… until blankets of smoke filled the sky, making it even darker, inside."

It always took time for Bruner's eyes to adjust to the dimmer light.

Favoring his left leg, Bruner pitched himself further into the veiled darkness, and used his stereoscopic rangefinder for support.

"Bruner, you all right?" Lomax yelled out over the din.

Lauren nodded.

He then became conscious of a new sound, as his left foot squished from the pool of blood filling his shoe.

Time and circumstances never allowed him the luxury of worrying about his two wounds again.

"Not once", he said.

Lauren had entered his battle station through what he'd always considered to be his own personal hatchway. "After all, it put me right in front of my rangefinder… the long optic tube used to sight targets."

"Jeez, that sucker's optics was strong."

The rangefinder resembled a super high-powered field glass. With it, Bruner could adjust the optics that, even miles away would place him standing next to, or in front of, an enemy target.

"Made no difference. Whether a plane's pilot or an enemy ship's crew, miles off… it felt as if I was right in the cockpit or standing on deck, next to the enemy."

"Think of our director as a small twelve by eight foot metal can", said Lauren. "…cut in half, and sitting on its side. The little cabins were brand new additions to *Arizona*… completed, in Bremerton, Washington, six months prior to the attack."

"Each director had three hatchways, another three, overhead, were smaller observation lookouts, and three drop-down observation windows, port, starboard and aft."

It housed six crew members, all sailors. *Arizona's* complement of 88 Marines had other assignments.

Constructed of heavy steel, the director sat on a rotating turret structure—a barbette—able to be cranked by hand within a full 360-degree radius, depending upon its placement on a ship.

"The plotting room's computer confined ours to about a one hundred eighty degree radius, just enough so we didn't shoot the crap outta' our own vessel during the heat of battle."

"My friend and drinking buddy, Alvin, had the responsibility to crank that sonuvabitch around for me to sight targets. Up front, our gun captain, Ensign Frank Lomax, called out instructions at his sighting post."

Inside, the director was pure chaos.

"And a hell of a lot of cussin' went on. But then, for the Navy… cussin' was standard issue, so-to-speak."

Lomax did his best to keep a lid on things. "But as a crew", said Lauren, "we were all young… and not yet battle tested."

Less than twelve hours prior, Lauren had been holding hands with a beautiful young woman. He had trouble unwrapping his mind from her image. And there was Alvin Dvorak, who'd saved a bus seat for him the night before, after spending his night getting drunk.

Bruner glanced across his rangefinder to Dvorak. "He looked a little green around the gills, after all the beer. He looked like he was sick.

"Alvin, you all right?" Lauren yelled over the clamor.

It wasn't so much what Dvorak answered back, "… because it wasn't important. Instead, it was his slight smile that told me that he would be all right, and that I could count on him."

The battle continued, outside. Inside, it was total disarray. Each crew member yelled to be heard. And sounds magnified as they echoed, inside, off the director's bulkheads.

"In the background… gunfire. Ours, and the enemy's. Outside, it sounded like a gunfight at the OK Corral… times a thousand."

"Agitated as hell… uncertain what to do first, we must've cussed every other word."

Machine gun rounds pinged off the director's overhead. Several rounds found their way through an open roof hatch, and bounced off the walls, "…like peas in a wash machine… before they dropped to the floor or disappeared out through another hatch. Damned lucky no one got hit."

The director's overhead stood shorter than Bruner was tall. "If you were short, you were able to stand up straight without bending over. You can imagine what it was like in heavy seas for the taller of us, but you got used to it."

"Lomax and Lott had no problem with its height. They were both under five seven. But Stratton, Zimmerman and I welcomed the overhead hatches, when we'd keep 'em open."

"Besides being six-one, I still climbed onto a horizontal riser pipe welded across the interior deck, near my rangefinder. It allowed me to pop my head up, anytime, like a turtle… just enough to let my eyes observe through the overhead."

"To look out of their top hatches, Lomax, Stratton and Zimmerman used moveable wooden boxes to give them extra height, up front."

"We all welcomed the overhead hatches… kept open most of the time. It helped keep a decent breeze going, on a hot day… and cleared the air, on Wednesdays and Saturdays after we ate beans and cornbread. But this wasn't a time to consider those benefits."

"Regardless, never occurred to me… the possibility of machine gun rounds finding their way through our hatches. We'd never been under attack before."

"Guess they coulda' killed any of us through the overhead, or through the hatchways. But we had so many other things to worry about."

"As any crew member called out what they saw, I'd leave the viewfinder… depending on its importance, and pop my head back and forth… in and out of the overhead. I'd view all that went on, up and down battleship row."

Four hundred yards down the channel, Lauren saw USS *Oklahoma,* now listed heavily to port. What didn't reach him was the knocking of men caught in its hull—hoping someone would come to their rescue.

Throughout the attack, Bruner's telephone-talker, Ronnie Lott, continued to ramble, "We're gonna' die!"

Lauren knew, like the others, that it was bad. Their only hope—not taking a direct hit.

"At first, our director had faced north, toward *Nevada,* with my hatchway to the south… at the sky platform."

"A couple minutes into the battle, Zeke Zimmerman stepped through my hatchway. He'd arrived late… no hat, and his t-shirt wrong side out. His name, stenciled on the shirt's inside back, now in the front, was visible from the outside… on his chest."

"Funny what you remember as you're getting shot to hell."

"As a rule, Zeke would've entered at his own hatchway, on the director's starboard side. But he'd climbed in the back… because my hatchway rested closest to the platform ladders."

Zeke's face was a mirror that reflected how terrified the crew was, caught off guard like they were. Out of breath, he bent down behind the rangefinder, to tie his shoes.

Bruner had begun to look through his optics, when Zimmerman spoke.

"On my way up," Zeke reported "…saw the ol' man… Admiral Kidd, standin' out on the bridge with his Marine, and his shot-to-hell leather chair."

"You wouldn't believe it. The old guy had his shirt buttoned wrong, with one side longer than the other… looked all cockeyed."

It occurred to Lauren, *Who the hell cares in the middle of all this?* Then he remembered his chance meeting with the Admiral not three hours earlier.

"What the hell took you so long to get here, Zeke?"

"Damn attack caught me all soaped up, in the shower."

Lauren almost broke out laughing, considering the statement came from the one crew member known to take at least three to four showers a day.

Zimmerman ducked under the rangefinder and took his place alongside Stratton, near the port hatch.

Bruner returned to his eyepiece, and felt the base of the director move on its circular barbette. He glanced back over to Dvorak, who used his brodie knobs to hand crank the cabin toward starboard.

Lomax, our gunnery officer, looked through a port in front of him, to determine the range and flight path of the enemy.

"Take us southwest around at two thirty-eight degrees, toward *Tennessee*", Lomax shouted. Dvorak cranked some more, then held his vertical wheel tight. The director halted in place.

"Next to Lomax, our sight-setter, Stratton, cranked a gauge in front of him and shouted his coordinates to our gun crews through his telephone headset."

Without looking, Lomax yelled to the back, "Bruner, see what you can sight and let me know."

"Sighting, sir."

"Truth be told", said Lauren, "his order was folly... with all the confusion inside our battle station. And with Lott, yammering that we were all gonna' die..."

Lauren bent his head over the optical viewer, and tried to sight the line of battleships—one in front of another, down the channel.

"For all the hundreds of times I drilled this, during maneuvers... and then, following Lomax's orders, I felt like a fool trying to sight *any* target. Hell, there were enemy planes flying past... all over us, swarming close like a nest of hornets."

Bruner shouted back to Lomax, "Our range is wide off the mark... the bastards are comin' in too low. And the high-level bombers way outta' range."

Continuous machine gun blasts reverberated throughout the harbor, as the pings created large divots in the ship's bulkheads.

"I was as nervous as Lott... and the rest of the crew. Truth be told, we were all wondering if we were gonna' die. But when faced with life, over death, the last thing you wanna' listen to is someone like Ronnie Lott goin' a little crazy."

"Don't know how many times Lott reminded us that death was on the way."

Bruner did all he could to shut Lott out. He bent over the rangefinder again to follow Lomax's orders, leaned his head into the rubber face-guard that surrounded his viewer, then came up again.

"The optics are black", Lauren blurted out. Can't see a thing. He checked it again." He pumped the rangefinder's hydraulic foot pedal, to raise it slightly, thinking maybe his optics were too low for his angle."

"Didn't change a damn thing," he said.

For a split second his mind didn't comprehend what had gone wrong. Had the lenses been shot out? Then it hit him. Bruner raised his head up, off the face-guard.

0801

"The leather protective caps covering the optics… were still attached outside." Lauren turned to his telephone talker.

"Ronnie! Get your ass out there and pull the covers off my optics."

"I ain't going out there." Lott retorted. "It's your rangefinder. You do it."

"Don't give me any shit, Ronnie. You want to live? Get your ass moving or I'll throw you outside, and feed ya' to the wolves, myself."

Lott continued to argue with Bruner.

Without turning around, Lomax interrupted.

"Lott! You don't get movin', right now, I'll let Bruner do what he said to you."

That got Lott's attention.

"He ducked under the rangefinder, and bolted outside," said Lauren, "…jumping down to the bridge wing without using the steps."

Lott pulled the covers off the closest optics to his left. And as if a base runner—heading from third to home—he circumnavigated the bridge catwalk; ducked under the starboard scope; snatched off the opposite covers and, at full-tilt, re-entered the director.

Lott reported to Lomax that the optic covers were removed. Then, he passed the same message to Bruner.

Without another word, he tossed the leather covers near Bruner's feet.

"Damn, that kid loved to piss me off."

0802

Attempting to avoid further confrontation, Bruner returned to his optics. But Lott couldn't resist opening his mouth, one more time, "...with some smartass remark."

Lauren clenched his fist and thought about punching him. But it wasn't a time for that.

He turned his head directly to Lott. A momentary sense of pity overcame him.

"Ronnie", Lauren forced a calm demeanor, "sit down and shut up. We'll be okay."

Despite deafening sounds outside the director, Bruner's voice appeared to calm Lott. He did as Bruner had suggested.

Lott backed off, slid down against the bulkhead's corner, found Lauren's old, fogging-out blanket, and collapsed on it.

"He seemed to quiet down, for the moment," Lauren said, "which was a godsend."

Lauren returned to his optics. His face rested against its rubber housing as he attempted, once again, to sight targets through his stereoscopic lenses.

He felt the director's motion, as Dvorak cranked it several more degrees to his right. Lomax called out to Dvorak whenever he wanted positioning to enable Bruner to sight a possible target. With each new command, their crew felt vibration, beneath their feet as the director's cabin moved into position. And the four, port side, 5″ guns move synchronously with it, below.

With each call of new coordinates, Dvorak was at the ready, hands tight on his two brodie knobs, ready to crank his vertical control wheel, while cogs in the gears carried the director's housing left or right.

Zimmerman's crank, near the right hatch, aimed the director up or down, to coincide with targeted enemy aircraft sightings. But Zimmerman had similar problems, as Bruner did, sighting fast-moving planes, maneuvering in and out of mastheads, or while coming in too low.

0803

Within seconds, Bruner's crew heard gunfire issue from their anti-aircraft gun crews, right below their platform.

In battle, on a Navy ship, all those in a crew can tell which guns are being fired, just by listening to their sounds. Bruner knew, straightaway, their port-side anti-aircraft guns were up and running, full out—replacing for a moment, the Marines' machine guns, up in the crow's nest.

"It was like music to my ears. And I thought, maybe, with a lot of luck, we might make it after all."

"But it was another false hope."

"Once we recognized the sounds of our guns… I swear, we all wanted to cheer… though, at the time, we were a little preoccupied, just trying to stay alive."

"I don't think that my smile had left my face, when our port-side guns began to sputter. It was like a car backfiring. And then, they just gosh-damn died out… giving the fight's round to the enemy."

"Our own 'peacetime policy' was about to kill hundreds of sailors and Marines."

Peacetime policy prescribed that any ship berthed at Pearl Harbor, with armaments—in particular, battleships, cruisers, and destroyers—be required to contain all ballistics.

Specifically, the policy required each ship to maintain what was referred to as twenty-five 'ready rounds'—always locked in an ammunition box, and set next to each gun.

In theory, this policy allowed gunners to have an emergency supply, for an attack, in order to get the guns up-and-running, until shells arrived topside. The projectiles would be sent up via an ammunition lift—similar to a grain elevator—from below deck.

Each projectile, to the anti-aircraft guns, weighed about 60 pounds. Well-trained gun crews, above decks, were needed to get them off the elevator, and into each gun in record time, in order to fire.

"As our guns started to peter out", said Lauren, "we all realized it at the same time. That's when the cussing double-timed."

"Shit! There's no shells comin' to the guns," yelled Lomax.

"Lomax was pissed. And by my thinkin', looked as scared as the rest of us.", said Lauren. "Given the situation, the tie-up of rounds comin' up sure didn't fill us with much confidence."

Dvorak sensed this. "Must be waiting for rounds to come up from below."

"At that moment", said Lauren, "I think we were all counting seconds... hoping against hope the guns would start up again."

"But, shit... it didn't happen and we, as a ship, were back to square one."

A thick cloud of black smoke blew in through the right hatchway. It first enveloped the crew, then was sucked back out as quickly as it had entered.

Choking on the smoke, Dvorak chimed in, "Looks like we're screwed, blued, and tattoed."

Lomax shouted to Dvorak, "I'm heading below, to find out what the hell the hold up is… we gotta' get ammunition to the guns if we're going to get outta this."

Bruner looked up as Lomax handed his binoculars over to Dvorak. He stepped toward the starboard hatch, at Bruner's right, then stopped and turned back.

"Good luck, you guys."

"Dvorak… you and Bruner are in charge 'til I get back."

He waited for a Japanese plane to pass over the ship, grabbed hold of the hand grips, and stepped onto the small ladder.

"One other thing", he yelled back, "be careful, and stay inside… no matter what happens, don't leave the director."

He stepped down to the platform, ducked air debris from an explosion that carried over from *Vestal,* then disappeared across the sky platform through black, wind-blown smoke.

"Neither Alvin nor I wanted to be in charge. We had no idea what to do, 'cause we couldn't initiate *anything…* with no shells comin' up to our guns, from below."

0804

Across the channel *Pennsylvania* took a hit, and blew up in dry dock.

"We all watched, in disbelief, as tons of wood pilings and what looked like body parts flew all over Hell's half acre. It was sickening to watch."

A great amount of action occurred, in so short a period, it was difficult to focus. Bruner kept trying to find one focal point to concentrate on, but his eyes kept going back to *Oklahoma*. By dialing up magnification on his viewfinder, he was able to place himself right next to the rolling ship.

"I could see its sailors yelling for help… up so close it was like being witness to a living horror show."

Bruner realized it happened so fast, men had to have been trapped inside. Then, through his stereoscope lens, a different enemy plane appeared than the one that had attacked earlier.

A Zeke attack plane—nicknamed "Zero"—joined the fight. Smaller than the bomber that raked *Arizona* when the attack first began, the Zero was a one-pilot attack plane. It carried no bombs or torpedoes and was armed only with two 20mm cannons and two 7.7mm machine guns. It was sleek, fast, and looked like it could turn on a dime.

"Japanese plane after plane strafed those poor bastards as they tried to escape *Oklahoma,* some by sliding down its side to the water. Some were being pulled aboard *Maryland,* berthed inboard at Foxtrot Five. They were scrambling up ropes, nets and ladders… anything the topside sailors were able to get over *Maryland's* side."

"It was gut wrenching… like watching a movie in three-D… I was so close, through my optics, that I'd see machine gun rounds ricochet off the hull and tear sailors apart. Then they'd slip down the side of the ship, into schools of swarming sharks.

"There were sharks all right. Lots of 'em."

Bruner watched as the sharks ripped into a sailor's body, "…and thrashed and splashed around like you wouldn't believe. I couldn't hold back the sick feeling it gave me, and puked my breakfast."

"As I puked, I turned my head toward Lott. He'd returned to his corner… once again moaning, and had pulled my blanket up to cover his head. Far as I know… didn't even hear me puking."

Bruner forced himself back to the rangefinder, and took another look at the harbor. He called out to Dvorak to crank back to port, four degrees.

"Our battle station was so high, I had a clear view that looked out over the repair ship, *Vestal*. I scanned up and down its decks… busier than shit… a whole lot of activity going on."

"Through my vantage point… my scope, it appeared they were attempting to cast off from us, as quick as possible."

Bruner continued to scan the channel. He'd call out to Dvorak to shift the director, accordingly. "I'd shout the degrees I needed. Alvin would brodie his wheel. And the director would respond."

"What a beautiful piece of equipment they'd added back in Bremerton, that summer. I'd guess a million dollars spent to add the bridge wings and two directors, in order to better coordinate our firing solutions between the plotting room and our A.A. guns."

"Just one big problem… in port, we coordinated the hell outta' firing solutions. Just had no goddamn projectiles to shoot at the enemy."

"Like the clock in my mother's dining room, my heart was beating so hard, I could almost hear the last seconds of my life tick by."

"Where the hell's Lomax?" Dvorak yelled out in frustration.

He still hadn't returned.

Bruner glanced at his watch and realized it had only been a couple of minutes since he'd left. He calculated that Lomax must have just reached the main deck—considering the continuing barrage of ballistics being thrown at the ship.

"If he was still alive, at that point, he'd be just starting to head below."

"I silently hoped he'd hightail it, and get back soon."

"Safe to say, after Lomax left, no one followed orders from Dvorak or me. Chaos was in full pursuit at our battle station… and I suppose in the starboard director, as well."

"Shit, after a time, *I* didn't care. We were all concerned only about staying alive."

"I guess", said Lauren, "that's why God gave us officers. As enlisted men, you were always bellyaching about them when they were near. But to be without an officer during battle was like a ship without a rudder. To have no ammunition to boot… well, it complicated our lives, ten-fold."

"So much crap was going on around us. Frankly, with my rangefinder, I was the only one with a box seat to the biggest fight there ever was."

"With the exception of Lott, our crew moved around, aimlessly attempting to figure out what was going on outside."

"Beyond our battle station, and from where I stood, World War II had just started."

"Until ammunition was delivered to the guns, the director's crew had nothing to do… or even try to do. We all felt helpless as hell."

Still, Bruner and the crew wanted to see what was going on outside their metal perch. Some stuck their heads up through roof hatches, yelling back descriptions of the ongoing battle.

"We all cussed up a blue streak."

At least twice, looking through his window-hatch, Stratton yelled out, "Get ready! A torpedo track's headin' right for us."

Instinctively, the crew held their breath—and grabbed hold of anything within reach to prepare for the hit. We were thankful none came.

"What Don had seen", said Lauren, "must've been headin' for *West Virginia* or *Tennessee,* in front of us. Or they were duds."

"Whatever they were," said Lauren, "Don saw them coming, and I'll always be grateful... he was the one crew member Alvin and I trusted to keep us informed."

The crew did what they thought was best to protect themselves, to stay alive. Some, however, miscalculated.

Lauren's friend, Zimmerman, in the pointer position, kept moving in and out of the port hatchway, on to the sky control platform, at Lauren's left.

Zimmerman's job was similar to Dvorak's in that he sat on a metal seat and, with an identical steering wheel, moved the entire director and its optics—vertically—up or down, depending upon the degrees Lomax would call out."

"But with no officer around", said Lauren, "it seemed Zeke moved between inside and outside the director way too much, considering what was going on out there."

"Zeke ....Hey, Zeke", Lauren called out, "Get your ass back inside, before you get it shot off."

"Either he never heard me, or didn't give a shit... 'cause he continued to duck in and out, to yell about action in the battle, from right outside our director."

Zimmerman had a mind of his own. He'd step outside of the director, and play "chicken" with enemy pilots and their machine guns, all the while looking about to spot whatever he might see.

"Get the hell back in here, Zimmerman," Dvorak shouted.

"Didn't do any good," said Lauren.

"We'd yell back and fourth at one another. Then, someone else'd stick his head up through an overhead, or out a hatchway, to get a gander outside."

"Stay at your station… 'til Lomax gets back", Bruner yelled. "What the hell you trying to do… get your head shot off?"

Turns out, I was as guilty as the rest, far as the overheads were concerned. Sticking our heads up through the hatch was all we *had* to do, without anti-aircraft shells at our port-side guns, below.

"Didn't do much good", said Lauren. "It was still pure chaos, inside and out."

"Don't know how many times Alvin and I yelled at Zeke to stay inside… did no damn good. With Lomax below decks, he didn't want to take orders from us… and did whatever he damned well pleased."

"We gave up trying… it was no use."

— —

Frank S. Lomax

Frank Stuart Lomax was born on 24 April, 1917 in Broken Bow, Custer County, Nebraska, to James Conrad and Lyle (Young) Lomax. His family owned and ran a stock farm, which put them in the middle class.

Frank graduated from the US Naval Academy at Annapolis, and was commissioned an Ensign on 6 June 1940. When he entered the Navy he was 5′ 6″ tall, weighed 127 pounds, had medium brown hair, blue-gray eyes, and a tanned complexion. USS *Arizona* was Ensign Lomax's first ship. **On December 7, 1941, Frank Lomax was 24 years, 7 months and 13 days old.**

"Frank Lomax was the gun captain of our battle station, the port-side anti-aircraft director, and I guess it was his fate to be with us. In order to gain experience, Ensigns were most often transferred from one Battle Station to another every three or four months and Frank Lomax just happened to be with us on that fateful morning.

Lomax was a quiet kind of officer, but when he gave an order he expected it to be carried out without any BS. Whenever I visit the Shrine Wall at USS Arizona Memorial, my eyes search out his name, after my friends Billy, Alvin, and Casper.

Frank Stuart Lomax, Ensign

USS *Arizona*

KIA

Chapter 13
TIME WARPS & NIGHTMARES

0805

Along Battleship Row, what crew members recognized most were the sounds of firing .25 and .50 caliber hand-held machine guns, coming from those up in the crow's nests.

If anyone had thought about it, while under fire, they might've realized that machine gun fire—from all ships throughout Pearl—would never have stopped the immense incursion of the Japanese Imperial Air Force.

With the exception of its aircraft carriers, the entire Pacific Fleet was moored in the harbor, and situated too close to each other for its own errant shells to avoid hitting American ships, ground facilities, or even Honolulu, fifteen miles away.

The range was too far for a battleship's primary armament—the 14 inch guns—and too cumbersome to fire, within the harbor, itself. Their purpose was to bombard beachheads, up to 20 miles away, or to broadside enemy ships.

"In the beginning, we managed to get off initial salvos," said Lauren. "All failed, when it came to hitting the Jap's high altitude bombers. Hell, they were flying over two miles high… like geese in V-formation."

"Reminded me of hunting with my brother, Clarence, back in Washington, as a kid."

"Difference was… we watched what few anti-aircraft shells we got off explode, well before they'd ever reach that elevation... but we could hope."

As far as Lauren was concerned, in his mind—in the heat of the attack—he kept waiting and hoping the cavalry—American planes from an aircraft carrier —would ride in and save the day.

"Didn't happen", he said. "But it was like I had a sixth sense, as I followed the attack through my rangefinder. Whenever I heard our crew call out something critical, I'd leave my viewer, step up on the riser pipe, and stick my head out the hatch, above."

At one point, Zimmerman popped back inside and yelled.

"A *Nevada* gunner's facing down a Jap…looks like he's got a bead on a plane, heading straight for us." He ducked back out behind the director, on the catwalk.

Bruner jumped to the overhead, and saw an enemy plane come in, across the channel.

It came in low, over the water and—at about a thousand yards out—dropped a torpedo. It appeared to be heading for either *Arizona* or *Nevada.*

"Torpedo launched!," Stratton shouted to his crew.

All held their breath as they attempted any level of readiness. It was uncharted territory for each of them. All appeared helpless—without any ability to shoot back.

Again, Zimmerman shouted through the port-side hatchway, "Someone from *Nevada's* raising a helluva ruckus."

"Torpedo just missed us, *and* the *Nevada,"* Lauren yelled down, into the director. Skimmed past *Arizona's* stern and headed just under *Nevada's* bow."

"Damn, we were lucky this time," shouted Dvorak, with relief in his voice.

Glancing over to *Nevada,* tied up aft of *Arizona,* Bruner's attention was drawn to its port-side boat deck, where the 5" Anti-Aircraft guns were located, amidships.

Time slowed to a crawl, during the attack, as if a frame-by-frame film. "What we saw, heard, did, or thought, happened in milliseconds," said Lauren.

"And I swear to God… if the movies ever get it right, it's when they show bodies under stress, in slow motion, in battle."

"During the attack, it was like our brains worked harder as we processed every possible action… sound, or occurrence that surrounded us, in order so we could survive."

"Not certain how to explain it, except that everything appeared richer to me… tighter-packed… denser than normal…"

"I might not be the smartest turnip on the truck, but I know this… I took in things I'd never have seen under normal circumstances. And what each of us saw and heard that morning was burned into our minds forever."

Bruner observed gun barrel smoke coming out of *Nevada's* forward Anti-Aircraft gun—trained toward the south channel—and sailors with their gun captains, feeding what ammunition they had available.

"Some shooter from the gun that was causing the most racket had a bead on this incoming bastard. After I adjusted the optics on my rangefider, my first thought was that the gun crew's shooter might have been a sailor I knew who was a crack shot."

Word spread and all the crew observed as this real-life gunfight unfolded, "…just like an old Western movie."

"We saw another torpedo plane come in low following the first and then saw him get ready to drop his torpedo, but for some reason he never fired. His mistake. Then the shooter on the *Nevada* was on this guy, firing, with one long burst after another. We called it 'cutting the fuse.' Damned if *Nevada*'s gun crew didn't hit the bastard coming at us head on. Then there was just a puff of smoke and a buch of flames and fire. The plane nose-dived into the water, and flipped… ripping its wing from the fuselage."

To Lauren, it was one of a few bright spots during the entire attack. Cheers rang out from his battle station and they heard the same from other ships, throughout the harbor, as the enemy went down.

Bruner's eyes were drawn toward *Nevada* again, standing taller on the riser pipe, much of his body exposed, outside the overhead. Returning to his rangefiner, Lauren adjusted his optics toward *Nevada*, and its gun crew came into focus, their gun barrell still smoking.

He thought he recognized the shooter—a sailor named Ray Cannon, who he'd met back in Long Beach, who'd given him pointers on how to target shoot—and win prizes for the girls—at the Pike Amusment Park.

"The guy was one helluva shot. A real cowboy from Denver who grew up on a ranch he had called the 'Diamond K.' "

Leaving his rangefinder and sticking his head back out the hatch, Lauren looked across the two ships' decks for a brief moment, just as his friend turned toward *Arizona* as he walked toward Nevada's rail. Lauren raised his hand and waved.

Ray Cannon, recognizing the wave, returned the salute. An instant later, both quickly took cover as another enemy Zero took aim at *Arizona* and began firing.

"Can't remember anyone saying a word, or asking who the shooter was I may have recognized, but I knew that enemy pilot didn't have a prayer… as a chance friend, from my days long ago in Long Beach… had caught his target while out hunting."

So, there they were, during the heat of battle, from one ship to another—recognition between two men, for just seconds, knowing they may never meet, again.

"It *was* the last time I ever saw Ray… other than, at times, in my nightmares."

Still, in that instant, Lauren was hit with a flood of

images from his days when *Arizona* was stationed in Long Beach:

Strolls on Rainbow Pier, on double dates; endless rides on the wooden Cyclone Coaster; shoulder-to-shoulder sailors and families passing the mechanical monkeys and dancing hula girls, the Spook House, and the fat-to-skinny mirror—with the air hose that blew up unsuspecting girls' skirts.

Parts of Lauren's young life as a sailor had flashed before him.

And he was resolved.

Billy and I'll hit the Pike again when Arizona returns to the West Coast… if we make it outta this alive.

In near succession, three more bombs missed *Arizona*. One produced a towering splash adjacent to the port-side, amidships.

"A torpedo hit us," Stratton shouted.

The underwater explosion was large enough to convince a number of crew members that their ship had taken a torpedo.

Lauren attempted to calculate the minutes Lomax had been gone. But the explosive distractions made it difficult.

"I hoped he'd get back soon, so I wouldn't have to keep wasting my breath on Zimmerman… who didn't want to listen, anyway. Shit, it was up to Zeke if he had a death wish. At that point I no longer gave a damn."

Bruner returned to his rangefinder in another attempt to determine what was happening up and down the channel.

"One thing I figured out, soon enough… we were sure as hell getting our ass kicked."

Mere seconds had passed before the entire crew, aboard *Arizona* felt a jolt.

And time froze in place, and we all held our breaths again.

Without warning, the first bomb to make a direct hit careened off Number 4 turret's faceplate, near the ship's stern. The crew heard a heavy 'slap,' as it burst through the deck by the captain's hatch, splashed past officer country, shot through three decks below, and then detonated.

The blast radiated fore and aft, sending a concussive shockwave, and shrapnel, in all directions.

"It knocked us so hard… if you weren't holding on, it would've brought you to your knees."

Divots appeared in the outer painted surfaces, as shrapnel took large chunks out of the ship's paint, some a half inch deep.

"Despite all that, I can't remember any one of our crew falling."

Bruner and the others felt *Arizona* shudder hard, as fires erupted in the wardrooms, officer's cabins, and down into the third splinter deck's staterooms, and beyond.

"Must've killed a hell of a lot of officers aboard *Arizona*", said Lauren. "…since it happened so fast, and many of them would've still been below. Hell, it was Sunday morning."

He glanced out through the port hatchway, to his left.

Zeke had grabbed the rail, surrounding the sky control platform, and "…held on for dear life."

Aboard USS *Vestal*, Lt. J. G. John Henry Birmingham had been on the bridge, when the attack first began. He raced down a ladder to sound general quarters, then worked his way to his battle station, when two bombs—intended for *Arizona*—hit the repair ship, port and starboard.

Birmingham had spent the night of 6 December having dinner and playing cards with his friend, SC 2/c Thomas Owsley, one of *Arizona's* cooks.

Thomas had promised John that when Birmingham's 4 to 8 watch was over aboard *Vestal* "…We'll be making cinnamon rolls for *Arizona's* crew. Come back over and I'll save some for you and your guys."

So it was with concern, for his friend Owsley, when the first bomb made a direct hit on *Arizona*—that Birmingham's attention was drawn across decks to the battleship's stern.

As he turned toward *Arizona* he witnessed a strange sight. Birmingham checked his mind, *and* eyes, to confirm what he saw. High above *Arizona's* afterdeck, hundreds—perhaps thousands of pieces of green paper had shot high into the air, "...and were drifting across the deck and over toward *Vestal*."

But it wasn't just any paper.

Aboard *Arizona,* Zimmerman raced back to the director's port hatchway.

"Hey, take a look, outside", he said. "Honest to God, its raining money. Swear ta' God!"

The aft bomb's concussion had forced an immense volume of air through the second deck's hallway, past Junior Officer's Country. It buckled steel and ripped through anything in its path, including the paymaster's disbursing office—where cash had been waiting for disbursement for liberty payments.

This created a vacuum that then sucked the money back toward the bomb's penetration site, and shot it up and out any breach produced by the strike.

Again, Bruner stuck his head out the overhead.

The sky was filled with bills, of all denominations. They fluttered through the air—and swirled through the holocaust, toward *Vestal*. As they floated down, most were caught up in the roiling black clouds, to be consumed in the burning waters and shipboard fires.

"It was a sight, I'll tell you," said Lauren.

Birmingham, aboard *Vestal*, and Bruner, aboard *Arizona*, both noted that no one paid it another mind. "....And no one on *Arizona's* crew... or aboard *Vestal,* that I'm aware of", said Lauren, "ever picked up that blood money."

"Those dollar bills were worthless, and blood-soaked," John Birmingham would later recall.

Other than Lott, who still sat huddled in the corner, none of Bruner's crew had thought a bomb could sink *Arizona*.

"Hell, during training and on maneuvers, we were schooled and made well aware that *Arizona* had armored decks. So we were pretty certain any bomb's damage would just be superficial."

If hit, they'd rescue the wounded, secure the hatches, flood the damaged compartments if necessary, and move on.

For another split second, Bruner thought of the many times he'd walked past the disbursement office.

And he wondered if the paymaster was inside when the enemy came knocking.

"It was customary for most assistant pay clerks to disburse leave money, by division. They'd move around, fore to aft, with their cash boxes full and a Marine. And they'd make sure any sailor on scheduled leave could get their money before catching a launch to shore.

"Each sailor would then sign the clerk's logbook, for the record. It was a pretty efficient system.

"Most of the time we were paid in ones, twos, and five-dollar bills."

Sitting in his molded metal seatback, Dvorak used old-fashioned muscle to crank one direction or another. "Always good at his job, there was no bullshit from Alvin, unless he'd been out drinkin' during liberty."

"Alvin!" Lauren shouted, "Bring us southwest, at two twenty-two degrees. Wanna' see if I can catch me some enemy comin' across from Ford Island."

"Two twenty-two, it is," Dvorak shouted back.

He put his entire body into cranking the vertical steering wheel. The gear-teeth grabbed hold inside the barbette, the director swung southwest toward the Naval Air Station, and on to face what little of Ford Island could be seen.

Then it stopped at the computer's locking pin.

"Far as she'll let me go."

"Got it," Lauren shouted back.

Stratton confirmed the coordinates.

The director now faced *Tennessee* and *West Virginia's* stern, berthed in Foxtrot 6.

Bruner's head was glued to the rangefinder's view piece. At once, he'd fine-tune matching knobs near each side of his face. But time and again, concussive explosions throughout the harbor sent vibrations across all surfaces, and sometimes knocked his optics out of focus.

"Shit!" he'd repeat, under his breath, then refocused, once more.

All Bruner could find were low-flying planes, with which he had to contend. Each one so swift, it was difficult to get a lock on them.

"Tryin' to bring what's happening into focus," he yelled to anyone listening. "Problem is, the bastards are too damned close for me to track… comin' in too fast. And the smoke…"

"Same problem, here," yelled back Alvin.

Due to proximity, Bruner and Stratton had to let the planes fly right through their range of vision. Bruner popped up through his overhead, to get a visual fix.

"Torpedo track coming in port-side," Zimmerman shouted, from the sky platform.

Stratton shouted, "This one's comin'. Brace yourselves."

Lauren pulled himself down from the overhead, but not before having glanced down over the forward decks. Bodies lay everywhere, as sailors and Marines—those who were still alive—made helpless attempts at getting shells to the guns, to retaliate.

Lauren found himself muttering, under his breath, "Shit, no, no, no…" Feeling powerless to do anything, he slammed his hand down on the rangefinder, in anger.

"Goddamnit!"

"Must've been a dud," Zimmerman shouted, outside.

"Alvin," yelled Lauren, "crank us south to two-thirty… I wanna' see those assholes comin' down Battleship Row."

"Two-thirty, it is, pal." Alvin's arm muscles tightened and he put the gears into motion, again.

The director bore to the south, toward the Harbor's entrance, near Hospital Point.

"As soon as the director came to a stop, and Alvin had called out the degrees I'd asked for… I'd return to my lens."

Dvorak climbed up on his wooden step, stuck his head out the overhead hatch, and watched for a moment.

Lauren's mind flashed to a better time, the night before, when they both rode the bus back to Pearl. Lauren felt Nikki's presence, and the memory of her fragrance overtook his senses.

Something more pressing brought him back.

"I was about to use the rangefinder, when two big explosions reverberated, nearby."

Dvorak brought his head back in and cried out, "*Oklahoma*'s just taken two more torpedoes… she's listing even more to port." Then, Dvorak's head was back out the hatch. This time, he climbed up on his seat, for a better view.

Bruner returned to his lens, and witnessed another chapter of nightmares as they unfolded.

The director's crew went silent. "We grabbed any opening we could find to observe *Oklahoma*, as she rapidly began to heel."

Haunting cries rose from *Oklahoma*, and from nearby ships.

"*Oklahoma's* turning turtle."

Its men struggled to hold on to the hull, as it moved from list to roll. Bruner watched sailors step over the railings and climb onto its hull, to avoid being pulled under and trapped, beneath.

"Straight out... the sight of that giant battleship through my lens... as she began to roll over, burned into my mind."

"Scared me shitless. Hell, although I joined the Navy, I could barely swim."

"Even Lott jumped up from his corner to watch."

"*Oklahoma* appeared so close through my optics, I felt as if I was standing along with her crew, while they scrambled over the exposed hull."

"It was the worst... and was amplified by all the gunfire and explosions around us. Something I've never forgotten," said Lauren, "...still appears like a neon sign in my dreams, and has always given me night sweats."

A loud woosh broke Lauren's momentary trance.

"I heard this sound come outta' nowhere... a woosh not on top of us, but close by. Then... *bam!*"

Zimmerman had ducked around to starboard for protection, then popped in, again.

"*Vestal's* just taken a bomb!" he said. "...think she's gonna' go down."

"By that time, I sure as hell began to wonder if Lomax would ever return."

"Things began to move faster by the minute," said Lauren. By this time… we all knew the battle was lost. You could see it written on our faces."

"Lomax hadn't come back. The planes were too close or too high to sight. No ammunition had been brought up to the double-A's. We were up shit creek."

"During this time both Zeke and Alvin shouted back reports of activity, on all sides. And my head popped in and out of the overhead, to confirm their sightings."

"There ain't nothin' close to fun, in a battle you know you're gonna' lose."

"All we could hope for was to stay alive until the enemy ran out of rounds, bombs, torpedoes… or fuel."

"It didn't appear that would happen any time soon."

— —

SECOND TO THE LAST TO LEAVE

Donald G. Stratton

Donald Gay Stratton was born on 14 July 1922 in Inavale, Webster County, Nebraska to Robert G. and Jessie (Rutledge) Stratton. Don enlisted in the Navy for six years on 16 October 1940, in Omaha, Nebraska.

At the time of his enlistment, Don Stratton weighed 150 pounds, was 5′ 10″ tall, had brown eyes, light brown hair, and a ruddy complexion. He reported to USS *Arizona,* which was his first ship, on 9 December 1940. **Don Stratton was 19 years, 4 months and 23 days old, on the morning of the attack on Pearl Harbor.**

"Don Stratton is a friend of mine, and as fate would have it, the two of us escaped Arizona together over a ship's line to USS Vestal, as part of what Military Historians call Arizona's Greatest Escape. Don and I have spent a good deal of our lives working to get Joseph George from USS Vestal, who was one of the two men responsible for saving our lives along with the lives of our crew, the Congressional Medal of Honor, which we feel he rightly deserves.

In the spring of 2017, the two of us working together traveled to Washington, D.C., me just shy of 97, to meet with the President at the White House, along with the Joint Chiefs of Staff and members of Congress to make this case and to let Joe George's family know that we have never forgotten his courage.

This journey has proven successful and as I write this note, Don Stratton and I have been informed by the Navy that due to our efforts, Joe George has been awarded the Bronze Star with Valor in order that this forgotten Pearl Harbor hero has been recognized.

Read the Full Story of *Arizona*'s Greatest Escape
Along With Viewing Rare Photos of the Attack by Visiting:
USS*Arizona*sGreatestEscape.com

Donald Gay Stratton, Sea 1/c

USS *Arizona*

Survivor

Chapter 14
DEVIL'S DISCIPLES

0806:00

At this time, the already cramped director picked up a new recruit. George Sanford Hollowell stopped on his way down from the crow's nest, and appeared at Bruner's hatchway.

"What're you gonna do?" he hollered.

"Scared the crap outta me," said Lauren, "comin' through my hatch like that. Sonovabitch came up, right behind me, stuck his head in, and yelled."

"Shit, as if I know," Lauren answered back.

Bruner heard the whine of another approaching Zero—and its machine guns. He reached for Hollowell's belt and pulled hard.

"Get your ass in here."

They ducked out of the hatchway to shield themselves against the bulkhead. And Zimmerman scrambled around the other side of the director, for cover.

No sooner had Hollowell stepped in beside Bruner, than machine gun rounds created more divots in the steel cube.

The kid's face blanched "...as white as his shirt," said Lauren. "Something I've never forgotten."

"But if I'd had a mirror, I'm sure my face would have looked just as ghostly."

"Can I hang out with you guys?" Hollowell blurted out. "Nothin' but Marines up in the nest. I had no gun up there, and nothing to do."

Lauren felt Hollowell genuinely wanted to be useful, somewhere.

"Don't know where the hell else I can go…" the kid said. "Or who to report to. Besides… I'd be torn to bits tryin' to get down to the main deck."

"The more the merrier," Dvorak shouted, above the din.

Glum-faced, Hollowell shifted by Bruner, and moved over to stand near Lott—still crouched in the corner. He glanced down at the lump under the blanket, and looked to Bruner. Lauren just shrugged.

Once again, Dvorak and Bruner attempted to get Zimmerman under control.

"He wouldn't come in from outside… just wanted to see it all, I guess. Don't know how the hell he avoided a hit."

Inside, Lauren continued to put up with Lott.

"The new guy, Hollowell, glanced at the lump, still moaning, under the blanket. He moved closer to my rangefinder, but said little."

A native son of Phoenix—proud to serve aboard *Arizona*—Hollowell, turned to Bruner and yelled above the clamor. "Let me know if you need anything done… if I can help do anything…"

Seemed to be a good kid, thought Lauren.

"See if you can talk Zeke, out there, into comin' back inside. I gotta' get back to my scope."

Hollowell, nodded and, without question, ducked under the rangefinder. He moved toward the hatchway and prepared to call out to Zimmerman.

Bruner glanced at his watch. Its leather strap had come loose out of the free-loop.

No time to adjust it, now, he thought.

— —

0806:15

High above *Arizona,* a bomb had given warning, with its recognizable whistle—heating up the air that surrounded its nose and fins. The missile nicked the ship, bounced off the anti-torpedo bulkhead on the port side, then detonated.

A waterspout shot up as high as the main mast. As if a rogue wave, it doused the entire superstructure and upper decks.

At the port-side catwalk, Zimmerman shouted out, "Wahoo!" as the spray drenched him.

Again, the vessel was jarred, and active crew attempted to reassemble at their stations.

"Alvin," Lauren shouted. "Crank 'er 'round, back more toward *Oklahoma*. It'll give me a better look."

Dvorak responded to Bruner's coordinates, on his wheel, so they could better respond to the onslaught—*if* Lomax could just liberate ammunition from the stores below.

Again, the gear's teeth grabbed hold. The steel cube swung toward *Arizona's* forward.

The crew jumped into action, once more, in an attempt to find a target that might be within range.

"Hell. If nothing else, we were getting plenty of practice."

Lauren leaned into his viewer, in another attempt to survey the channel's attack.

0806:30

Originating off aircraft carrier, *Hiryu*—barely seen with the naked eye, at 10,480 feet elevation—a B5N2 Nakajima high-level bomber, led a V-formation of 5 Kates, over Oahu's Kahuku Point.

Along with 44 other high-level bombers from *Kaga, Soryu,* and *Agaki,* each squadron bypassed the southwest tip of the Koolau mountain range, then approached Pearl Harbor's entrance over the Western-Pacific side of the island.

Each Kate carried one Type-99, No. 80 Mark 5, 1750-pound bomb—including a 50-pound burst-charge, packed inside its tip. It was covered with 4 inches of machined-forged, armor-piercing steel.

Two miles above Oahu, Lieutenant Shojiro Kondo, the Nakajima bombardier for lead pilot Tadashi Kusumi, found a target and commenced release of his payload. It contained 132 solid pounds of toxic, pale yellow cast crystals that formed the explosive, TriNitroAnisole.

Starting its descent, the warhead picked up speed and moved with purpose—averaging over 377 feet per second. Its kinetic energy increased, as it sought the target.

Within 26 seconds, it would be found.

Aboard *Arizona,* a haunting noise accompanied the distant hum of 49 approaching, high-level bombers.

For the crew, time froze in place, as they took in all that surrounded them. Other sounds disappeared. Nothing else seemed as consequential, to the crew, as what might be approaching from the heavens.

Movement of the port-side director, distorted Lauren's rangefinder. His view was limited to blurred action, in the channel.

He wondered if his buddies had similar thoughts about possible outcomes. *Would they be sitting at Smith's Union ever again, commiserating over beer? Would tomorrow be a time for reflection and making better decisions about their lives, and how best to lead them? Or, will we even be around to think about 'what might be next?'*

0806:40

Bruner and the others looked to the overhead, and waited for any sign that might give them hope.

A heavy splash in the water... a near miss or bounce off the torpedo blisters. Something, anything—except a direct hit.

But the sound became more intense and disquieting.

It came, at first, from very high, then closer, in direction, as if on a bead to blast open the gates of hell, below.

"It was a long way… away sound", said Lauren. "….Like the roaring whoosh of a colossal javelin, it got louder and louder as it approached."

0806:43

One-by-one, the tension increased, as time stretched to the limit.

To a man, they scrutinized each other's faces, searching for recognition and reassurance—confirmation—*any* sign to signal in a countenance that this one would miss. That this bomb would not be "the one."

0806:50

Lauren returned to his optics, to locate any sign to contradict their concern.

The plotting room's rangekeeper may not have been able to compute this quadrant in time, mathematically. But in terms of physical moments, seconds were split like hairs.

The human mind absorbed thousands of elements—through each god-given sense—and it slowed, for *Arizona's* crew, as though time itself had been sedated and stretched to its limits.

Milliseconds became microseconds. Microseconds stretched as if they were pulled taffy.

No longer was the woosh sound important.

One thousand seven hundred and seven pounds of destructive power hurtled from ten thousand feet, to find its mark.

0806:56

Off to the right, in the same starboard direction Dvorak had cranked the director, a enormous collision met with *Arizona's* forecastle—producing a two-foot long hole in the armored steel deck.

"Those who designed and engineered *Arizona,* decades before, to prevent bomb penetration", said Lauren, "had never met the Japanese."

In 1910, during *Arizona's* design phase, what engineers thought to be thicker, reinforced steel—to stay the piercing of a deck—didn't take into consideration a plane whose seventeen hundred pound payload could be dropped from a height of over ten thousand feet.

No one suspected kinetic speeds that would defy an early 20th Century engineer's education—and his need to forecast an expanded use of their knowledge of physics.

A hundred sixty feet aft of bow—just forward of Turret Two, near the starboard paravane—the bomb breached what was believed to be solid, impenetrable steel.

And *Arizona's* entire world altered, forever.

In a matter of seconds—as if a Great Dane had been caught in a heavy downpour—the entire ship convulsed and tried to shake off the intruder.

Arizona shuddered fore to aft.

One-by-one, the men aboard ship felt the first thrust.

Time dissolved, shallow breaths were taken, and hearts paused to calculate possible damage, as the missile plunged below decks.

And the director's crew held a collective breath as the bomb took seven seconds to locate its sweet spot.

0806:57

To Bruner, "…it was like a horrific accident on a busy highway, that just wouldn't stop. Sounded as if two trucks crashed, head on, right before us. And it jarred the whole damn ship."

0806:58

Each deck penetration conjured vivid, indelible impressions on the minds of the crew, each strike more violent than the one that preceded it. While the converted, high-altitude bomb pierced the decks, below, it marked time as it waited for its delayed fuse to ignite.

0806:59

Metal twisted against metal, one deck after another.

The demolition continued through the main deck's crew berthing areas, then drove into the second deck, past the carpenter's workshop, the laundry, and the surgeon's exam and operating rooms.

With each penetration, a loud "clunk" echoed back, from below. Sensed throughout the ship, *Arizona* shook and convulsed repeatedly—as a serial killer forced its way through each deck level.

"We couldn't help but feel it."

"Don't know about anyone else… but if there'd been enough time to think, the sounds were so close, we would've had chicken skin, head to toe. It was that frightening."

0807:00

Momentum slowed as the bomb forced its way through the third and splinter decks, tearing apart its bulk provisions store and the supply department's main issuing room.

Both were Kitty-cornered from the sailor's detention cell—the brig—where a scrappy, drunken sailor, out of West Texas, while on leave the night before, had been held for general court-martial, under a charge of murder.

Whatever type of bomb had been dropped, the crew had no choice but to listen and wait for it to come to a stop.

Finally, the bomb rested, deep below, at the first platform deck.

And all of the prior damage would be insignificant, up against what was to come.

No one could predict how destructive it might be. In microseconds, Lauren pondered how bad it would hurt his ship—a prize among America's great battleships. It had, in due course, been awarded to him, after completion of basic, and "...through the luck-of-the-draw."

One bomb and two near misses, before this... and we're still afloat...

In their own silence, they waited and braced for an evil spirit to rise out of the depths. But it didn't come.

In their altered timeframe, the sounds just stopped.

Inside the director, they each looked to the corner, where Lott had buried himself.

"Even *he* stopped moaning," said Lauren, "and appeared to be listening from under the blanket."

For one split second, the men allowed a moment of elation... and dared to smile... in hopes it might've been a dud.

"She didn't explode," Zimmerman yelled, from outside. "Thank God the bastard didn't explode."

"There's a reason survivors refer to that particular missile as 'the lucky bomb.' ", said Lauren. "But there's a hell of a lot of irony in its nickname, too."

"A lucky blow… the Japanese pilot and bombardier might argue it was skill, in light of *where* it struck. For us… it was a sucker punch to the head *and* gut."

"If you'd stood in a passageway, outside the forward hatchways on the first platform deck, where my best friend Billy Mann was, at the time… in particular, you'd see engraved and embossed label plates, with designated letters 'F' or 'M'… and a compartment or tank number to classify the purpose of any room or cavity.

"Where that lucky bomb hit, the letter 'F' designated fuel or diesel oil compartments; 'M' was short for 'Munitions'… most anything to do with storage and handling spaces for ammunition.

0807:01

In the forward section of that deck, where the bomb came to rest—near frame 40, "…the compartments contained munitions materieal a sailor *wouldn't* want an explosive warhead to meet up with," said Lauren. "Unless you were the enemy.

"Shit… forget about our own bomb and catapult charge magazines stored there… the mine-charge mags, and other smaller explosives. What would send us skyward was right where my best friend, Billy, manned his post… at the forward hatchways to the explosive black powder magazines."

Deep below decks—at Billy Mann's battle station—the warhead met, near dead center, with 1.3 million pounds of stored black powder, for the 14" and 5" guns. There were thousands of stored rounds, intended for the anti-aircraft machine guns—surrounded on both sides of the hull, and below that, by 1.5 million gallons of diesel fuel oil.

At the most forward peak-tanks—located below on the second platform deck in the hold, and within the double bottom—were storage canisters and tanks loaded with 12 tons of gasoline, designated for reconnaissance aircraft.

At once, the men understood what they had forgotten to fear the most: A massive explosion—way down deep in the bowels of the ship. And they sensed something ruthless and grim was about to happen.

"All we could do was wait for the devil to show up, from below… to make his personal appearance."

"And we didn't have to wait long."

0807:02

While obscured, the bomb found its blast seat, as a .02 second delay fuse ran its course. The heat from the primary explosion released energy in the enclosed spaces, found below decks. And it sucked in any excess oxygen, as it produced a mixture of carbon dioxide and moisture, drawn from the air.

In an instant, the combined brew created a super-heated atmosphere that expanded as it searched for its point of egress—and total combustion.

Sailors on the sky control platform, and throughout the ship, next heard a loud, muffled sound.

WUMP!

At the speed of sound, the initial flame's head began its climb to the surface.

Across the harbor, just northwest of Battleship Row, sat Hospital Ship USS *Solace*. Navy doctor, Erik Hakansson, had decided, that morning to film the majestic harbor setting for his family. He stood at the starboard railing, before the attack began, with a handheld film camera.

And he felt compelled to keep the camera aimed down Battleship Row.

Unseen by human eye—at the time—his camera captured an unconfined, single, visible flame that leapt from deep below decks, sprung out through the bomb's entry point, wrapped itself around turret one, then disappeared, as all remaining air was sucked back into the void to feed the monster.

Less than half an instant, later, in the confines of the second platform deck—where all the air had been depleted by the first detonation—a massive closed chamber was created that would carry out the enemy's strategy beyond even their own wildest expectations.

And a cataclysmic chamber of evil incarnate distorted and disfigured *Arizona*, as it blasted upwards and forward.

The starboard magazines ignited, within; morphed into super-heated expanded gases; then, triggered another explosion of the port magazine's cordite stores.

In unison, the ship's hull bulged its port and starboard sides outward. Compressed air bellowed upward through *Arizona's* stack and shot a gigantic column of black soot and smoke straight up, hundreds of feet above waterline.

Then a louder, more forceful explosive roar followed.

The bomb's load of packed TriNitroAnisole—a "moderate" explosive in and of itself, was equivalent to around 107 sticks of dynamite. But when combined with 1.3 million pounds of explosive black powder, and over a million gallons of Bunker-C diesel fuel and aviation gasoline, the explosive power was equal to more than 525 tons of TNT.

At once, *Arizona* leaned forward, as it retched to vomit back whatever it had swallowed. And a convulsive vibration shook every rivet and bulkhead in its hull.

Resembling an angry stallion, millions of pounds of explosive thrust sent *Arizona* rearing and kicking into the air.

As though ignition had been triggered on an enormous rocket, *Arizona's* skin blew open and vented a propulsive force, so enormous, that it raised its thirty-seven ton hull over thirty feet above waterline.

From the port-side director, Stratton shouted out, "Whoa Nelly."

"Seemed as if I was back on the Long Beach Pike's roller coaster," said Lauren. "Felt it in the pit of my stomach and in my rattled brain."

"Up we rose, then down. Quickly but… to our senses, it decelerated, as if in a slow motion sequence… if that makes any sense."

"There was heavy cussin'," said Lauren, "as our ship continued to buck high in the water. I swear… all of us called out to God, in one way or another."

"*Arizona's* hind legs reared up outta' the water, just before the fires of hell ascended."

Following orders from Bruner, Hollowell had just called out to Zimmerman through the port hatchway, "Hey, you, get the hell back in here."

Zimerman had already pivoted to Hollowell's voice, and started his race for the hatch. But as he reached the door, the bucking ship sent him flying to the bridge wing's catwalk

He grabbed hold of the railing, pulled himself up, and jumped for the hatchway handles.

At that moment, Lauren was still bent into his optics. "The ship's bucking threw me off balance. For whatever reason, I gripped the range finder, tightened my eyes to the rubber face guard, and continued to look for God-knows-what, as I rode it back down.

Mid-ship, the bow tore apart, as if ripped paper. And *Arizona's* entire forward interior section of decks pancaked—and was catastrophically destroyed.

"Hell, it just pulled away from itself and split apart like Tinkertoys."

Huge metal shards, mechanical assemblies, human torsos, and body parts were sent aloft, hundreds of feet into the air. They were scattered in the water, aboard nearby ships, and onto Ford Island—tossed as if unwanted jetsam.

Without warning, the conning tower and forward turrets collapsed and the foremast began to tilt forward.

With purpose, the beast began its rise to the surface.

"It was a demon outta' Hell," said Lauren. "And it put a hurt on us that'd last a lifetime."

The ship gave vent to a massive fireball that shot over 500 feet above the waterline. It spread and gutted the forward section of the ship; rose past the superstructure deck; climbed the main mast; and, without discrimination, shred and disintegrated the limbs of ship's officers, Sailors, and Marines, caught anywhere in the vicinity.

Aboard *Vestal*, Lt. J. G. Birmingham, and many near him were slammed backwards, against a bulkhead, but not before he witnessed the immense fireball cross over to their ship's stern, then retract to its flame's center point, aboard *Arizona*.

"It was like someone had lit a monstrous wooden match, as it's tip exploded outwards," said Birmingham. "You know... the kind you'd use to light a fireplace."

"But this one was colossal, leaving behind a towering flame that roared like a mad grizzly, and engulfed anything in its path."

The concussion from the main explosion, was intense—a force so large that, without discrimination, it blew officers and sailors off the decks of *Arizona, Vestal, Nevada, Tennessee*, and *West Virginia*.

Arizona slammed down hard.

Combined with the explosive force, it cut through the harbor's water supply line that fed Ford Island, and created a ten-foot tidal wave that plowed onto its banks.

What had occurred erased that moment from Lauren's mind for over seventy-five years. He struggled to describe, from his perspective, what had brought on seven decades of silence, night terrors, and cold sweats.

"At first we'd heard far off rumbling sounds that grew louder, as they rose from the depths of our ship."

But by the time the monster reached topside, the sounds had morphed into an ear-splitting scream, as if "… all of the Devil's disciples had risen from below. And they were mad as hell."

As if a gale force wind blew from a giant blacksmith's bellows, "…that's when an enormous black mushroom cloud vented upwards, right behind my rear hatchway… and shot vertically through the uptake stack, hundreds of feet above our ship."

With lightning speed, the gigantic fireball followed behind, and ascended out of the bomb's crater, beside Turret 2, with an explosive, thunderous roar.

Venting toward port, then starboard, the violent concussion blew many of *Arizona*'s and *Vestal*'s crews off its decks and into the water. Fires that had burned on *Vestal* were blown out by the blast's force.

Body parts and chunks of steel landed on Ford Island. And anyone caught forward or amidships were either incinerated or sent into the burning, oil-covered water.

Many, fortunate enough to be on deck, aft of the death blast, were knocked overboard—but to safer waters, if they could beat the sharks to shore.

"No one could've predicted the size of this thing," said Lauren.

With his eyes at first focused on the optics, Bruner witnessed what appeared to be a total blackout—then, the brightest light he'd ever seen.

Almost blinding him—after first reflecting off the lenses—it was as if, following two million years as an extinct volcano, Ko'olau had come to life, again—right below *Arizona*.

The expanding wave of intense heat caused his exterior optical glass to explode, as the blast created its own hurricane force winds that propelled the monstrous fireball outward and skyward.

"Hollowell had just ducked under my range finder, to call Zimmerman inside," said Lauren.

"That's when it hit."

"And," said Lauren, "it happened in the blink of an eye."

Hollowell just managed to shout, "Hey, Zimmerman, better get your ass..."

The fireball engulfed the entire superstructure—where sailors had climbed to their battle stations, less than ten minutes prior.

It encircled the main mast; shot across to *Vestal*; and was sucked back to its point of origination. Left behind was a deafening howl, out of the enormous fire that ensued.

The captain's and admiral's bridge—and those inside, were incinerated as the explosive fire enveloped the starboard director, shot over the sky control platform, wrapped itself around the port-side director, and then climbed the main mast and beyond, as it chased the acrid, black, mushroom cloud—and created the perfect fire storm.

Hundreds of screams blended into a high-pitched wail as the explosion, and its subsequent repercussions, tore into steel and human flesh with the compulsion of a serial killer.

And a thousand men would, in time, take their last breaths.

The powerful blast first entered the director through the starboard hatchway, where Dvorak sat—in a direct line with the incoming fireball—hands tight on his steering wheel's brodie knobs.

The concussion and fireball hit him first—full force—while it raced starboard to port. As if a rag doll, Dvorak was at once lifted from his position, and slammed back, hard, against his fixed metal seat.

The force then caught Stratton in the face and chest; grabbed and slammed him against the bulkhead and, according to Stratton, "…rattled me around like a piñata."

"I thought I was going blind, from the fire", Stratton would tell Lauren, years later.

On the platform, Zeke had already decided to head back inside. He managed to grab hold of the hatchway handles just as the blast raced through and circumnavigated the director.

The force of the concussion hit him in the back, and face-on. As if a spirit's presence had seized his body, it grabbed at Zimmerman's torso and bent him forward, then backwards. The impact ripped his grip from the door handles, sucked him into the flames, and dispatched him, hard, against the platform's railing.

Inside, Hollowell was propelled backwards, across the steel cube. His head slammed against the range finder with a forceful blow, and his body was dumped next to Lott—who had pulled Lauren's blanket tighter across his own head.

The hellish fireball had sucked oxygen from the cube, shot across the steel shell, and merged with a second blast of flames through the port and rear hatchways.

As if in a boxing match—in a futile attempt to protect his face from being hit by the fire and heat—Lauren held tight to the range finder. Instinct caused him to raise his right arm around the viewport, for protection.

But the conjoined fireball circled around the interior and assaulted his body. It upended Lauren, sucked him down, and battered his head against the range finder's floor pedals.

Lauren was thrown hard against the forward bulkhead, and landed at the base of Dvorak's chair.

"Imagine... we were caught in this metal cube, dressed only in our white shorts, t-shirts and caps... and every cubic inch, inside, had ignited in flames. If someone had watched from outside, it would've appeared more like a crematory oven... with our bodies, inside. The difference being... shit, we were being cremated alive."

"At the time, it felt like firecrackers and flames had torn at my body... yet, I was detached, with *no* ability to control the consequences."

As if flames from a dragon's mouth, the enormous fireball retreated, and was sucked back out the hatchways—to implode upon itself.

But the bomb had served its purpose. And the fireball disappeared as swiftly as it had rolled through the director.

The entire ship forward of the main mast had been demolished. Left behind was a massive wake of destruction.

Outside the director, an intense inferno raged around the crew.

With each successive explosion, a new containment section would breach, below decks, as additional munitions heated up and blew through their weakened bulkheads.

Arizona, as big as it was, again heaved into the air, fell back to the water and rocked up, down and sideways. With each successive explosion, it ripped itself apart at the seams.

Horrendous sounds split the air and reverberated across the harbor. Popping rivets, bursting pipes, and screeching steel, accompanied the explosions. Transverse bulkheads were wrenched from beams, and twisted metal pipes were torn apart, as if soft licorice.

Without further warning, the bow split from amidships.

Arizona's main mast, and its superstructure deck, began to sag more—then, without ceremony, leaned ever so slowly forward.

— —

SECOND TO THE LAST TO LEAVE

George S. Hollowell

George Stanford Hollowell was born to George Arthur and Lorena Harriet "Hattie" (Bowen) Sanford on 9 July 1920 in Phoenix, Maricopa County, Arizona. He graduated from high school in 1938, and enlisted in the Navy on 21 January 1939 in Phoenix. When inducted, George was 5′ 5″ tall, weighed 137 pounds, had brown eyes, light brown hair, and a ruddy complexion.

George Hollowell reported to USS *Arizona*, which was his first ship, on 11 September 1939 at San Pedro, California. **On 7 December 1941, George Sanford Hollowell was 21 years, 4 months, and 29 days old.**

"George Hollowell was a spotter for Arizona's forward 14-inch gun turrets. His battle station was in the crow's nest of the main mast high above my battle station. I had never met him until the attack began. He came down the ladder from the crow's nest and asked if he could hang out with our crew, hoping to escape certain death. Fate did not see it this way.

George Hollowell was standing next to me, just two feet away when Arizona exploded, and its concussion and fireball racing through our battle station caught Geroge and threw his head against the Director's Bulkhead. He was KIA that morning and I have thought about him often as I wrote my book. God rest his soul."

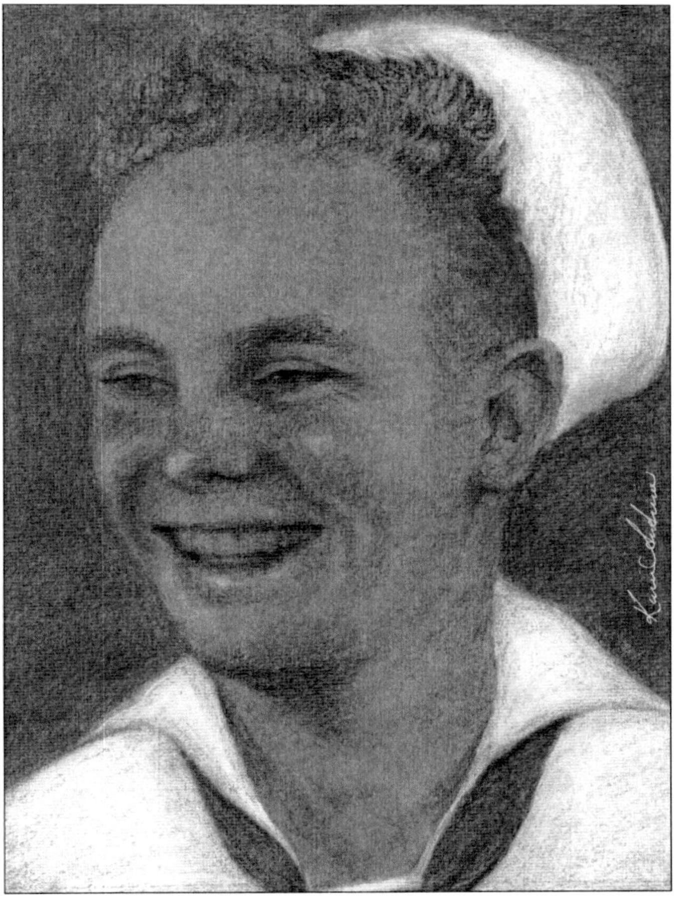

George Sanford Hollowell

George Sanford Hollowell, Cox

USS *Arizona*

KIA

Chapter 15
THE FRUIT BOWL

7 December 1941
McCleary, Washington
10:05 a.m. Pacific Standard Time

Lucille and John Kellerman sat at their dining room table, as they had on many Sundays—after she had pulled John to early church service. Relaxed and at ease, the sound of five-year old Mary-Lu playing upstairs competed with John's rustling newspaper pages and with the ticking of a small clock on the dining area hutch.

The family had finished a light meal.

Unlike Mary-Lu, Lauren and Clarence had moved on into adulthood. Lauren had joined the Navy in 1938. His older brother, Clarence, had moved out and married.

Lucille rose from her chair and headed for the kitchen, dishes in hand. John sorted through the *McCleary Stimulator*, Sunday Edition, to catch up on news.

McCleary, Washington was a quiet lumber mill village. For ten years, following the 1930 Census, its sign on the town's edge stated "Population 1,150"—a coincidence for the Kellermans' house. Lauren Bruner's pre-Navy address had been the same number. When the 1940 census was published, their McCleary precinct's population had increased by just twenty.

Company-owned, by Henry McCleary, the village was tucked at the north-western edge of Capitol State Forest, between the state capital, Olympia—15 miles east—and Aberdeen, 27 miles west. Smaller villages encircled an area that made up the remaining region of Grays Harbor County.

The two-story Kellerman house was about thirty-five by thirty-five feet square—larger than homes of other families who had struggled to put roofs over their heads during the Great Depression. To a young child like Mary-Lu, a home could seem larger than it was. But it was still small enough to make it a cramped home, when someone desired privacy.

"Before I left for the Navy, in thirty-eight, we all just accepted what we had," said Lauren. "After all, the Depression was in full bore, prior to World War Two."

The Kellerman family hadn't given much thought to whether they lived a sparse life.

Lucille's previous home with her first husband, LeRoy Bruner-Daniels, was much different. In 1920, LeRoy began working as a "shingle weaver" at the cedar shingle mill in McCleary. They rented a small rundown clapboard house, provided by the company. In 1925, however, Leroy became quite ill. Diagnosed with tuberculosis, and sent to a sanitarium, he was kept busy, making reed baskets.

Lucille was able to step into LeRoy's job, in order to feed her children that, by then, included five— Dorothy, Clarence, Lauren, Pauline, and Chester.

Without their father around, they managed to subsist on vegetables and fruit from their garden, and on salmon and trout caught by Lauren and Clarence from nearby creeks.

Two years later, LeRoy died, at age 29, from Cedar Lung Disease—contracted, over the years, from inhaling heavy doses of cedar dust in the shingle mill. His illness, misdiagnosed as tuberculosis, was considered the lumberman's equivalency to coal-miner's black lung disease.

Ironically, it appeared that all workers who contracted CLD were "misdiagnosed" with tuberculosis, and sent to the sanitarium—if they didn't die first.

Upon LeRoy's death, the company decided they had to give Lucille's job to a man. His widow and children were instructed to leave the premises. To Lucille, it was just the way it was.

"But my mother was an attractive woman," said Lauren. "A 'looker,' as they referred to beautiful ladies in those days."

"She had little trouble finding a second husband to help put food on the table, after that."

Her second husband, John Kellerman, worked long hours planing fir doors at the Henry McCleary Lumber Mill. A small but feisty German, Kellerman had been a longtime bachelor.

Following her first husband's death, Lucille had thought Kellerman quite capable of providing a more secure life for her. It would also provide a way for her second son Lauren to return from living with his cousin Flora and her husband, Burton Troxell.

That extended family arrangement had followed the failed attempt at living with a couple of elder "Holy Rollers" and, later, with one of two dairy farmers—the first of whom used the equivalent of slave labor to run a secret moonshine distillery, on the side.

All, with the exception of Lauren's experience with the Troxell's, "...had left a bad taste in my mouth."

John Kellerman married Lucille, and, together they bought their new house.

Upon their marriage, Lucille brought part of her family and household goods together, and furnished their new home with whatever had survived through difficult times.

In their new home, the kitchen was situated behind the dining area. Lucille and John's bedroom was downstairs.

Two small bedrooms took up the second floor. Unlike most of their neighbors, the Kellermans' bathroom had indoor plumbing.

"This was like heaven, to me", said Lauren. "I'd used outhouses for years, while living with Flora and Burton, before *their* separation. And at another dairy, owned by a Swede family, where I lived and worked through the week during my first two years of high school, in exchange for food and school clothes. Right after I graduated out of elementary school, in 'thirty-one."

"It was my first real job, and boy, was I proud. Caught the school bus at the farm Mondays through Fridays, then went back to my cousin's house for the weekends."

"Truth be told, I looked forward to it, 'cause my dog, Bozo, was always waitin' for me. He was a Collie-German -Shepherd mix. Sure loved that dog."

The Kellermans heated their house with a small wood-burning stove. Fired by cut wood from across the creek, out past the back property. It sat against a wall in the front living room, near the dining area. The stove's chimney rose up through the first-floor ceiling, through Clarence's old upstairs bedroom. It provided scant heat to mix with whatever rose from the first floor.

Even after Clarence moved out, Lauren never moved into his older brother's bedroom. On cold nights, old blankets provided warmth that the chimney could not dispense.

Among Lucille's most cherished heirlooms, brought with her from her previous house, was a large fruit bowl. It was one of the few cherished items handed down, after her mother passed.

And it occupied the center of an always-draped lace dining room table.

The bowl was a thick, clear centerpiece of etched glass that, without fail—regardless of economic hardships—was brimful with fresh, seasonal fruit from their garden, or from bartering with neighbors after shopping at the village market—bought if times were good.

Depending on the season, apples, cherries, oranges, and plums provided an array of colors, in an otherwise subdued interior.

Lucille treasured her centerpiece fruit bowl. It had survived so many calamities over the years, and was symbolic of the promises life might grant, despite austere periods and hardships that dogged her family.

John Kellerman turned his newspaper, and folded it in half. He continued to read a story about British and Dutch pilots sighting Japanese invasion ships at Singapore.

Kellerman set the paper down to drink from his coffee cup. He looked to Lucille who had returned from the kitchen. Her wide grin accompanied a fresh-baked gooseberry pie.

10:07 a.m. Pacific
0807 Hawaii Standard Time – Pearl Harbor

While sitting on the table, suddenly, and without warning, Lucille's prized fruit bowl burst into chunks of etched glass. A fall harvest of golden and red apples plunged from their shattered glass bed, rolled and dropped off the table, and rolled across the floor with a ferocity matched only by Lucille's scream.

The gooseberry pie slipped from her hands and gravity did the rest. It crashed to wooden floor slats, splattered back up to the tablecloth, and onto Lucille's Sunday dress.

In spite of a crackling fire in the wood-burning stove, Lucille Kellerman felt cold. In an instant—but for the ticking of the clock—the room fell silent.

Lucille's gaze was drawn to the clock. She turned pale and looked into John's eyes.

"Something's happened to Lauren," she said. And Lucille collapsed to her knees.

— —

SECOND TO THE LAST TO LEAVE

Lucille I. Bruner

"My mother, **Lucille Iowa Smith Bruner**, was born on 26 December, 1897, and was ***42 years, 11 months, and 12 days old on the morning of the Attack on Pearl Harbor.***

After my father died, when I was six, Mother gave me away and rarely over the next seven years wrote or came to see me. Hell, it was the Depression, and she couldn't feed us. Although I begged her not to send me away, she did anyway, and I only saw her during those seven years when I got into trouble.

When I was 14 and starting high school, Mother asked me back to live with her and her new husband John Kellerman. I had to think about this long and hard, because she wouldn't let me bring my dog "Bozo." In the end, it was my brother Clarence who convinced me to give moving home one more try.

I spent my high school years living with my mother before I joined the Navy in 1938. When John Kellerman passed away, Mother married again, but I never met the guy. Some time later, as I was fighting the war in the South Pacific, I was notified that some stupid kids racing their cars had killed my mother and her then-husband while they were walking into town. I tried to get leave to go home, but it was denied. We were at war and this was the Navy."

Mrs. Lucelle Kellerman

Lucelle Bruner Kellerman

Lauren's Mother

Chapter 16
WHIRLPOOL OF DEATH

0809

Donald Stratton was in a state of shock. It was as if a thug had thrown him against the forward bulkhead. Anticipating the fire's blowback and, despite reeling from extensive burns, Stratton's instincts caused him to reach outside—in an attempt to close the port hatchway.

"The ship was ablaze", he reported, "and I thought we'd get hit, again. Didn't want the fire to come back inside."

With his burned left arm, Stratton leaned out to pull the door closed.

The skin on his hands and body was still burning and, like Bruner and Dvorak, was hanging in strips.

Stratton grabbed the hatch and pulled hard. "I managed to dog one of the handles down… thinking we might be safer from the growing flames."

But while taking the precautionary stance, upon touching the white-hot door, Stratton burned his right arm and hands, again.

At once, he cried out, pulled back, and sagged to the deck in excruciating pain.

Moments elapsed and, despite the roaring fires, a newfound, death-like silence took over the director. It was as if someone had pushed a mute button inside Lauren's steel world. And for a time, his mind wandered inside a fog-like state—not knowing if he was dreaming, hallucinating, or preparing to let go of the silver cord.

He felt caught in a space, where the earth stood still, where it halted it's spinning, and where his body and mind were engaged in a struggle between a decision to die and a need to live. For Lauren and the others, this particular point in time may have provided each their own encounter between choosing life and allowing it to escape—that decisive moment when mind and body shake hands and agree to part ways—or fight on.

The subdued quiet merged to cover the onslaught, and helped to tolerate the heat from flames, raging outside their temporary haven.

No one moved for what seemed like hours. Yet it had been no more than minutes.

"Seconds, actually."

Lauren's hearing had diminished after the bomb's deafening concussion. And there was a heavy ringing in his ears that wouldn't stop.

His mind eventually surfaced to face reality.

"My forehead hurt and I recalled hitting something hard as I was thrown toward Dvorak's station."

The air was stifling, choking, "…and hot as hell. But compared to what we'd just been through… shit, it seemed like a moment in paradise. Even with the flames raging outside."

As he lay on the floor, unable to move, a disgusting stench made him retch.

"I thought I was gonna' puke again. It was that bad."

Lauren realized he had trouble with his eyes. The entire director appeared blurred.

Then his fingers came into focus, "…nearly charcoaled to the bone… skin hanging off, but somehow still attached to my hands."

"Damn, they hurt like hell."

"I looked at my hands, and saw what I'd smelled… and it was me."

"Besides stomach-churning smells of burnt flesh and hair, the air was filled with another foul stench. I recognized it as burning rubber… the soles of our shoes."

Beyond the burns and the hurt, there was something else. Hidden away—next to his memory of past odors—were other things that reeked. Foul smells had taken over. A stink of decay that was accelerated by the oppressive heat.

His foggy mind attempted to clarify what turned his stomach.

The odors had swirled around Lauren's battle station, and entered, as if uninvited guests. To him, it was a vile odor "…a thousand times worse than anything I'd ever smelled. It just came in the director and attached itself to each of us."

"Goddamn, it was bad."

"Honest to God, I thought maybe someone had crapped in his pants, because we were all so damn scared. But that wasn't it either."

Lauren forced himself up on his elbow and, hot as it was, managed to rest against the forward bulkhead.

Searching his mind for a source of the repulsive odor, he glanced around the director. Stratton, like everyone else, was in shock—frozen in place. No one appeared to move.

"I knew that strong odor was something I'd never want to smell again."

Then it hit him "…like another round from a enemy plane."

"Death… our director, and everything in it reeked of death."

To Lauren, the entire steel cube smelled similar to road kill—the kind found when he grew up, back in Washington. A rotting, dead badger or raccoon—mixed with the scent of cheap perfume, like that sprinkled into a casket. It created a pungent odor that bit at his senses.

"There's death," said Lauren. "And then there's death by fire… where every fiber of a burned body or corpse has already begun to decompose in extreme heat and humidity almost at once."

"There we were, inside our director… all of us, except for maybe Lott, contributing to a foul-smelling stew of men being baked alive."

It radiated off burned sailors—many of whom had been torn apart by explosive projectiles or airborne shrapnel.

The overwhelming scent of human blood, inside, and beyond Lauren's director "…was godawful and sickening beyond belief."

Wet and drying blood, shredded organs and bile, charred bone, and cauterized skin, all conjured up a mix of odors that reeked beyond Lauren's imagination, "…and it crawled like a giant beetle, right up my nostrils and into my brain."

It was real, and Lauren realized that his body had contributed to the blood bath.

He experienced a visceral reaction to the concoction that mixed with the heavy smoke, blew through hatchways, adhered to bulkheads, and stuck to their skin.

Still, that instant was just a part of the ongoing crisis.

It was then that a realization hit Lauren. Though buried deep within, it would erase his past, and bring him to a new level of understanding about his life.

"There I was, charred like forgotten meat on the grill. My entire body was being cooked at a temperature my mind couldn't make sense of."

"For the past three years, Billy and I had been living the life in paradise, together, with our buddies and shipmates. And in all my time at Pearl… beyond giving my best, as a member of the Fire Control division, my only interests had been drinking, playing cards… and chasing pretty girls."

"But we'd heard stories, coming out of Europe, of British infantry soldiers who'd been burned alive, in their armored tanks, during battle."

"And rumors had circulated that many of their light infantry tanks were known to be 'death traps.' "

"Hell, it never occurred to us that we'd had to be concerned with their problems here, in Hawaii."

"And all at once, it dawned on me… those burning tanks weren't any different than what we were going through, inside our metal coffin."

"So far, I was still alive… but paradise vanished, that day."

"At that point, I realized fate had changed my life, once again. And it all came home to roost."

"There we were… thrown, in an instant, into combat. Without any way to fight back. We were roasted past well-done… burnt to a crisp."

"And God, it was hot. Scorching hot."

"The soles of my burning work shoes were roasting. The steel walls of our director, roasted. And my hands… hell, they were like burnt strips of bacon."

"We all were burnt to hell, except for Ronnie Lott."

"The rest were either burnt toast… or dead."

"So death had found us, after all… mixed with the heat of battle, and the sinking of *Arizona*. And my crew scattered around our cubicle… and outside… shit…"

"I could hear them begin to moan. And I could feel death all around me."

"And the screaming… I can still hear the screaming from below decks. Even today… sometimes when I wake from a nap, I still hear them."

"At night, triggered by my dreams, I've caught myself making a beeline to wash off the smell. But the stench doesn't leave me."

"It has never left me."

"After all of these years, I still can't wash it off … or outta' my mind."

Inside the director, Lauren attempted to focus, once again, but a filmy substance filled his left eye. He wiped it with his arm, and discovered smeared blood.

"It had run into my eye from where I'd hit something."

Lauren skimmed his forehead, with a burned finger, and came across a large gash—just above the left eyebrow. "Still have the scar."

Then, he checked his leg wounds.

"I felt heat… but couldn't detect pain, as much. My injuries were just wet and sticky. And it appeared the fireball had somehow helped to cauterize my leg wound, from that bastard pilot who tried to kill me."

"Fortunately for me, my right eye wasn't filled with as much blood, and I was able to focus enough to land near Dvorak, just above me."

Dvorak appeared shell-shocked, "…still half in his seat, close to me… his head crumpled over the steering wheel."

"Muffled moans and cries surrounded me… some that could well have been my own."

"At first I thought the sounds came from my crew, but there were too many cries… hundreds, all running together as if calling out, at once, above the sounds of battle… all trying to talk … at the same time."

"In my dazed condition, I heard voices screaming for help, yelling their own prayers… or begging for relief."

"I swear I heard someone yell out for God to take him, right then and there."

The sounds got louder, and converged, from all directions. To Lauren, their cries echoed up, from below, as if tormented souls of the netherworld—husky, throaty, guttural sounds—or moans from a watery graveyard.

"I tried to speak, to say something… anything. But I couldn't."

Neither could anyone else. Each man in his own world, attempting to figure out if they were alive—or in hell.

For the moment, Lauren had lost all clarity, as he rested on the blazing hot floor—against Dvorak's seat—unable to get up.

His eyes wandered up to Dvorak. The cubicle was filled with dense smoke. Then, something registered in Lauren's mind. Smoke was emanating from his own skin. He glanced at each sailor and realized almost everyone's body was smoking, at the site of their burns.

"In my daze, through the fog of blood in one eye... and through the smoke, I attempted to focus on Alvin. I glanced up and realized... he had no ears."

"Shit, they were just... gone."

"Damn, he looked real bad. But appeared to be breathing."

To Lauren, the cries and moans overpowered the massive blaze and aerial bombardment going on outside. For a few moments, his mind floated in and out of consciousness. It seemed to help him escape the pain.

The moans and cries brought back visions of the elderly Pentecostal couple, where he and his brother, Clarence, had been sent to live, after their father died.

"I was a small kid, then. Five or six, when mother gave me away. The first time was with Clarence. After that, I was on my own. Life was shitty, back then. Just like now. When would it end?"

Clarence and Lauren had been sent to live with an elderly couple. And the sounds that arose off *Arizona*, reminded Lauren of those days—during the Depression—when they were forced to attend tent revivals, where participants uttered similar mournful sounds.

The brothers, not understanding it was considered a derogatory term, would call their caretakers, "Holy Rollers."

"It got us into a world of trouble. So much so, that the old couple took us back to Mother within two weeks."

"Crazy, but that's what popped into my mind as I lay on the hot steel deck… attempting to focus my eyes and mind."

"Damn, as a kid I hated those tent revivals and their shouts, moans, and violent body movements. Since the attack, I've always associated that with *Arizona's* dying."

Another explosion brought him back to reality.

Lauren attempted to move, then realized his hands and face were still burning, where they touched the steel deck.

It took all the strength he could manage to stand up and "…avoid laying on the hot griddle."

The rangefinder's housing was still intact. Lauren used it to steady himself, as he rose from the floor.

With one blood-filled eye, he surveyed the damage and began to check for those, in the director, who were still alive.

"There was little that wasn't either red or white hot to the touch."

Near Lott, Hollowell was bleeding profusely, from the head.

"I thought maybe Lott was dead, under the blanket. Then, my one good eye caught his body move underneath."

0810

At first, Lauren hadn't realized Lott was still under the blanket, and that its movement "…was from him shaking."

"Hollowell was close to Lott, and his blood was running onto the edge of my old blanket."

"By the time I got up, from the floor, Ronnie had still not come out. I knew Alvin was alive, but his ears and burns scared me."

By then, Don Stratton was beginning to move again.

"I saw his eyes follow me across the deck. Compared to Alvin," said Lauren, "Don looked pretty good at first, until I saw his arm."

Upon closer inspection, Lauren could see "...he was burnt toast, as well."

The fireball from the ship exploding had passed through the director's port and starboard hatchways, where Dvorak and Stratton had been at their posts.

Stratton's clothes were burned away, and in tattered strings. "His skin," said Lauren, "looked as if it had just melted off him."

"All our hair was gone."

Lauren could see Stratton's charred hands, "...and the bloody pulp of one mutilated ear."

The searing heat continued to overwhelm.

Still, not a word had been said.

"We've got to get outta' here, and off the ship," Lauren choked out the words.

Lauren's eyes were drawn to his friend, Zimmerman, lying out on the catwalk. And that moment became a major contributor to decades of night terrors.

Zeke laid on his back, in a grotesque position—just off the director's hatchway door—his right arm still reaching out for the pull-up handle, from when he'd been caught by the fireball.

"He was burnt to shit... black almost... not moving or breathing. I knew he had to be dead as I looked out to the door."

Lauren leaned out and looked down at what was left of Zeke.

"The fireball had pretty well stripped him of most of his skin and clothes."

"For the first time, that morning, I began to cry. But tears dried from the intense heat, as soon as they'd stung my burned cheeks."

How in hell could Zeke be dead? I'd just tried to wake him for mess a couple hours ago.

"Still, to this day, I remember Zeke's body. Not warm, like you'd think a living body would be... but smokin' like a stove pipe. It was creepy."

From inside the director, Ronnie Lott came out of his silence and started babbling, as he had before the bomb.

"As if any of us needed that shit," said Lauren.

Dvorak spoke up for the first time, and yelled as best he could to Lott, "Shut up, Ronnie."

"That was the first thing Alvin had said… and it did the trick," said Lauren. "I can't remember Ronnie opening up his mouth again. At least… not to complain. I think Alvin scared the piss outta' him."

Lauren figured by the way Zeke was lying outside the hatchway, that the fireball and concussion must have caught him full in the face, "…in all likelihood as he tried to duck back inside the director, miscalculating his timing."

"Shit… I kept telling him, but he didn't wanna listen."

"Turned out to be one of the worst serial nightmares I've been forced to relive throughout most of my life."

"Death, and its smells… I sometimes still touch and taste. It's been a pain in the ass most of my life, to recall these scenes."

"And if I ever believed in purgatory, before one can enter heaven… what we all experienced that December morning was its twin."

"From that day on, I've never been certain I'm headed for heaven. But can always hope."

Lauren didn't know if it happens to all when they experience close encounters with death, but at this point in the battle of Pearl Harbor—standing at the threshold of his director's hatchway—time slowed, again.

"I suppose I felt it necessary to wrap my head around the fact… that I was going to die."

0811

The sounds in Lauren's battle station had taken on a different tone. No longer did loud talking or cussing permeate the air as it did, minutes before. Lauren would describe it as "deathly quiet."

"Just our moans… that had taken over and joined in the choir of the remaining crew aboard *Arizona*."

Lauren now stood, shaking, as he glanced at his left wrist to check his watch for the time.

"Hell, my watch was gone… leather band and all was burnt off my wrist."

His entire arm was "…just pure charcoal, from fingertips to shoulder."

Shit!

He scanned the director's floor.

"I loved that goddamned watch. But I could barely see, given the blood in my left eye… and the smoke and heat, inside and out."

Lauren looked for the watch for a moment longer, then gave up. "It was obvious my high school graduation present had been blown to smithereens."

He felt his head, and for his cap.

"Where the hell is my cap?"

"Screw the cap," I thought "Where's my hair?" All I could feel was burnt skin where my hair was supposed to be.

"Must've been burnt off in the fire, or so I thought at the moment."

Lauren attempted to breathe in and was hit with a fit of coughing. The others were beginning to do the same. Their seared lungs made it difficult to breathe—even in short breaths.

"It became a real chore, especially with the sweltering air inside."

Without a word, Dvorak climbed shakily out onto the Sky Control Platform, on the starboard side. He realized right away it was a mistake, as he tried to breathe, and choked.

The fire had shifted closer.

"He reappeared in the hatchway, quick as a wink."

"When he climbed back in, Alvin looked more like the walking dead."

He tried yelling to Lauren, and anyone else who might listen, "*Arizona's* going down. The trade winds are fanning the fire and smoke, and it's moving toward us."

"This way out is no good", he said. "Fire's comin' up, starboard, 'round the catwalk."

He looked to Lauren, "Can you see?"

Lauren nodded.

"Rubbing my eye made it somewhat better. I wiped the blood away again, on my hand, across what was left of my t-shirt. The blood was sticky."

"It was then I took stock of what little clothes I still had on, and compared them to Alvin's. He and Stratton were in the same boat."

Their t-shirts were tattered, burned, and filled with holes. Lauren's heavier shorts were a little bit better off, but not much."

"Not so many rips or burn holes."

"I think the rangefinder somehow blocked me, a little, from the fireball. But … what started out less than an hour before, as the uniform of the day and summer whites now bordered on unrecognizable. Black, burned, ripped, and caked with blood."

"Lott was the only one of our crew," said Lauren, "who looked almost the same comin' out, as he did goin' in."

"I swear to God, because Lott had covered himself with my old blanket, he was pretty much untouched."

"Shit… he even had his cap on and it was pretty damn clean, too."

Dvorak moved to the port hatch, and yelled for us to move out, in order to find a way off the ship.

The men began to follow Dvorak out the hatchway. But Stratton stopped short, deciding they needed to check on Hollowell. Stratton realized he was burned pretty bad and, instead, yelled over to Lott to check on him.

At first, Lott refused to look at the burned body, lying next to him.

"No use," said Lott, "he's bleeding all over."

"How the hell can you tell?" said Stratton, "you haven't even looked at 'im."

Stratton held his ground and commanded Lott to make certain Hollowell wasn't breathing, before they would abandon him.

Ronnie bent over Hollowell and yelled back "He's a goner."

With his severe burns, Lauren was beginning to experience intense pain. Like most of the crew wearing shorts, his legs were burned from his thighs to his ankles.

"My t-shirt had caught fire. And my back, both arms, and right side were charcoaled. My right arm hurt the most."

"So was the right side of my face."

"All the hair on my head was burned off, and my right ear was scorched, pretty bad."

0812

"Having to step over Zeke's burned and twisted body in order to leave the director was difficult for all of us."

Dvorak left the director first, followed by Stratton. Then, Lott realized his crew was leaving, and scrambled under the rangefinder's tube, "...in a helluva hurry."

"I believe he thought we'd leave him behind."

Lott pushed his way past Lauren in order not to be the last out. Bruner inquired, once again, if Lott was certain he'd thoroughly checked Hollowell.

Lott reported he had, and that "...Hollowell's head was caved in on one side."

"Looking down one more time at Zeke, laying at my feet as we exited... I was damned careful not to step on him."

"His face was burned almost completely black and, like the rest of us, except for Lott, his hair gone."

"In my dreams, I see his blue eyes... always open, just like they were that morning... his cap tipped half-way back off his forehead, when off the ship. The bar girls loved him."

Outside, between the smoke and flames coming up from below, the ordeal continued for the men.

"I've never smelled anything near as bad as it was. Outside, the smoke reeked, even more, of diesel fuel mixed with death. And I'm certain each of us had our own idea of what death would be like. But no one said a word about it, after being barbequed."

"We all must've thought if we didn't say the words 'dead,' or 'death,' or 'dying,' then it wouldn't latch onto us."

"For sure, that's what I believed."

Soon after they had left the director, two sailors raced across the sky control platform from the starboard director—their mirrored anti-aircraft crew.

One of the sailors, Larry Farquhar, Lauren knew well. From Washington State, Fire Controlman 2/c Farquhar grew up less than 30 miles from Bruner's mother's home.

"Larry's and my parents were friends. They'd get together to play cards on occasion... so, during those times, Larry and I'd be thrown together. Never thought of us as being close friends, growing up."

"But I'll tell you... when he walked back into my life that morning, Larry became the closest thing to being back home... at least for the moment.

Home it wasn't, but Lauren was "...sure as hell happy to see Larry. I'll tell you."

The sailor who was with Larry was Gunner's Mate Earl Riner "... a quiet kid with big ears. But a nice guy."

"As they approached us, we moved away from Zeke, outside the hatchway, and closer to the director's bulkhead to shield us from the smoke and fire."

Dvorak spoke up, "What happened to the rest of your crew?"

Larry looked to Lauren.

"The fire got 'm all," he said. "Of the six in our director, four were caught outside when the ship blew."

Dvorak nodded toward Zimmerman, lying dead, outside.

"Same for Zeke," he said.

"Truth be told, Larry and Earl looked pretty well toasted, about as bad as we were. Not surprising, considering the explosion came up from starboard first.

As the men gathered around, "...we were all coughing and choking like hell."

"Do you guys have any plans to get off this powder keg?" Larry yelled above the ongoing battle.

How the hell do we know? Lauren first thought. "You have any ideas?"

"Thinkin' I'll try and make the swim to Ford Island," Larry shouted back.

"How the hell you gonna make it down from up here?" chimed in Alvin. "Chances are, the ladders are no good, broke and blown to smitherines."

"Thinkin' I can handle climbin' down what's left."

Alvin shrugged, and suggested they move closer to Larry and Earl's starboard director.

"Let's see how far the swim might be. Getting to the main deck from up here could be tricky."

"I'm thinking it's real hell down there."

In spite of the unbearable heat and fires that encircled their crew, the six men headed toward the platform's starboard side.

Just then, another sailor came down the crow's nest ladder—cussing and yelling for their attention.

"At first, I couldn't remember ever seeing the kid before. But that wasn't new, considering *Arizona'a* size, and the number of men on board."

The sailor jumped the last three rungs of the ladder, to the platform. He rubbed his burnt hands on his shorts.

"Shit that was hot ...Name's Kuhn," he said.

"Seaman First Class Harold Kuhn ...A spotter, up above, for Gun Turrett 1 and 2."

Lauren saw his hands. "They were redder than hell and starting to blister, coming down the hot ladder."

"Can I fall in with yous guys?" he shouted above the din. "Have no idea what the hell t' do."

At first, Lauren thought he talked funny, with his accent. Harold was from Bronx, New York.

"And damn proud of it," he had always said, when teased.

"Kuhn was a little shorter than I was" said Lauren. "I'd say, about five-ten or so. But you could see he was about a hundred-sixty pounds of muscle."

"Hey, can I tag along?" he asked, once again.

Upon hearing his accent again, Lauren recalled he *had* met Kuhn before—during a night of poker.

"As Alvin said... the more the merrier", Lauren quipped. "But we can't guarantee anything."

"The kid's face was ghost-white. Like ours, but with the exception we were burned and he wasn't, for whatever reason… just his hands. He was still wearing a cap, like Lott. The rest of us weren't.

"To this day, still can't figure out how Ronnie still had his hat."

"The seven of us… a ragtag gang of survivors, moved literally 'hot-footing it', so-to-speak, starboard, following Larry. But it got even hotter as we approached the Ford Island side of the ship… between the charthouse shack, in the middle, and their director."

"Within a minute, we were stepping over the rest of the bodies from Larry and Earl's crew."

"They were spread out every which way. Deader than a busted nail head… twisted and burned almost beyond recognition."

As the men approached the dead, Larry spoke up, over the roaring fires, "Kept telling these assholes to stay inside, but they wouldn't listen… now they paid the piper."

"Earl Riner never said a word," said Lauren. "But I could see tears running down his cheeks."

Lauren couldn't help but think of Zeke and how he and Alvin "…told him the same damned thing. He, too, didn't listen, and ended up paying the price."

— —

Fred "Zeke" Zimmerman

Fred "Zeke" Zimmerman was born on 10 May 1921 to Frank George and Mary Edith (Burrows) Zimmerman in Cleveland, Stutsman County, North Dakota. After completing tenth grade, Fred left school to join the Civilian Conservation Corps (CCC) as his family was large and needed his help.

Fred enlisted in the Navy for six years on 24 January 1940 in Minneapolis, Minnesota. He was 5' 9" tall, weighed 142 pounds, had light brown hair, blue eyes and a ruddy complexion.

Nicknamed "Zeke" to his friends, he reported to USS *Arizona,* which was his first ship, on 26 March 1940. **On 7 December 1941, Fred Zimmerman was 20 years, 6 months and 27 days old.**

"Zeke was a friend of mine, and the closest member of my battle station crew to me, other than Alvin Dvorak. We shared the same crew quarters, and I remember the morning of the attack I was razzing Zeke to get up and out of the sack. Less than three hours later, I was looking at him burned and laying dead with his blue eyes open and staring up at me. His death has always been a recurring nightmare throughout my life."

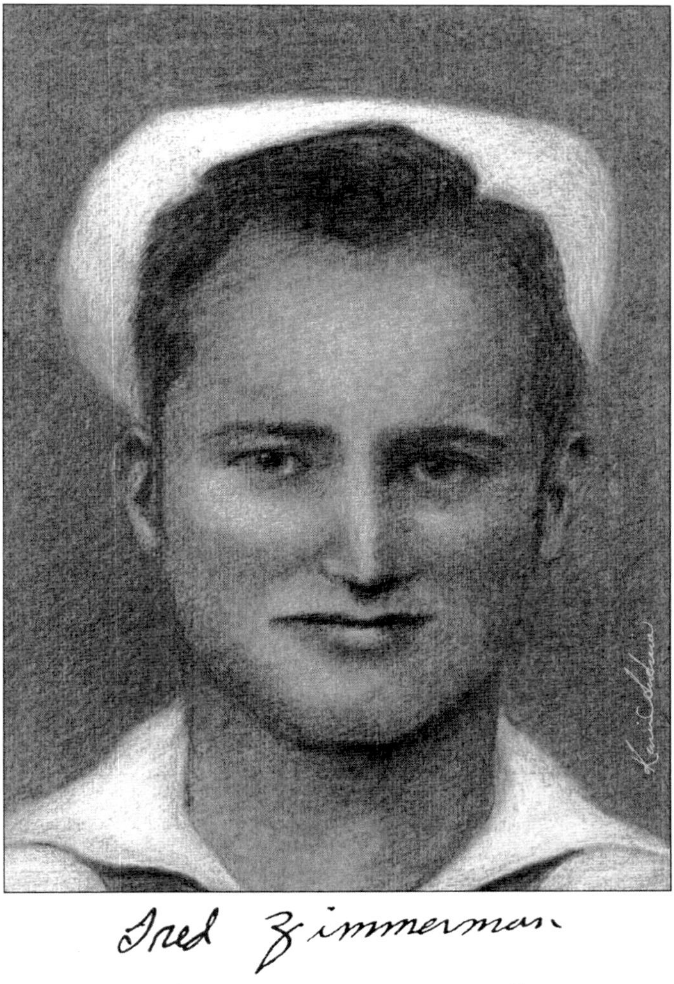

Fred George Zimmerman, Cox

USS *Arizona*

KIA

Russell A. Lott

Russell Ardell Lott was born on 19 January 1920 in Kingsley, Iowa to Arthur William and Leola E. (Fryer) Lott. He came from a Navy family, as his father was a U.S Marine who served on the battleship USS Maryland in World War I.

After completing the 11th grade, Russell enlisted in the Navy on 14 October 1937 in Des Moines, Iowa. When he enlisted, he was 5′ 7″ tall, weighed 149 lbs, had light brown hair, blue eyes, and a ruddy complexion.

He reported to USS *Arizona*, which was his first ship, on 4 June 1938. Known to his friends by the nickname "Ronnie," **he was 21 years, 10 months and 19 days old on 7 December 1941.**

Russell Ardell Lott returned to USS *Arizona* when he passed away and was interred back to the ship, where he now restes in Gun Turret #4 on 10 August 2003.

"Ronnie Lott was pretty much a loner, and I didn't know him well outside the crew of my battle station. He was the telephone talker for Gun Captain Stewart Lomax and myself to the ship's plotting room. Ronnie escaped Arizona along with our crew as part of Arizona's Greatest Escape. After the war, I'd see him occasionally at one of Arizona's reunions, but we were never close enough to share a beer."

Read the Full Story of *Arizona*'s Greatest Escape
Along With Viewing Rare Photos of the Attack by Visiting:
USS*Arizona*sGreatestEscape.com

Russell Ardell Lott, Sea 1/c

USS *Arizona*

Survivor

Chapter 17
LARRY & THE WALKING DEAD

Death still lurked at every corner, as the seven sailors made their way over to the starboard rail, facing Ford Island.

Nightmares of walking across the sky control platform with Larry, and those that followed, have never faded.

On the way over to Larry's starboard director, toward the rail, Lauren noticed there was less smoke and fire burning on that side of the ship than there was on the port-side.

"Not what you'd expect, when you think about it," said Lauren, "considering that the starboard side was more of the entry point for the lucky bomb."

The two men walked over to the railing and looked out toward Ford Island. It was as if they'd gone to a movie. As they watched, enemy aircraft continued to strafe, bomb, and fly over the airfiled.

Bomb explosions sent debris flying high into the air. Much of it headed toward Battleship Row.

"At one point", said Lauren, "a plane's wheel landed in the water between *Arizona* and the shore."

"Made a hellofva splash, and narrowly missed men in the water… some living, many already dead."

Arizona shifted in the water, again, and the men leaned into the railing, for support.

"Shit… careful! These rails are hotter than hell," Larry shouted.

Lauren pulled both hands off the rail. "Took a second for me to realize that my charcoaled fingers were still burning. I looked at 'em with a new hurt, after that."

"Larry and I were both transfixed by what was going on below us. It was godawful Hell."

Arizona continued to sink. Lauren felt it shift downward. "With my imagination running wild, I figured we might sink below the water line. Didn't occur to me that the harbor here was shallow compared to the middle of the channel."

His eyes were glued to the water, as some crew members jumped over the side, from aft.

"I was slowly starting to panic. As a kid, I was never a good swimmer. And I just barely passed the swimming test in basic training. As Lauren put it, he "…never expected, in a hundred years, that once I got assigned to a battleship, that I'd ever be required to get into the water."

"Hell, everyone from my older brother, Clarence, to Navy recruiters, told me it was impossible to sink a battleship."

Where the heck were these these guys, now?

The distance between *Arizona* and the shore was about 50 yards. But to Lauren, looking down from at least 70 feet, to the waterline, "…it might as well've been a mile".

Lauren spotted fuel from the ship seeping into the area, heading toward shore. He watched it slowly creep over the water, as it turned from dirty brown to an oily black.

Looking below and aft, fires raged on decks below. The water between *Arizona* and Ford Island was, by comparison, somewhat free of fire, at the moment.

Then, out of nowhere, from forward on the main deck, a sailor raced out of the flames, his clothes totally ablaze.

"The poor guy was screaming his head off," said Lauren, "and must've been blind from the fire. Don't know if he fell overboard or just jumped, hoping the water'd put an end to the pain. But…"

"I swear... as he hit the water, burning like he was, it started a chain reaction, with all the leaked fuel that had spread over the surface."

"Holy shit!" Lauren screamed in disbelief, as he watched these new events unfold. His crew turned to look below.

The sailor's burning body immediately touched off a fire that slowly fanned out across the water,"...between our ship and Ford Island. It began to catch up with the men who'd been swimming through the oil, for shore. They'd been pushing the fuel away from their mouths and eyes when the flames began to sweep over the water, to engulf them."

"It was as if an arsonist had poured gasoline over an old warehouse floor... struck a match, and casually tossed it in."

"More than once, we saw swimmers' heads consumed by fire. They'd already been soaked with fuel... when the fire spread, it moved so quickly, it basically advanced right over their heads and faces. "

"We were hypnotized, as men screamed out in sheer pain. Others just gave up and slipped below the surface. It was a nightmare."

Bodies floated everywhere—most laying facedown. "One dead Marine, close to the ship still had his eyes open, and seemed to look straight up at us".

When the water ignited, it caused several men who still had it in them, to take off swimming even faster for shore. Some could only dog paddle, "...like me," said Lauren. "And they got tangled up in the oil and fire. We watched some slip below the surface. And there was nothing we could do."

When the lucky bomb hit, some bodies had been thrown against the rocky shoreline of Ford Island.

"One guy was half in and half out of the water. His head looked like it was split open like a coconut… blood and brains spilled out onto the rocks."

Lauren turned to see if anyone besides Larry was still standing with him. They'd all returned for the port-side director across ship, except for Larry's crew member, Earl Riner.

"As Earl had approached the other side of the ship, he'd stopped near one of the bodies from his starboard director. The sailor lay spread-eagled. And Earl was puking his guts out… some bouncing off the dead man. I could hear him, crying and screaming between the puking."

"In between, he kept yelling 'the whole world's on fire.' "

"I felt guilty… almost like I was spying. Then, Larry said something that pulled me back to another reality. I turned to Larry, then wished, after that, that I hadn't. Larry pointed below and told me to look at the decks."

Lauren attempted to lean out over the red-hot rail, careful not to get burned more than he already was. The main deck resembled a warzone graveyard—much like the fields of Gettysburg. Bloodied and burned bodies... body parts lying all over the deck as far as he could see—most of them, still smoking. The constant smell of burned, human flesh and hair—rising to the mast—made him retch. He quickly turned back to the sky control platform.

Out of nowhere, Larry spoke up, with a question so out of context, that it was unsettling.

"Remember, Clutch Butt… that officer's good lookin' wife who took hula lessons over on the island?"

"What?"

"The times we used to watch her take hula lessons… through the binoculars."

Lauren had to think. This was not something that would have come to mind.

"Yeah… I remeber those days." Lauren's voice drifted off.

"Wonder if she and her family are alive."

Lauren was adrift in too many other thoughts, and Larry's attempted story got lost somewhere after he mentioned the binoculars.

"The wind kept blowing smoke and shit our way," Lauren said. "And I'd do whatever I could to cover my mouth and nose with my hand."

"The left hand, of course. My right arm was burnt to a crisp, and blistering really bad from raising it automatically to protect my face… when the fireball raced through the director."

The smoke became thicker, as larger flames took over the decks and bulkheads, below. It all began to rise much faster, from below. "The loud roar from the fires mixed with the attack still going on were almost deafening."

"Having made the mistake of looking down to all the death and destruction… this was definitely why, from that moment on, I never liked funerals. No matter whose funeral it was."

To Lauren, standing high upon the sky control platform, looking down, was as if he'd been standing on the edge of a mass grave.

"Trouble was", he said, "some of these dead still walked, and cried out for help, before they either fell, or just laid down on the shattered and pock-marked deck."

"I realized, as I gazed out over *Arizona's* main deck, this would surely be the biggest funeral I'd ever attend… that is, if I even made it off the ship… and didn't become a part of the funeral, myself."

Larry yelled at Lauren and interrupted his thoughts.

"You wanna try and swim for shore?"

After what he'd just witnessed, Lauren thought he *had* to be joking.

"He wasn't," said Lauren. "He was dead serious. And I felt right away that, if I tried to make it across the water, I'd end up dead, too."

"Hell, no," Lauren said. "We'd never make it."

"Look, I figure it gives us a better chance at living, than if we stay up here and get cooked like shish-kebobs, all over again."

Lauren was stumped. Larry had a point. As he looked around, he saw flames growing larger, and coming up from all sides. He still hesitated.

"I can't, Larry. I've always been a crappy swimmer. I'll never make it… especially with my burns in that saltwater."

"Okay, pal. But I gotta' give it a try."

"Good luck…"

He turned to face Larry, but he'd already gone. Lauren watched him run to the side of the platform, and move down the first set of ladders. Despite the clamor, he could still hear Larry yelling and cussing.

"Damn, Lauren… the rails are hotter than hell."

"I was tempted to go to the edge, to see if he made it into the water. But the heat from the fires was too hot, and I knew my body couldn't take much more."

It was the last Lauren figured they'd ever see each other.

"I headed back toward the port-side director and walked through the smoke… dodging flames at my side of the ship. I had to step past the dead bodies and Carl's puke, in order to rejoin my remaining crew."

"I pretty much figured we were lost… and I was on my way to being dead."

As he moved from one side of the platform to the other, half way across, he passed a small metal charthouse, used for the big gun spotters—and heard voices.

Lauren stuck his head in the hatchway.

"It wasn't difficult to recognize Ronnie Lott's voice, in the darkened space. The kid was scared shitless, just like the rest of us. He just showed it more than some."

Stratton and Lott stood—in shock—along with Kuhn and Earl Riner from the starboard director, all in an attempt to avoid the flames, smoke, and smell of burnt flesh.

"Not that the smells didn't surround them in the confined spotters area. There were three dead guys inside who didn't make it through the massacre".

Lauren realized the stench was multiplied by the hot enclosure, and it made him retch.

"No one was talking, except Lott. And it appeared no one was listening, either."

"Where's Dvorak?"

Stratton pointed toward the port director.

Lauren turned to leave, then yelled back, "If you just sit here, crying in your beer… when Alvin and I find a way off this dead man's ship, we're gonna leave your sorry asses."

"That, by God, got their attention."

Lauren didn't look back, but he could hear they were following close behind.

The men arrived back at port-side, overlooking the channel. Lauren glanced at Alvin who, in spite of his massive burns, moved briskly along the edges of the burning platform, looking for anything or anyone who might come to their rescue. Lauren realized, at that moment, Dvorak *was* in even worse shape than he thought.

"Alvin didn't complain though. Just turned to me and spoke… his voice raspy, like mine, from inhaling all the shit from the fire and smoke."

"Where's your friend?"

"Farquhar?"

Dvorak nodded.

"Not comin'."

"I could tell by the pain that showed at that point that he really didn't care. He was mentally focused on the numbers… and getting the hell off our perch."

There are countless reasons why Alvin Dvorak has always been Lauren's hero.

"Hell, he saved my life."

But right then, as Lauren watched Alvin standing there, moving decisively at the edge of the inferno—burned over so much of his body—he realized how resolute and determined he was, not only to survive, but to help save all of us from certain death.

"Shit, Alvin Dvorak is what Navy traditions have been built on, for centuries… and why sea-going songs are sung."

"This was a man intent on getting off the dying *Arizona* and saving all our butts. He constantly searched, through smoke and flames, for a way off, still thinking, despite being half dead."

Arizona still shuddered as she continued to settle into her grave. "And each time she did, it still scared me bad."

Stratton led Riner, Lott, and Kuhn to where Dvorak and Bruner stood. Lauren turned to them as they approached. He saw his old blanket, left behind, out on the platform, "…sorta bunched up near the outside wall of the director."

"How the hell it got there, I don't know. Had to've been Lott… the only one who used it."

Then, he saw Hollowell's blood on the corner of the blanket, already coagulated from the heat.

Lauren turned toward the director to see if Zimmerman was still laying dead near the door.

"For just one split second, I thought maybe, just maybe this had all been a bad dream."

From port-side, looking out into the channel, the men witnessed "...even more destruction, fires... and frequent geysers, when bombs splashed. And there was even more oily smoke, getting worse by the minute."

"It was blinding, and my eyes hurt like hell. I kept blinking, and rubbing sticky blood from my eyes."

"Didn't help much".

As they stood along the burning-hot rail, the morning trade winds occasionally whipped through and cleared the smoke, for moments at a time. It allowed them to get a glimpse of what was out there.

"Then, the goddamn stuff would blow right back in and over us. There were times we'd lose each other, standing side-by-side, and were scared shitless to move, for fear we'd fall right over the rails, onto the burning deck."

"Hell... we had little sense of balance, during those moments, because the ship was settling, and we could hardly tell up from down."

This all took place in a matter of minutes.

Several times, someone would yell, "Jap plane coming in at one o'clock." And they'd all duck into the director, as fast as they could.

"Each time," said Lauren, "some of us would have to step over Zeke's body while we dodged incoming rounds."

"We'd hear machine gun rounds hit and ricochet off our bulkhead and director's roof, just as we'd make it back inside."

"We knew the battle was far from over. And that the enemy was still intent on adding us to their list of kills."

"But as soon as we heard a plane pass overhead, we'd jump down and run back to the rail again, hoping to catch a break."

For a time, the men moved slightly back toward the platform's center, to avoid the heat that emanated from the flames.

"Then, from out of nowhere, we heard a loud crack out between *Arizona* and the quay. We turned in that direction, just as a six-inch manila line broke and, like a gigantic rubber band, shot back toward the ship's side." The rope had been pulled tautly by the ship's sinking, so tight, the tension had to give.

"The damned thing snapped and shot right back, across the ship, in our direction."

"Instinctively, the men ducked, even though it was not close. The snap and crack is what scared you."

"Hell... how much more of this do we have to take?" Riner shouted.

"Standing there, just waiting to catch a break, I couldn't help but wonder if Larry had made it off the ship... or drowned in the oil fires, on the way to shore. I tried to second-guess my decision to stay behind. 'What if,' I kept askin' myself."

"About then, I figured I probably wasn't gonna make it, anyway, and wondered just how death would find me... and what it'd feel like."

Why the hell did all this happen?

Instantly, memories of Nikki flashed before him.

"Just my luck. After finally meeting the right girl."

Lauren attempted to recall Nikki's smell, but couldn't. He thought of the softness of her skin. But there were too many deadly distractions in his life at the moment. And his thoughts faded quickly.

Alvin broke Lauren's revelry.

"Hey you... keep a sharp lookout for more Jap planes, comin' down the channel."

"Here was a man," said Lauren, "hurt the most, among us. Yet he had the good-God sense to consider the safety of his crew."

"We sure as hell looked like six blackened crows… way out on a limb, by ourselves. The enemy pilots were still shooting at anything, moving or not. It would've been easy for 'em to swing around and come hunting us… guns blazing. That's the things going through my mind."

The sounds of war were magnified by their plight. Gunfire was served directly from the enemy, accompanied, in the background, "…with explosions like you wouldn't believe, still happening thirty minutes after the attack first started".

Then—from their port-side, hidden somewhere in the smoke—the survivors heard muffled sounds of engines. The sounds broke through all the noise, and reverberated between hulls. Then, it hit them.

"Sonofabitch! *Vestal* was starting her engines and preparing to pull away from our death ship."

Each of the men scrambled to see anything they could, through the roiling smoke.

Stratton pointed to the main deck. "*Vestal's* still tied to *Arizona*, but her lines are taut as all get out."

"Think she's straining to pull away," said Lauren, "not wanting to be pulled into our grave."

"Someone's going to get killed when those lines snap" said Kuhn.

No one wanted to answer. They were caught between enemy fire and possible death, by abandonment—or from the potential whip-crack of their own cable moorings.

"Don't know what they call the phenomenon", said Lauren, "when you shouldn't look at something… but you do anyway. That's exactly how it was with me, and all the rest of us, too."

"There was so much death everywhere, seventy feet or so below us. Should've never taken in what we did, but we just couldn't help it."

"Shit, I think we all thought we were gonna die, anyway. So we figured we might just as well keep on looking and watching for anything that might turn the tide in our favor."

At that point, the crew spotted a launch, picking up survivors in the water. The crew all screamed together, as loud as their burned throats would permit.

"But no one heard us," said Lauren, "or couldn't do a thing for us, from where they were."

Didn't even look our way. It was disheartening as all get out. We felt lost and forgotten, high up on our perch.

"Of course, everyone was in shock and trying to take care of themselves. At least the living were."

"Only once, did I see a launch's helmsman appear to look up at us, as he swung around just aft of *Vestal*. We could tell his boat was already overloaded with living and dying men."

"Must've heard one of us yell out, because I remember him looking up. And just as he did, another smoke cloud enveloped us, as he rounded *Vestal."*

The last image that stuck in Lauren's mind, for decades, was when he saw the helmsman looking back up and "… sorta shrugging his shoulders, probably trying to say, 'What the hell can I do. Can't do a thing for you, buddy."

"I was pissed at the guy," said Lauren, "but couldn't blame him much. How the hell could one helmsman save six guys seventy feet up, in the middle of raging fires…."

"We were on our own. And we all knew it."

Suddenly, Lauren was overtaken by thoughts of his friend, Billy Mann. He hoped against hope that Billy didn't get caught up in the blast. But the realization hit him hard.

The black powder magazine was his battle station.

Maybe he got a late start heading down there. Maybe he was stuck in the head… or in the shower like Zimmerman. After all, it was *Sunday morning.*

"I could only hope, though I knew it to be highly unlikely. Billy was a hell of a runner. Quicker than me. And he would've been the first to the magazine with his big ring of keys."

Still Lauren continued to hope. He tried to think of the last time they were together. "But I couldn't even do that… and it made me mad. Sometime Saturday afternoon, I knew that, for sure."

Lauren's eyes continued to wander back to the main deck, as he searched for another way of escape. But all he could take in were charred bodies, "…strewn all over each other. Like someone had shaken out boxes of burnt wooden matches, all over the decks."

Most everywhere he looked, no one moved. Clothes and hair disintegrated. Some still on fire.

"Faces and ears like Alvin's… all burnt the hell off. Just laying there, one on top of another."

"I'll tell you it was damned awful."

Then he'd see one or two crewman "…walking any which way. Burnt to hell, but still walking."

"They couldn't have seen where they were, or where they were going. Most had one or both arms stretched out in front of 'em. No hair, no eyes. Faces charcoal black."

Some turned round and round, in circles, "…as if a dog trying to find a place to lie. Hell, these were the walking dead of *Arizona*. Zombies, if you believe in those things."

"I guess I did, at the time. Saw them with my own eyes. All looking for someone to help them. Hoping for a hand to reach out… my hand… any hand."

"I wanted to help them. God, I wanted to help them. Every one of us wanted to. For God's sake, they were *Arizona*'s crew. But we couldn't do a damned thing. Us, way up in the main mast. Them, down below. Might as well've been miles away."

Some were lucky like my friend, Lou Conter, who was aft on the ship when the bomb hit. Those further away from that fireball… those were the luckier ones.

"The closer to us, and everything forward… holy cow! It was a world of the walking dead."

It was difficult for Lauren to come to grips with so many images flooding his mind. How to survive and get off the ship was first and foremost. "But any hope for rescue," said Lauren, "this late in the game, was looking bleak."

He looked past *Vestal,* both forward and aft.

"The harbor, as far as I could see, was filled with even more bodies and body parts… everywhere. The few that I saw, who managed to stay afloat, were being picked up by ship's launches."

Some made it before the oily fires consumed them.

"Or before the sharks arrived."

"Sonofabitch," Dvorak uttered, under his breath.

Lauren had been standing next to him. So it wasn't like he was yelling or anything.

"Thing was, Alvin didn't swear much. So that's what really got my attention."

Lauren followed Dvorak's eyes straight down to the main deck. A burned crewman had tripped, fallen forward, and was hanging onto *Arizona's* port-side deck's edge—caught between it and the repair ship.

"We couldn't see if he was a sailor or Marine… not sure which, because his uniform and hair were burnt off."

"He screamed out something, but we couldn't hear what. Could only see his lips move, from where we were, so high up."

"'Help'… it must've been."

"Two of *Vestal's* sailors saw him, and ran over to save the poor guy's ass. But as Alvin and I watched the guy caught in that rat trap between the two ships began to slip."

"Burned badly and, I'm sure… with little strength left to hold on, his hands finally gave way… just as *Vestal*'s two sailors had reached him."

"His rescuers jumped toward the railing, but the poor guy slid down between the two ships, and fell into the inferno. They peered down helplessly, between the ships, but the crevice was completely filled with smoke and fire."

"There was nothing they could do."

The two men aboard *Vestal* turned in resignation, and headed back to fight for their own lives. Neither man saw Lauren's crew—or even looked up—before the smoke concealed us, once more.

As quickly as the smoke had moved back in, there was another clearing between the two ships. And Dvorak started to shout and wave his arms wildly.

"Where he got the energy and voice to yell, at that point… I'll never know."

"At first I didn't grasp what he was doing. Then I saw what he saw… one of the biggest goddamn sailors I'd ever seen. Hell…to me, he looked like Superman. But right then and there, I knew he might be our hero, because he saw us. Wasn't wearing a red cape, but he was holding a huge red fire axe."

"Hey Vestal, up here! Hey Vestal," we kept shouting. Then the rest of our crew began chiming in, with what must've been our last ounce of strength. At that point, we knew if that sailor didn't help us… we were lost.

— —

Lawrence A. Farquhar

Lawrence Albert "Larry" Farquhar was born on 16 March 1921 to George Archibald and Ina May (Briggs) Farquhar in Sanders, Montana. He enlisted in the Navy on 13 September 1938 in Seattle, Washington.

Lawrence's friends knew him as "Larry." When he enlisted, he was 5′ 10″ tall, weighed 144 pounds, had blue eyes, brown hair, and a ruddy complexion. **On 7 December 1941, he was 20 years, 8 months, and 21 days old.** Larry survived the attack and made the Navy his career and rose to the rank of Lieutenant Commander before retiring.

"Larry and I knew each other as kids growing up in Washington State, as our parents would often play cards together. You might say that my knowing Larry was one of the reasons that convinced me to join the Navy in the first place.

Although we knew each other we never hung out together unless we saw each other at Smith's Union Bar and shared a beer.

After Arizona blew up, Larry crossed over to my battle station from the Starboard Director, looking for a way off of the ship. Despite my arguing against it he decided to try to swim to Ford Island through the burning waters which to me wasn't a good idea. In the end, both his ears were burnt off because of the burning oil."

Lawrence Albert Farquhar

Lawrence Albert Farquhar, FC 2/c

USS *Arizona*

Survivor

Chapter 18
ROPE & ESCAPE

"Hey Vestal. Hey you aboard *Vestal*."

"Up here."

At first, it seemed hopeless to get anyone's attention from the ship moored outboard to *USS Arizona*.

First launched as a fleet collier—the now designated cruiser-division repair ship had been converted in order to service battleships. On Saturday, 6 December, *Vestal* had replaced USS *Nevada* that had been moored next to battleship *Arizona* on Friday, 5 December.

Vestal's orders: Repair *Arizona's* evaporator filters in the boiler room, prior to its scheduled sailing for Long Beach the following week.

Less than ten minutes into the battle, *Vestal* took two bombs that started fires aft and amidships. She was in a fight for her own survival, after one of several bombs put a five-foot hole in the bottom of her hull.

Many sailors on *Vestal's* deck had been blown overboard from the immense concussion that radiated from *Arizona's* fatal, forward blast. The battleship had already begun to settle. It was with some irony, the concussion had knocked out many of *Vestal's* fires that had raged above decks. However, with fires still burning aft and below decks, *Vestal* had begun to list.

0816

After the explosion and fireball, the six remaining sailors including Lauren, Alvin Dvorak, Don Stratton, Ronnie Lott, Earl Riner from the starboard director, and Harold Kuhn, from high in the the crow's nest, remained.

Lott and Kuhn weren't burned much. Lott, because he took cover under Lauren's old blanket; Kuhn, because his position in the crow's nest had somehow protected him, as fire engulfed the ship.

"Besides us, we left three others dead," said Lauren. "My friend, Zeke Zimmerman… our pointer, and the sailor, George Hollowell, who'd found his way to our crew from the main mast's crow's nest. Came down to join us just after the detonation of the powder magazines."

It appeared to Lauren and the others that both Zeke and Hollowell died as a result of the explosive concussion.

"Hollowell hit something sharp that opened a gash across his face," said Lauren. "Hell… the entire director was nothing but metal. And Zeke tried to come back inside, and was thrown back from the hatch door to be charred and burned to death... out on the platform."

"Damn, he'd come close to getting back inside."

Then there was Ensign Lomax, who got caught by the explosion somewhere near the main deck. This then was where Lauren found himself, with five of his surviving *Arizona* crew about twenty minutes into the attack, Sunday morning.

"There we were. Six men… most burned, and all of us still being incinerated, as if we'd been sent on a path to Hell."

"We were left standing outside the director, on the sky control platform, over seventy feet above water… but getting closer to the water by the minute as *Arizona* settled."

Dense, black smoke continued to swirl around the men, and made it difficult to breathe or to see.

Dvorak, though, assured the rest that he'd gotten the attention of that big sailor aboard *Vestal*. But from where Lauren stood, the ship appeared to be moving away from the dying *Arizona*—and its few survivors.

Like the rest, Lauren thought for a moment about jumping, but knew he'd never make it to the water. It was a good thirty feet or more, straight out, from the sky platform to the edge of the main deck.

"Before *Vestal* began to move away, just two or three feet separated it from *Arizona*."

"You'd need to be a champion long-jumper to make it past the deck's edge. No one could ever hit that mark perfect, miss both ships, and land in the water. Then there was the fire burning on the water."

"No way."

In Lauren's mind, the thing that settled it—about making an attempted jump—was hearing Lott yell out and swear something. Lott pointed to the ship's aft where, for a brief moment, they'd heard one horrific scream above all the rest.

Someone from the aft mast had tried to jump, intent on making it to the water.

"He didn't," said Lauren, "which was a lousy idea in the first place. And Lott was trying to tell us what he saw, between his cussing and moaning."

"For a moment I thought he was fulla' shit… didn't think anyone as high up as we were would be dumb enough to try and make the water, even if I'd thought about it."

"Then I realized in momentary panic, like all of us were in at the time, our minds played funny games. Who wants to willingly burn to death? In their minds, it must not have been an option."

Still, Lauren found Lott's story hard to believe until the wind shifted and the smoke cleared the fantail.

"I heard something, kinda like the sound of an overripe tomato hitting a wall, before I heard someone else yell as he jumped."

They all looked aft, trying to see what had taken place. Just then, a third sailor jumped from near the same spot.

"We could hear this guy wail, all the way down, until he hit the burning deck with the same squashed-tomato sound."

"Goddamn that was awful."

Lauren wanted to throw up, but couldn't take his eyes off that last sailor and where he landed. From Lauren's position, it appeared he made it a lot closer to the water than his friends. "But in the end," said Lauren, "he still didn't make it."

And it was just one of a thousand recurring images Lauren tried to put out of his mind over the years.

The smoke shifted again and Lauren took his eyes away from the jumpers. "That's when I got my first real glance at the destruction and death on *Arizona*. If I coulda' cried, I would've. But all those tears and fears were buried right then and there."

Lauren glanced over the length of the repair ship. There was *Vestal* as it nested alongside—moored stem to stern to *Arizona,* fires raging fore and aft. Lauren had seen her numerous times that weekend.

For whatever reason, he noticed she was painted a darker shade of Navy Gray than *Arizona*. The contrast between the two was stark.

"How bizarre was that… to notice such a thing in the heat of battle?"

But that's the way it was in the midst of a fight. Images were snapped up, processed through the optic nerve, and were developed and indelibly imprinted, as if a sped-up precursor to instant Polaroid snapshots—for the mind.

Lauren and the rest of the crew defied the enemy as they looked out into the channel. Beyond *Vestal,* for moments at a time—each time the smoke cleared—they witnessed unimaginable sights. As if lightning strikes that lit up the night, to reveal hidden monsters, the crew saw total destruction of the harbor.

Debris and lifeless bodies shared space in the burning oil and diesel fuel. It was a horrific scene that made no sense. They'd then disappear, again, into the billowing smoke.

Lauren was lost in thought.

How in hell could a little country like Japan catch us completely off guard, and with our pants down?

Time-shifts occurred in sequences. Witnessing an event, death, or a harrowing incident, would slow time to a crawl, as such events were seared into Lauren's mind. But real-time sped up as the crew ducked incoming planes that spit death from above.

Waiting for help, adrenaline pumping—and time now at a complete standstill, Lauren saw things on deck he didn't want to see or remember.

0817

Explosions and fires throughout Battleship Row created unnatural winds—as if miniature cyclones. They'd race up and down the channel, and blow the black, greasy smoke away from the crew, for moments at a time. The men stood in desperation—in an attempt to get their bearings—high atop the slowly tilting main mast.

There was just enough clearance through the haze to see the channel. Just then, an enemy Val flew in low, over the water, and disintegrated before their eyes.

"I'd heard more firing from one of *Nevada's* machine guns, as the gunner set his sights on the plane. Wondered if it was my friend again. The Val was coming in at just about the same height over the water."

"He was a hell of a shot." Once he started firing, it wasn't but a moment before nothing was left.

Seared into his mind were pieces of the enemy plane—including a propeller, being thrown around "...like tossing pieces of a toy plane in the air."

Lauren felt the ship continuing to settle and beginning to pitch forward. He began to slide and reached down to steady himself.

"I grabbed the rail, and let it go as fast as hell."

"Damn, it was hot."

"Imagine, how most of us had skin, on our hands, already burned off... some to the bone. Despite adrenaline, still pumping through our veins... burning my flesh, again, on searing hot metal, was a pain I'll never be able to describe. I can still perceive the sensation, even today."

It was around this time, Dvorak and the others moved up there shouting across to *Vestal*, again, in an attempt to get anyone's attention. Although it continued to list, *Vestal* was still afloat and moving away into the channel, from its position, alongside *Arizona*.

"*Vestal's* getting up steam... tryin' to pull away from *Arizona*," said Dvorak. "A tug's come over to help pull it outta there."

The men looked to the ropes.

The lines, holding the two ships together, were pulled like overstretched rubber bands. As *Arizona* continued to sink deeper into the harbor, it continued to pull *Vestal*, "...a hell of a lot smaller ship," down with it.

"Then," said Lauren, "we saw this big guy again with a fire axe begin to chop the mooring ropes that held our two ships together. This sailor was so damn strong, as he ran along *Vestal's* deck, taking just two or three chops to sever each line."

"Like striking cobra heads, each snapped back toward us."

In a matter of moments, *Vestal's* sailor approached the area directly across from the sky platform. We all shouted as best we could across the deck, still trying to get his attention.

"Hey you… on the *Vestal*. Up here."

"How the hell any of us found our voices," said Lauren, "between choking and coughing from smoke inhalation… not to mention seared throats, I'll never know. But all of us overcame that obstacle, because we had to."

"Didn't take long for us to realize Alvin was yelling to that particular sailor again… and the whole of us started shouting along with 'im."

It seemed as if it took forever for that big guy to look up to the platform, "…even though we were all screaming our heads off, between explosions, mortar fire, and machine gun rounds."

The sailor slashed the crew's final hopes, as he cut the last line holding the two ships together.

"My heart sank as I watched the Navy tug begin to pull *Vestal* away. And I saw those around me sick with dismay."

By then, *Vestal* had slid away from *Arizona*, and was gaining momentum.

"To top things off… new fires and explosions kept rocking that ship. And we knew if *Vestal* died, we'd sure be dead as well."

"The rest of us gave up yelling for a moment, coming to believe that we were being left behind."

Completing his rope-cutting job, though, was distraction enough for the sailor to hear their cries. He looked across, and up to the sky platform, to see Dvorak *still* yelling and waving his shredded arms.

"Alvin *never* gave up," said Lauren.

"Up here," Dvorak shouted. "Up here!"

"Then," said Lauren, "the big sailor waved his fire axe, to show he'd seen us."

Regardless, Dvorak kept shouting—even suggesting in some way that a line be thrown over, as a means to escape. "What the hell, I thought!"

Wind continued to blow smoke down from the ship, and onto *Nevada,* behind them. It made little difference as wind travelled from ships, in front of *Arizona,* and blew the rancid smell of death upon them.

"As we waited for that big sailor to do something, anything" said Lauren, "we measured with our eyes to see if *Vestal* had come to a stop or was, inch by inch, still being drawn away from us… taking away our only chance to live."

Continual explosions of ammunition and black powder—set off by *Arizona's* fires—still rocked the ship.

"Now, I don't want anyone to think we just stood there… no cares in the world… just twiddling our thumbs. On the contrary, besides *Arizona* edging into her grave and tilting hard forward… which made it difficult to stand upright, fires aboard and below not only kept burning, but raged even more as the minutes ticked by."

"Each time explosions rocked the ship, some of us would be knocked to our knees. Our tendency was to grab hold of something, so we wouldn't get thrown over the rail. Problem was… there weren't nothin' to grab onto that wasn't burning hot."

0818

His pain distracted Lauren. He glanced down to check his burned hand, and his eyes caught movement on the main deck, fifty feet below. What he saw began what he'd always refer to as "…the worst of his nightmares." From that moment on, throughout the rest of his life, Lauren made unsuccessful attempts to bury any thought of them.

Without touching the hot rail with his bare hands, again, Lauren leaned over to look toward the bow, then astern. His eyes followed the main deck, forward, over the part of the ship already nosing into the water.

He felt they were sinking fast. Though the fear of turning turtle like *Oklahoma*—two ships forward of *Arizona*—was always in the back of his mind, he knew, due to settlement, it was now impossible.

Yet, that fear still held and wouldn't let go.

"What I saw gripped at my mind, like a vise. *Arizona's* main deck was completely destroyed… nothing but twisted metal. And the dead lay everywhere."

"On the port side of the ship, several men… all who'd been burned during the explosion, jumped overboard, fore and aft of the smaller *Vestal*."

"But the fools jumped directly into burning oil. They'd come to the surface as the hot oil attacked… and attached itself to their heads and faces."

"It was godawful, terrible. I could hear them scream and cry out for help… chilling, high-pitched screams I'd never heard before... but over with almost as quickly as they'd begun."

Then they'd just slowly sink into the water… joining hundreds of *Arizona* crew members, already in the channel.

Looking down at what was once an immaculate teak deck, Lauren realized "…it'd been downright torn up… destroyed. This was the very same deck I'd spent countless hours holy-stoning with my division, and on other occasions, sitting around, playing acey-duecy or poker… or maybe just writing a letter home."

"But goddamnit, it was a mess now… littered with bodies and blood… shredded by the large teak splinters that'd hit 'em like shrapnel."

"And I realized, then… my entire life had changed, in less time than it took to play a softball game."

"Make no mistake. As I looked along the deck, most of the living… those who made it off the ship… or survivors, as they called us, had either been thrown or jumped over the side, following the fireball. Some made it. Most didn't."

"Fire burning on the decks and cherry-hot wreckage of our ship was one thing. But when I saw the waters of the harbor on fire… throwing off such intense heat… it was something else. Twenty-one years old, and no one ever told me water could burn."

Then, there were the men's bodies—some still thrashing about on deck in their final death throes, others blindly wandering, but most, feeling pain—crying out in high-pitched screams or moaning in strange, guttural sounds.

"They didn't resemble, in any way, the men I'd worked with… almost all burned beyond any recognition as being human. Some clothed only in their skin… burnt black and charcoaled."

"The old expression… 'Died with their boots on,' came to mind. For whatever reason… I suppose, due to their thickness… their work shoes didn't burn off completely."

The burned men continued to moan as they walked—a horrific chorus of men crying out for help. Arms outstretched, either to help guide them, because they were blind, or because it was too painful for their arms to touch their bodies.

Lauren hesitated, and found it difficult to further describe what he witnessed.

"Because they couldn't see," he said, "they'd walk along the deck until they'd fall overboard, into the burning oil. Others tripped over bodies on deck… never to get up again. And once down, they'd stack up like cordwood."

"God-awful."

"One sailor, in particular, walked what was left of the deck, almost right under us… now sixty feet below. He must've heard our screams to the sailor, aboard *Vestal*. This guy was burned beyond recognition… no hair, no clothes and, like Alvin, no ears."

Just his boots.

"He heard us yelling, and he looked up… no eyes in his sockets… hands outstretched and, with what was left of his mouth, he kept repeating something…. But the poor soul was so far below. With the deafening sounds of battle surrounding us—even up on the sky platform, we had to yell just to hear each other."

"Always thought that young sailor was trying to scream out 'Help me' over and over… though I couldn't be certain."

"In my mind, that's what I believe… and it's haunted my dreams, thousands of times, ever since."

"But then, this fella', with his head pointed toward our yelling… tripped over another dead crew member, and became one of the mounds of bodies, scattered over the deck."

"I wanted him to get up and save himself, but he never moved again."

It occurred to Lauren, that those men were the walking dead of *Arizona*. "But by the grace of God, I'd just barely escaped becoming one of 'em."

From that day on, Lauren refused to watch horror movies, of any kind. "Hell," he said, "I'd seen my friends turn into the real thing… men who became the walking dead. And I never wanted to be reminded of it again."

"In the end, though…my dreams wouldn't let me forget."

"Understand... all these events took place within just minutes. The attack hadn't stopped. Several times, someone in our crew would yell, 'Jap plane coming in, one o'clock!' or six o'clock, or from some other direction. And we'd all race into the director."

"Each time, though, when we re-entered the director... it became more difficult, because of Zeke's body, layin' right there as we dodged incoming rounds from those damn machine guns."

"And it just seems so sad, even today, that with each fleeting moment, stepping back and forth over Zeke, how terrible I felt inside... like we were disrespecting the dead."

More than once, during their rush to safety, they'd hear rounds hit, and ricochet off the director's roof and sides. And they realized they'd probably be lying there, close to Zeke, if they hadn't moved fast enough.

"To me, it just underlined the fact... this fight was far from over. The enemy was still intent on adding us to their list of kills."

The strafing runs occurred multiple times. Often, the attack planes could be heard through the smoke. But as soon as the crew heard a plane fly past, they'd hurry back outside, to continue any attempt to get off *Arizona*.

"It was during one of these fly-bys, I wondered if Larry had been able to avoid the shrapnel and make it to safety, between the time he left us to the times we were strafed."

It was between one of those rakings, Lott yelled out, again.

"Lookit the sharks out there... near the ship's side.... Sonovabitch!" He pointed down between *Arizona* and *Vestal*.

The men looked below, as the water began to thrash.

"Most of us were cussing," said Lauren. "For me, seeing the sharks sealed the deal. Not only was I a poor swimmer, but also I was still alive… and it'd take a lot to get me into that water."

"You'd think I woulda' put two an' two together, about water and the Navy, when I joined. But the recruiters convinced me not to worry… no one could've seen this coming."

"Then a wild thought occurred to me, at the time… those guys, floating facedown, didn't give a shit. They'd already passed on to a better place."

But in that moment—the world appeared to Lauren as if it had met its end. *Hell… anything would be better than here*.

Looking down at the aft deck—through all the smoke—Lauren's attention was now drawn to several sailors. He watched them walk around, in pure shock, "…clothes and skin burnt completely off of 'em. Their skin in ribbon-like strips," he said, "and the strips were still burning."

"But worst of all…"

Lauren stopped and tears welled up. This was the stuff of decades-long night terror… this was what had locked up his throat for over seventy-five years, when insensitive reporters asked the one forbidden question, "What did you see?"

For decades, words could not express the horror his own mind would not let him speak. Then, almost as if marching in step with a slow motion clock, he spoke with courage about sights he'd witnessed, on the afterdeck.

Scenes that were seared into his mind, forever.

"Two men came out of the…what I call 'the Marine section' – where the sinkage got started."

"But… these two guys walked out from there. They just… sauntered out, their backs to our platform's rail… and stood there, near the stern, lookin' like they were talkin' to each other, in their whites… caps still on, as if nothin' had happened."

"And I remember thinkin' 'thank God these two guys made it out okay.' "

Cheeks stained wet, Lauren began to draw on years of hidden memories to describe what came next.

"After a while they turned around and… were comin' back in my direction. And they were like a… what'da'ya call it? An old black and white negative. White uniforms, from behind… and from the front… shit, everything was black… and still burning. From their t-shirts, right on down to their… peckers."

"Yet… by God they were still alive."

"They got all the way back into the… hell, I don't know how far they got, but… they had to be in shock. Even *they* didn't realize they were just walkin' zombies."

"I'm certain the sailors went down with the ship… to cooler waters. God rest their souls."

— —

What had seemed like an eternity to Lauren, and to the others—watching each of the various events pass by—occurred in a matter of seconds and minutes. "It wasn't like just watching one accident happen, in slow motion," said Lauren, "at the intersection of Main Street and Vine. We all took in *hundreds* of incidents. Perhaps thousands… without our minds comprehending them, at the time."

"It wouldn't be 'til days, weeks or even months, later, that those grisly scenes would creep back into our minds… to haunt and follow us to our graves. Today, they call it

Post-Traumatic Stress Disorder. But in those days… hell, we had no idea what that was. We held it all in and just… didn't talk about it. Not even to our wives."

"You know…" Lauren stopped, mid-sentence. It had become very difficult for him to speak further of these atrocities, after so many decades of keeping them to himself. He sat in silence for quite some time.

Tears glistened across his timeworn cheeks. They had developed, in silence, as he considered not saying another word.

Is this the 'cathartic moment' the doctors said I'd eventually meet up with?

He took a breath and gave out a deep sigh. With a quiet resolve that he'd come to know over the years, Lauren Bruner spoke, once again.

"Ya' know…. Other than Alvin and *Vestal*'s big fella'… I don't think any of us had an idea as to the plan they were hatchin'."

— —

0819

Aboard *Arizona*, the smoke shifted, once again, and they saw the man who turned out to be *Vestal's* boatswain, holding his fire axe—yelling to its bridge.

"I sure as hell felt better after he turned around and ordered someone to hold that ship steady… and to stop the tug from towing *Vestal* back out into the harbor."

To the crew's amazement, the tug ceased pulling *Vestal* away.

"Turns out," Lt. J. G. Birmingham, from *Vestal's* crew, had later said, "that tug captain had served aboard *Vestal* years before. So he would've done anything asked of him by *Vestal's* crew."

The repair ship came to a stop—but with a wider chasm that separated the two vessels. Immediately, more of the burning oil found the void and spread into the new opening between the two ships.

Dvorak was right, though. Someone heard his hoarse screams.

With a new rush of adrenaline, they all chimed in. Despite thick smoke that clenched at their throats, as a vise, they cheered with fresh hope, as loudly as choking lungs would permit.

The man waved back and threw down his axe.

As he raced to the ship's rigging, this big sailor picked up a monkey fist, tied to the end of a heaving line—then sprinted back to the ship's rail.

Hell. Even from the sky platform, this guy looked big.

He watched the man cover *Vestal's* deck in giant strides.

Then, Lauren recalled one of the guys—couldn't remember who—shouted, "Hey that's *Vestal's* fighter. Won money on him Friday night, at the smoker. Name's George."

"The boxer?" someone asked.

"Yeah… Joe George. A heavyweight. Knocked out his opponent in the last round."

"Shit…" another chimed in, "If anyone can toss us a line it's that guy."

"Damn straight," the men chimed in.

Suddenly, there was a renewed sense of hope.

Boatswain's Mate Second Class, Joseph Leonidas George—this heroic six-foot-tall, twohundred ten pounds of solid Franklin, Georgia muscle—had placed country first when, in 1935, he chose the Navy over a football scholarship to Auburn University. During the 7 December attack, though, he had raced from bow to stern—as if a football hero, traversing his ship in cleats—to furl the awnings, uncover surface guns, fight fires, and sever mooring lines to *Arizona*, at the bow.

Somehow, amidst all the smoke and explosive clamor of bombs, torpedoes, diving Japanese Vals and Zeros, with their strafing machine guns, George had heard voices scream for help from across the water. It was a haunting sound that arose from the blackness and echoed between the two steel structures—both of which listed after taking ordnance, prior to and following the massive explosion aboard *Arizona*.

George's attention had, at long last, been drawn to *Arizona's* main mast. A chance break in the acrid smoke exposed six men, as George recounted afterward, "... stranded on the ship... trying to get off... surrounded by fire."

At that point, the twenty-six-year-old fighter faced two choices. To follow orders and cut *Vestal* loose, or to selflessly place his career on the line and save six sailors from certain death.

Standing on *Vestal's* superstructure, near the silvering shop—where he'd earlier smoldered a fire and furled back the forecastle awnings for the broadside surface guns—Joe George had watched shallow-running torpedoes ride the water. But Fate passed them on to other targets.

There stood George, a pugnacious but easy-going enigma of a man, who would later describe himself, when it came to making decisions, as "...one of those kids (who) just lets nature take its course." Yet, on this day, the sturdy boxer—with a strong build, penetrating eyes, and a firm, unblemished nose, despite his chosen sport—wasn't going to accept a technical knockout.

Arizona was settling fast.

"That part of *Vestal's* deck... the superstructure," George would later report, "was about the only part of the deck... even with *Arizona*" that could allow an attempt at rescue.

"Although her main deck was maybe lower than ours," he said, "she drew more water."

"It was then, that big old farm boy of a sailor," said Lauren, "yelled back that he was gonna help get us off… and not to worry."

Back on *Arizona,* one of the guys quipped, "Yeah, easy for him to say. He doesn't have anything to worry about." But we all knew he did. And the crew of six still doubted *Vestal* was their way out—their way off the fiery, settling death ship.

Lauren and the crew secretly prayed for a miracle.

Bruner glanced at Alvin Dvorak, next to him, who "sure as hell looked toasted." But it didn't stop him from continuing to yell, "Hey, throw me a rope. Over here."

Vestal's boxer deftly maneuvered the heaving line—with a lead-ball weighted monkey-fist knot tied at the end.

George twirled the heavy monkey-fist a half-dozen times, ankle to shoulder, to build centrifugal speed. Then he let the rope soar. In no time—as if a massive flying poi-ball—it sailed right over the crew's heads.

Improbable as it seemed, Dvorak—this man with ears burned off and little skin left on his hands—grabbed the line, mid-air, and hauled it in.

"Without a moment's rest," said Lauren, "and I'll never forget this… *burned* hands tight on the lifeline, Alvin began to pull up the slack. Our crew moved in to help, and pulled as fast as we could, as if our lives depended on it… which they did."

"Damn," he laughed, "if that wasn't the understatement of the year."

At last, the clothesline-sized, monkey-fisted rope George had thrown transitioned to a heavier, one-and-a-half-inch ship's line. The smaller, incoming line had been tied to a thicker mooring line, to allow for a toss across what Lauren has always called "the Valley of Death."

"Pull!" Lauren yelled to the others, "Before, *Vestal* leaves or we turn turtle."

They had just watched *Oklahoma* turn turtle, right before their eyes.

And who would've ever thought?

But Lauren knew better than that—as far as *Arizona* turning turtle. She was sinking fast. Straight down. He could feel the motion at his feet.

"In no time at all we had the end of *Vestal's* heavier line."

"Keep pulling!" Dvorak ordered, "I need enough extra line in case something breaks, or we lose the connection. Don't want it slippin' into the hellfire, below."

The six pulled and heaved rope behind them.

Dvorak gave an order to stop and, on the double, they helped him tie the ship's line between two stands at the platform's rail.

"Badly injured, or not, Alvin sure as hell knew what he was doing."

Amid the clamor, Lauren shouted, "What knot you gonna' use?"

Looking up, and with a slight smile, Dvorak answered, "Damn well not gonna use a slip knot."

It was the one smile Lauren would see that morning. Other than Dvorak's burned-off ears, it would be the last thing Lauren most remembered about Alvin, in those final minutes aboard *Arizona*.

Concerned, the crew watched as he tied the bowline, "...or bolin, as they used to say."

But Lauren put his faith in Dvorak. After all, he was the expert—and their boatswain.

Then, the rope's cord began to smoke, at the hot posts and rail tie-offs.

"None of us said a word about it," said Lauren, "hopin' each other didn't notice, I'm sure. But it scared the shit outta' me. All along prayin' the hot metal wouldn't burn through the rope as we attempted to cross."

Just then, over the din of battle, they heard the barrel-chested George shout from the *Vestal*, "Hurry up!" They ain't gonna' hold 'er much longer."

"We all knew we had to haul ass now... or not go at all," Lauren said. "*Arizona's* fires were out of control... and climbing fast."

Winds had shifted and the hot, acrid smoke—already burned into their nostrils, eyes, and mouths—moved behind them. The sky was still filled with enemy fighter planes, as the crew looked across to their anxious rescuer.

One fighter plane, in particular, maneuvered down the channel, machine guns roaring. They couldn't tell if it was headed straight for *Vestal*, or for them.

At the last moment, the pilot chose to play Russian roulette with *Vestal*, rather than just six guys out on a limb. Lauren was certain the pilot figured he could kill more with a bigger target.

Aboard *Vestal*, George saw the plane coming. From *Arizona*, it appeared to the six as if Joe George had turned to face the enemy—straight on—just like when he'd boxed and fought his opponent in the ring, two nights before.

Terrified for their one rescuer, they watched machine gun rounds start at ships aft—ripping, pinging and bouncing off *Vestal's* armored deck.

"And there was George," said Lauren, "right up 'til the last second, staring the pilot down."

"Even we could see the pilot's face He was that close."

"Then, by God, at the last moment, George did something he'd never have done in the boxing ring."

"He took a dive!"

"Hah, hah," Lauren laughed, "behind something solid."

"Of course, it happened so fast we all thought he'd been hit… our lifeline gone."

But again, just like the fighter he was, Joe George stood up, all business. He turned back to *Arizona,* waved, and bellowed, "Let's go. Get moving!"

Even then, the sky platform's railing glowed red, as it continued to dip forward ever so slightly. Somehow they'd have to traverse it to grab onto the line. Lauren looked around. Lott still held on to Lauren's old blanket, that he'd kept in the director. He grabbed the blanket from Lott's hands, draped it over the railing, then looked to Dvorak, who nodded agreement.

"Let's get movin'!" ordered Alvin.

0820

The moment had come to leave *Arizona* for one final time. Standing there, escape within their grasp, no one jumped at being the first to cross the line to safety.

"I'm sure we all thought it was a helluva long way down and across. If you slipped, it would've been a direct shortcut into Hell's fire and brimstone."

No one thought about who'd go first. "What broke the ice… and I'll never forget it, was Harold Kuhn. "He stood right up and volunteered."

"Look, yous guys," said Kuhn—Big Guns Spotter and Seaman First-class. "I'm not burned like mosta' yous. I'll go first and give it a try, to make sure the line'll hold."

Dvorak looked to the crew. No one objected. The Guns Spotter nodded to Dvorak and, as if an automaton, stepped to the hot blanket, climbed over it, and started across the line, hand over hand—"forehanded," as Joe George would later describe it.

Kuhn dangled above the hellish water—filled with death—and what by then was charged with sharks that had entered the harbor, looking for breakfast.

The men shouted encouragement, all the while hoping the rope would hold.

Dvorak monitored his knot. He noticed it had begun to smoke.

By now, some of *Vestal's* crew stood next to their rails—watching and yelling encouragement to *Arizona's* stranded men.

Kuhn got half way across—a good fifty feet—and Seaman First-class/Sight Setter, Donald Gay Stratton winked at Dvorak, and then started across.

No one was ordered to go in any particular order.

"By now we were yelpin' out cheers faster than an enemy's machine gun rounds," said Bruner. I turned back to see who'd go next, and noticed the rail-covered blanket was starting to smolder.

Shit, don't flame on us now.

Lott chose to precede Gunner Mate Earl Riner, from the starboard director.

Both struggled to reach the other side.

"What we didn't figure on was the bobbing of the two ships. It made the rope… and those on it, dip closer to thousands of gallons of burning oil."

Then the hemp line, itself, began to smolder, over the water.

Over 66,000 cubic feet of scorching heat had poured into the yawning chasm between the battleship and the repair ship. With each dip of the rope, the rising flames tortured the men.

There was still no telling if crossing to *Vestal* would be the surest route to safety. Fires raged in it's own belly, berthed outboard of *Arizona's* blistering shell.

"We had *no* alternative," said Lauren.

Joseph George, a master with knots, had also tied off his rope's end to the ship's railing. For extra insurance, as if two solid steel posts, he and Dvorak—both holding identical ranks, as Boatswain's Mates 2/c—had wrapped the extra rope, near the tail ends, around their waists and up their arms, to make certain the line didn't falter. Dvorak, more so, as he was now concerned about the hot rail burning through their tied-up end.

"How he ever held on, like that, I'll never understand. For Christ's sake… he was burned well over two-thirds of his body… his arms charred like barbequed ribs."

One survivor after another reached *Vestal*—each dragged over the rail by two or three sailors.

"Not Joe George," said Bruner, "because… like Alvin, he kept his eyes on the most critical line holding the two ships together."

It appeared, for a brief time, that the Japanese attack planes "had pretty well shot their wad, and had left for their carriers," said Lauren. "The channel had somewhat quieted, and a lull had settled in."

"Then it changed."

The already wounded Earl Riner had completed two thirds of his trek, across the seething waters, as a second-wave attack plane headed on a direct path down the channel. Earl stopped and was transfixed.

"From both ships' railings," said Lauren, "all of us yelled for him to get the hell on with it."

Riner looked back to *Arizona*, then to *Vestal*; saw his progress and "He musta' gotten a quick shot of adrenaline, seeing that Jap plane… 'cause he doubled his pace across the remaining rope just as a machine gun began strafing… I swear to God… right where Earl had been hanging, two seconds before. Didn't hit Riner, but the bastard's tail gunner's rounds must've hit the rope."

The men held their breath as they watched the hemp line snap a couple of twine wrappings. There was a chorus of cussing, from both ship's rails—followed by rousing encouragement for Riner to "…get your ass over here."

Riner made it to the other side without further incident. But once over the railing, he collapsed to the deck, spent, having realized how close he'd come to death.

"Finally, there was just Alvin and me."

Aboard *Arizona,* as if banshees on a rage, fire licked at the two men while heavy smoke swirled around them.

The platform jolted forward, as steel girders melted below. Lauren and Dvorak braced themselves and stared at each other.

"Alvin, you go first," Lauren said, "You're in worse shape than me."

"You go Bruner. Wanna' make sure my knot holds."

And that's when Lauren Fay Bruner became "the Second to the Last to Leave USS *Arizona*."

Lauren crawled over *Arizona's* railing, and the smoking blanket. He was careful to lower himself onto the long rescue line— by then, almost as hot to touch as any part of *Arizona*. He hoped vapors, rising from the line, were caused by condensation, rather than from heat.

Then, he spotted the shot-up, loosening braids.

Lauren knew time was getting short. He glanced over, once again, to *Vestal*.

What he saw was disturbing.

Joe George, the boxer, was vehemently arguing with someone who looked as if he'd fallen overboard and had made it back up the side. In the heat of the argument, Lauren and the others watched George pick up his fire axe.

In his dispute with an officer, Joe George refused to cut the rescue line, as ordered, until he could save *all* the lives of the six men, stranded aboard *Arizona,* including the last two.

Orders had earlier been passed down to "get the ship underway." Prior to spotting the six crew high atop *Arizona's* sky platform, as Petty Officer in charge of *Vestal's* rigging, George had been ordered to throw off the lines to the battleship. However, due to the continuing attack, he had decided to sever them with a fire axe.

Lauren and the others watched, as a dripping wet Executive Officer, John Toole, raged at George for cutting the lines—perhaps thinking it was a waste of ship's line, which could be saved and utilized later on. As probable was the fact that George—the natural hero he was—had countermanded orders to facilitate the saving of additional lives, despite all the devastation that had occurred on and around his ship.

Following *Arizona's* massive explosion, George had assessed there was no one aboard that ship capable of heaving a giant hawser over its side to release the doomed ship from its ties. Aboard *Vestal,* a bomb had burst through each deck, aft, and another had opened a five-foot hole in its hull.

Its stern was already down.

To George, John Toole's outrage didn't make sense, with nobody aboard *Arizona* to throw ropes off. "We had bollard to bollard and bits to bits to tie up," George had argued back.

Unless *Arizona's* crew would cast rigging off the bollards, and pull them through the chocks, *Vestal* wasn't going anywhere.

George had later reported, "…The only man I saw alive on *Arizona,* after I threw the line over [to the sky platform]… was one man laying down on the [torpedo] blister, gasping. And he was on fire… fighting for air, as he choked."

Following his verbal altercation, with the XO, George yelled to Lauren.

"Come on, get moving," he shouted, above the roar of two approaching Zeros headed down Battleship Row. Lauren watched as the planes strafed floating bodies in the water, then hard-banked toward Ford Island—their guns still spitting out death.

"Can't keep holding the ship."

"Severely burned or not, it was either stay onboard, to be finished off by the raging fire and smoke, or to take our chances at living… going over the rope."

When faced with that moment of reality, there was no choice, for the last two burned men, but to attempt the crossing.

"Throughout our entire ordeal," he said, "Alvin never left his tied line… making certain it held until just he and I would have to be on the line together."

Joe George didn't have to shout again. After Lauren started out, Dvorak released the wrapped rope's end from his arms and waist, and checked his knot one more time. It was smoking more than ever.

"Right behind you, Lauren," he yelled hoarsely.

Half way across, Lauren glanced down to the hell-fire.

So, this is how it feels to be barbequed alive.

From sixty feet up, he felt the heat of Hell and witnessed more grisly scenes of body parts surrounding dead and dying sailors—most that floated face down. Many were burned beyond recognition. Others being devoured by sharks.

"Given our circumstances… and bad timing, what with the second wave of Japanese attack planes still hitting

Battleship Row at full force, negotiating the rope was a physical challenge, beyond any belief… and the one of the most difficult things I've ever had to do."

At times, despite Lauren's charred hands, he was able to hold the line tight, while at other times his fingers would slip, "…and my hands would be loose as a goose."

Aboard *Arizona*, where Dvorak had tied the ship's line to the hot rail post, the rope smoked even more. More fire had reached the platform, and it licked at the men's lifeline.

Concerned, Dvorak glanced back at the railing. Within the knot, a bit of twine popped and, as if a small wick, began to glow, then burn. A very small glow, at first—it grew—and more bits of twine gave way to ignition.

Nothing about traversing the rope remained constant. *Vestal* was in ceaseless motion, treading water while it moved with the current. Channel waters churned madly from bombs and torpedoes. And large schools of Tiger and Galapagos sharks—the most aggressive of the reef sharks—had entered the wild frenzy below.

Lauren understood the irony of the shark attacks beneath him. Tiger sharks' teeth were the ones sold in Chinese shops on Hotel Street.

They're supposed to bring good luck...

The sharks became more of a motivation than the fire. "Each time I looked down and seen them sharks, I'd hold the rope even tighter… didn't want to end up among the food chain."

"Amazing what the body and mind communicate, when your adrenaline runs at full tilt."

Below him, and out into the channel, men continued to die while attempting to swim through the viscous, fiery oil, sharks, and enemy fire. Sailors tried, without luck, to push it away from their faces. "Just didn't work,"

Lauren recalled. "The oil on the water would stick to the swimmers' skin. The fire did the rest. It's a scene I'll never erase from my mind."

Abruptly, within fifteen feet of *Vestal,* Lauren's hands and arms became weak and tired—and he began to slip. "They hurt like hell," he said. "Behind me, toward *Arizona,* I saw Alvin had started to cross. I knew I couldn't stop. Yet, something strange was happening to our rope.

"The line kept dipping and jumping. I could barely hold on." He looked over to *Vestal's* bow, then out toward the channel.

"Launches carrying survivors were swerving around bomb geysers and dodging machine gun strafing, coming from the low-flying Zero's and Val fighters."

"*Vestal* was bouncing from action in the water."

And it was settling and listing fast, from its own wounds.

"Tired," said Lauren, "…hands and arms about ready to give up… my supply of adrenaline abruptly running out."

For a brief moment—a hundred eighty-eight pounds of wounded muscle—barely hanging from his burned fingertips, Lauren thought he might not make it. It may have been easier to just let go.

But it wasn't in Lauren's character.

Then came the sailor's shouts of encouragement, as he approached *Vestal's* port-side rail.

With one last burst of strength—and a loud scream of resolve—Lauren forced a leg up over the rope, to distribute weight—and to just hang on.

Suddenly, his mind turned off all sounds, and in full concentration, told himself to focus on the goal. Gone was the din of enemy planes, bombs, strafing guns—and the screams. Absent was the burning oil, the bodies, the sharks, and the smell of death.

Hanging nearly upside down, Lauren could only see the four sailors who preceded him. Then, gathering sailors from *Vestal*—some with hats in hand, wildly motioning him to the railing.

His resolve was set in stone. In his very quiet sea of tranquility, Lauren continued the last fifteen feet, pulling himself across the rope, in his hanging position.

As soon as he was pulled over the rail to the deck, though spent, Lauren turned back to watch Alvin's approach. More cheering arose amid the clamor. And Lauren quietly joined in, to buoy up the one man who wouldn't give up.

"Come on, Alvin," he whispered under his breath, "come on, buddy." It was as much a prayer as a challenge.

The men held their breath as twice, the weakened, braided strands began popping loose, midway.

Despite being burned over most of his body, and ears missing, Dvorak never stopped. As if he were eighteen and just out of boot camp, he forced one hand in front of the other, with a determination and spirit that refused to bend.

Encouraged by louder cries, from the sailors, Alvin Dvorak made the crossing to wild shouts of joy.

"And due to his leadership and encouragement," affirmed Lauren, "we all did."

"How, in his condition, he ever made it… I'll never know.

"I knew *I* was hurting. Yet he was worse off than me. And he just… kept going. Never once, did I hear him complain."

Vestal's captain, Cassin Young, who had originally given an abandon ship order, had been blown over the side. Some say it was during *Arizona's* massive explosion—but then swam back and climbed onboard, to counterman the order.

Upon witnessing rescue of the sailors from *Arizona*, he triaged the six men. Immediately, he ordered crew to hustle Bruner and Dvorak—the most seriously wounded—to the ship's launch for transport to the hospital ship, USS *Solace*.

0840

Prior to being shepherded to the gangway and escorted aboard *Vestal's* launch, Lauren glanced over to his ship, and sadness overcame him. *Arizona's* quarterdeck was fully awash, the ship entirely engulfed in flames.

He then looked back, just in time, to see the All-Navy boxer Joe George cut the last thread of their rescue line from *Arizona*.

"Again, with the fire axe. One swing of his massive arms did it."

At once, on the other end, *Arizona's* knot burst into flame, ruptured, and tore away from its post.

The entire rope snapped hard, flew into the air, and disappeared in the fiery waters.

"At that moment, I fcalled out to George."

"Hey. Thanks."

"It was the last and only thing I ever said to him."

"Joe George turned and looked directly at me... but never said a word."

— —

SECOND TO THE LAST TO LEAVE

Joseph L. George

Joseph Leonidas George was born on 8 October 1915 in Franklin, Georgia to Moses Leonidas and Fannie (Morris) George. He enlisted in the Navy for four years on 25 July 1935 in Columbus, Georgia.

When he enlisted, Joe George, as he was called by his friends, was a stocky 5′ 11″ and weighed 169 pounds. He had blue eyes, light brown hair and a ruddy complexion. While serving in the Navy, Joe became an accomplished heavyweight boxer who fought, representing his ship USS *Vestal,* just two nights before the attack. **Joseph George was 26 years, 1 month, and 22 days old on the day of the attack.**

"Joe George is an American Hero and the second of two men who saved my life during the attack on Pearl Harbor. It is because of Joe George and Alvin Dvorak and their heroic efforts that I have been able to lead such a long and happy life.

Both of these men deserve the Congrssional Medal of Honor for their valor during the attack. I know this to be true."

Joseph Leon George, BM 2/c

USS *Vestal*

American Hero

Harold J. Kuhn

Harold Joseph Kuhn was born to John Alfred and Katherine (Stradinger) Kuhn on 9 June 1922 in Bronx, New York. He completed 11 grades of school and enlisted in the Navy for six years on 23 July 1940 in Portland, Oregon. At that time he was 5′ 10″, weighed 133 pounds, had brown eyes, light brown hair, and a ruddy complexion.

Harold reported aboard USS *Arizona,* which was his first ship, on 1 October 1941. **When the attack on Pearl Harbor occurred on 7 December 1941, Harold Joseph Kuhn was 19 years, 5 months and 29 days old.**

He was one of six sailors trapped in the port-side anti-aircraft director, and because of that, became a member of *Arizona's* Greatest Escape. Due to his having the fewest injuries, Harold volunteered to cross the ship's line to USS *Vestal* first in order to test the line in order to see that it would hold for those who followed.

"I didn't know Harold Kuhn all that well, as he had joined our crew during the attack, coming down from the crow's nest in the main mast, and I will always remember his New York accent, even during our battle between life and death. Harold Kuhn stood with our crew and never failed or complained. He was a good guy and I am proud to have known him."

Harold Joseph Kuhn, Sea 1/c

USS *Arizona*

Survivor

Chapter 19
"SHIT! A ZERO AT 11 O'CLOCK"

0845

The second attack wave had fully begun.

Though the first wave had approached from the northwestern side of the island, the second wave hit from the southeast.

One-hundred-and-seventy-one Japanese planes struck in three groups. One, to complete their assault on cruisers, lined up along the East Loch-side of Battleship Row; another, to bomb hangars and aircraft on Ford Island, Barbers Point, and on Kaneohe—along with aircraft and hangars at Hickam Field.

The third group—mostly Zero fighters—was assigned to defend the attack planes, and to strafe anything that moved, in the harbor.

Five minutes earlier, battered and crippled, *Nevada* had just slipped away from Quay Foxtrot 8. The plan was to get underway—to escape, southwest down the channel, and break for open water.

"As it passed us, I silently cheered and wanted to clap my hands. But they'd just started to go from numb... to a raw pain that hurt like hell. Despite it all, I was damn proud of the *Nevada* and her crew."

0850

Two Japanese Val dive-bombers tore over Pearl Harbor's already destroyed channel. They banked sharply to the west, strafed targets of opportunity along Battleship Row and split-banked, to prepare for a return run down the channel.

From within the gates of Hell, a twenty-foot, open-air Liberty launch from *USS Vestal* slipped past horrors that only Dante might have described. As though ectoplasm slipping through a dark membrane, the small boat slowly evaded burning patches of oil as it skimmed, almost blinded, through dense, black, choking smoke.

After Bruner and Dvorak's launch had cleared *Vestal's* port-side gangway, at approximately 0845, the repair ship's last forward lines were severed. Captain's order was given to get underway, and the waiting tug resumed pulling *Vestal's* bow clear of *Arizona*.

With no steering gear to maneuver the channel, *Vestal's* crew would manage to pilot their ship, using its two engines, to head north of Ford Island. It would be intentionally grounded, twenty-five minutes later, at McGrew Point, across the East Loch—in a direct line with Battleship Row.

Meanwhile, Bruner's launch passed other victim-delivery launches, and dodged hundreds of burned, skeletal remains—most from USS *Arizona*. The difficulty was in navigating fast enough to evade attack, but slow enough—out of respect for the dead. As minutes passed, pain took hold. And to Lauren, it seemed as if they were moving at a snail's pace.

The fires, and resultant dense smoke, complicated maintaining such a course, and prevented determination of those who might still be alive.

Resembling expendable jetsam, layered across the water, smoldering bodies and body parts were pushed from here to there. Bomb geysers and maneuvering launches created a constant backwash of wakes between the embattled ships on Battleship Row and the Southeast Loch of the harbor.

Black oil splashed over floating limbs, torsos, and other floating objects. And it coated the sides of every craft it touched.

Less than an hour into the attack on Pearl Harbor—the greatest Naval loss in America's history—it appeared, to Lauren Bruner, to be the end of the world. Or what he thought it might look like.

Lauren—burned over seventy-three percent of his body—and his fellow crew member, Dvorak—over eighty percent—sat motionless on hard wooden benches. As though a secret smoker's tabagie, they were huddled together, joined in their suffering.

Dangerous and unpredictable explosive fires blew into the harbor sky. Burning infernos fed on their own fuels and created new weather systems—as they whipped water vapor into the air, then converted it to steam.

Stinging soot and ash fell throughout the channel, as the winds created strong updrafts and more wind to fuel the fires.

Something directly ahead caught Lauren's eye. There, among a floating congregation of torsos, a shark—awash in oil and diesel fuel--tore at the body of a fellow sailor, laying face down in the water.

Did Lauren only imagine screams coming from the sea? He instinctively forced himself to look down, away from the burning channel.

Pearl Harbor was still a very dangerous place, fifty minutes after one of the first Japanese pilots tried to kill him as he approachedd the director's rear hatchway.

The air reeked with engine exhaust, rancid burning oil, and other fumes that seized at Lauren's and Dvorak's lungs. The stench competed with sickening smells of burning flesh, iron, steel, and timber, as their victim delivery launch navigated through a slipstream of mercy.

More times than not, on this ledge between death and salvation, Lauren wanted to puke over the side of the launch. An hour prior, Lauren had planned to join his best friend, Billy Mann, for Sunday church services on *Arizona's* forecastle. He had just put on clean—shorts, t-shirt, and cap—in preparation for the day.

Without warning, Lauren's body forced puke up, and he retched vomit over the side.

"Those who've served in the Navy know that the launch in which we sat was for the lowest of sailors… often assigned by the Captain to run errands, or as a liberty launch."

"Alvin and I sat on hard wooden benches. They crossed the launch in rows, from one side to the other, just in front of the coxswain."

No one spoke.

0855

The coxswain was locked into situation awareness, while he navigated the two burned sailors through the treacherous harbor waters.

The hookman rode, standing forward—his pole at-the-ready to draw the launch close enough to their destination "…if we were lucky enough to get there." Now, as gently as possible, and with respect, he pushed aside sailor's remains, to clear a path to the hospital ship, USS *Solace*.

Throughout the harbor, the attack continued to unfold. Lauren could only watch as planes approached from the east to strike, again. They'd fly in low, then rise high, from just above the water. Each turned aggressively for their assigned targets, dove fast, then continued to bomb or strafe whatever was left.

"We could only hope our launch was too insignificant a mark."

"Alvin and I didn't talk. No one did. We were all lost in our own thoughts… wondering if we'd live or die."

"It was night terrors in the making," said Lauren. "And one, that even now—after seventy-five years—still creeps into my mind. Even when I attempt to bury it."

To Bruner's left, receding from view, he saw Battleship Row, and what remained of *Arizona,* ablaze and dying. Smoke filled the sky as high as one could see. To the south of her were other ships, all vastly damaged. It appeared to Lauren as though a selfish kid, in a rage, had stomped on them.

Not far up the line, eyes rested on *Oklahoma,* as she laid, fully on her side—her starboard keel above water; her mast stuck in harbor mud, forty feet below the water line. Lauren had watched her take repeated torpedo hits from fighter planes, and from a small Japanese sub that had, with stealth, slipped into Pearl.

Now, in the midst of battle, crews of men— hoping to hear survivors, inside—pounded on *Oklahoma's* hull, with hammers—the sounds of which were lost amidst the pounding of Japanese armament, throughout the harbor.

"At the time I thought they must have all immediately drowned. Later, I'd learn that over thirty crew were freed from *Oklahoma's* keel, a couple days after. But numerous men lived inside total darkness, for as many as seventeen days, before death called them."

Another of Lauren's recurring nightmares.

On the starboard side of the channel, to the right of the launch, were the "tin cans"—the sailor's name for destroyers.

Many were severely damaged. But it was easy to make out their guns doing their damnedest to answer the enemy—more so, during the second wave of the attack, than in the first.

"If anything, it might have given me cause to smile… and I'm not sure if I did… hearing our sailors and Marines let the enemy know Americans never gave up. Even when we were down on the mat and the referee had counted to nine… but never quite said 'ten'… we *never* gave up."

From behind, the coxswain yelled, "Oh, shit! A Zero at 11 o' clock."

Abruptly, Lauren was pulled back to reality by the grim sound of fighter planes. He and the hookman looked back toward *Solace*. Dvorak's eyes rose to the sky.

The enemy aircraft emerged through parting smoke, as though spit from the hospital ship.

"I figured we were dead… and instantly thought of my mother… suddenly wishing I hadn't been so troublesome to her, as a kid."

The fighter headed straight into the channel, bearing down on the launch. Machine guns roared to life over screaming engines. Water exploded in a trail of rounds that traced their path toward the launch.

And Lauren next wondered what death was going to feel like.

"I don't remember being scared, at first… just my thoughts about mother… and death."

Just as death approached the small launch, destiny intervened once again.

"The enemy changed course and immediately swerved off to our right."

Confused, amazed—and still alive—occupants of the launch watched the plane veer-off to chase *Nevada*. She was the only battleship still able to leave her moorings, and had become a primary target as she headed for the harbor entrance—determined to make it to open water, and to take the battle to the enemy.

Then it occurred to Lauren, *This was the third time, within the last hour, someone… or* something *had intervened to save my life.*

First it was my buddy Dvorak, up on *Arizona's* sky platform, now sitting next to him. Then the big sailor, George, aboard the *Vestal*. And now the crew of *Nevada,* who had derailed the Devil as he bore down on them.

"This was the worst day of my life but also, up to that moment, my very best. I was still alive."

Nevada had just approached Dry Dock #1 when the Zero joined a swarm of Val dive-bombers that were attacking near the 10-10 dock, minutes earlier. "They went at her with everything they had," said Lauren.

The Japanese pilots had hoped to sink the battleship and block the channel. "Even if they had," said Bruner, "the harbor was over four hundred yards wide, at that point, and it would've been near impossible to totally bottle it up.

In his condition, it was difficult for Lauren to follow the attack on *Nevada,* behind him. "As it turned out… I found out later just how lucky *Nevada* had been that morning."

Unlike *Arizona,* with it's forward magazine loaded with black powder… *Nevada* had previously emptied its main magazine of older main-battery shells, in favor of a newer projectile that was to have been loaded in the next morning.

During the bombing and strafing attack, on *Nevada,* 5 bombs were direct hits on *Nevada's* Number 1 turret; a second-deck penetration; one near the galley; and a direct hit on the port-side director "…the same battle station I had aboard *Arizona,*" said Lauren.

"But what saved their ass was the lack of black powder in their magazines. When one of the bombs hit a gasoline storage tank, it caused massive fires onboard. But it never ignited the forward magazine… as there was nothing in it."

Ultimately, *Nevada* was able to ground itself across from Hospital Point and the channel at Waipio Peninsula, "...but, I learned later, not before taking out three Japanese planes," said Lauren.

Looking forward, and trying to keep focused, Lauren was aware he and Dvorak were in really bad shape. Without a mirror, he had no idea how bad. Bruner could only judge how severe his injuries must be by looking at Alvin.

"And then there were my hands and legs," said Lauren, "Charcoaled… similar to a blackened steak, forgotten on the grill."

"I knew I must've looked like hell. And my body was running on pure adrenaline."

Still, it sent throbbing pain that parked in a distant fragment of his mind.

He glanced again at Dvorak. *Alvin's* sure *gotta be injured more than me, with his missing ears.*

But during this surreal existence, nothing seemed certain. Lauren reached up to touch his own ears—to make certain once again that they were still there. He was relieved to find them intact.

At that point, Bruner and Dvorak's adrenaline began to subside. And Lauren wondered if they'd make it.

"Even this long into the battle the enemy was constantly near."

The skies were still filled with enemy aircraft of different sizes. Though the air attack appeared to have initially slowed, there were signs that another wave had begun, as seventy-eight dive bombers and fifty-four high-level bombers swooped in from Oahu's eastern side—to drop new payloads.

By the second wave, new, smaller fighter planes, with only one pilot, joined the battle. Thirty-five Japanese Zeros approached, with orders to strike at any American planes that had managed to get into the air. But seeing few, they began to look for targets of opportunity.

Like bees, after being disturbed, Zero pilots were relentless as they tracked down and killed any American, in sight. "They'd fire rounds at almost anything that moved," said Lauren. "Even the dead."

"Guess they thought it was funny."

"I saw several of those bastards smile as they flew past, dealing death like a deck of playing cards."

"And from that point on, in my heart… I knew if my life were spared… like every other American, I'd help take this fight to the enemy's doorstep… and make them pay."

"I'd found my destiny… and I'd let no one take it away from me."

The problem was, Lauren figured that he and Alvin might die from their wounds and burns, or from the enemy, above—before they could reach help. He saw the mercy ship, *Solace*. It lay in a straight line in front of their launch, moored out from the north end of Ford Island.

Lauren turned his attention from the skies to their approaching objective.

Less than two hundred yards to go.

Greasy clouds of black smoke continued to fill the harbor. An unnatural trade wind carried it down the channel and spat tremendous heat directly into their faces.

Hospital Ship USS *Solace* came in and out of focus through the thick haze.

Is it really there? Lauren questioned his mind. *Or is it a mirage?*

Then, *Solace* appeared, again.

Lauren turned to Dvorak. "Look, they're taking us to *Solace*."

"Yup," was Dvorak's only reply.

"Funny how things can change life in an instant," recalled Lauren.

Lauren and his crew had often seen *Solace* from high atop their perch, in *Arizona's* forward gun director, in better days.

"We figured we were too young and healthy to ever need services from the ship with the giant red cross on its hull."

To them, the ship was there "…to care for sailors with swine flu or some such disease."

"But now, how the tables had turned."

0855

Violent swells and explosive torpedo wave action had caused black, oily muck to infect the base of *Solace's* outer hull—just as it had covered other vessels in the harbor. But to Lauren, the closer the launch came to *Solace,* the more its huge red cross resembled that of a church. All white from stern to forward "…except for that big ol' red cross painted on its side," he said.

"To me it was the most beautiful church I'd ever seen."

Although other launches dropped off the burned and wounded, it seemed to take longer for Lauren's hookman to pull them alongside *Solace*—closer to the gangway landing that went up to the quarterdeck.

Several launches were ahead of them. But the line kept moving.

0923

Finally, Bruner and Dvorak's launch reached *Solace's* gangway that led up to the quarterdeck—and triage. One corpsmen by the name of Jim Underwood jumped into action, to help them off the launch and come aboard the mercy ship. Lauren had no sooner stepped from *Vestal's* launch, than the hookman pushed it from the gangway. And it was gone.

He nearly lost balance as he looked up the steep gangway, to the ship, and was steadied by Underwood. He attempted to remove his thoughts from the horrors that continued to unfold on Battleship Row—now behind them.

It was all he could do to stare up the daunting steps they'd have to navigate. He'd climbed gangway steps thousands of times, yet these stairs almost appeared intimidating. Sheer adrenalin propelled both men on their climb, as each hung on to the railing.

"With help from Underwood, Alvin lifted one leg after the next.... zombie-like. Don't think he realized how badly he was hurt. I somehow followed pretty much under my own power, even though I was dead-beat."

It had occurred to Lauren, there was little difference between he and Dvorak, and the two sailors he'd witnessed on the stern of *Arizona,* prior to his escape.

"But with most of my clothes burned off, I was too weary and drained to think about if I were going to make it."

In line, the two slowly approached the quarterdeck, behind other burned and wounded who had already made it to the main deck. "It was '*step, wait, and hold on to the rope for dear life. Then, repeat.*' "

"To divert my mind from the continuing attack... and from the pain, I counted steps, as we made our way up."

"Lost count, somewhere after nineteen. ...Alvin was in front of me, unsteady and being helped. Even with help, he nearly fell twice. As we climbed, I kept asking if he could make it."

"I got no answer. He just kept moving."

So did Lauren—into the waiting arms of what he would later describe, as "…an all-in-white angel whom I thought must surely have been sent by God."

The Chief Nurse, LCDR Grace B. Lally, USNR, along with a doctor and a corpsman, met them at the top of the landing. As they had with hundreds of others, that morning, the team performed immediate triage, to determine level of injuries.

Nurse Lally was dressed in a crisp white uniform and hat.

"To me", said Lauren, "the nurses all looked like angels."

Stretcher-bearers stood, close by, ready to carry victims to assigned rooms. Or, in Lauren's case, to an open passageway—as all 400 beds were already filled.

0934

Many victims were ambulatory. But the triage team determined Lauren Bruner and Alvin Dvorak were in very serious shape.

"Within seconds I was made to lie on a stretcher, given a shot of morphine, and a tag was attached to my big toe… The attending nurse pulled out a lipstick from her pocket and marked my forehead with a red 'M'…"

"The mark indicated I'd already received my shot of morphine."

Lauren's drug took effect almost immediately.

After being assigned a triage spot, in the passageway, another "angel in white" cut off what remained of Lauren's burned clothing.

"In my morphine state, I could hear echo chamber-like sounds of scissors cutting through my blackened dress whites, and sounds of whispers, between nurses and corpsmen, as they pulled away the material that had fused to my skin.

"I was totally naked when they moved me to the ship's hallway."

Though Solace was overflowing, that morning, many of those brought on board would not make it through recovery. The dead were wrapped in sheets, and unceremoniously stacked, one on top of another in the mess hall.

Alvin Dvorak was moved, first, to an actual wardroom. "And I hoped", said Lauren, "we'd be able to recover, together, over time."

Bombs continued to drop. And strafing planes pressed on against any target left standing.

"Turned out to be a dangerous and daring time that will stay with me, through eternity."

— —

Alvin A. Dvorak

Alvin Albert Dvorak was born on 3 April 1918 in Tripp County, South Dakota to Joseph and Emma (Mach) Dvorak. Tragedy struck the Dvorak family early, when both of Alvin's parents died within a week of each other from Spanish flu, which was sweeping the country.

After his parents' death, Alvin went to live with his grandparents, John and Barbara Mach. He enlisted in the Navy for six years on 12 November 1937 in Minneapolis, Minnesota. When inducted, he was 5′ 8″ tall, weighed 162 pounds, had blue eyes, brown hair, and a ruddy complexion.

Alvin reported to USS *Arizona*, which was his first ship, on 9 July 1938 while the ship was on maneuvers in the Territory of Hawaii. **On 7 December 1941, Alvin Albert Dvorak was 23 years, 8 months, and 4 days old.**

"Alvin Dvorak was my friend and my hero. He helped save my life and the lives of our crew along with Joseph George on the morning of the attack. Alvin was responsible for orchestrating Arizona's Greatest Escape, as he was the one who got Joe George's attention on USS Vestal in orderto carry out the escape.

Only by the grace of God did I survive and Alvin did not. My friend passed away on Christmas Eve, nineteen days after the attack on a commandeered military transport to the west coast. Alvin Albert Dvorak was the Last to Leave USS Arizona."

Read the Full Story of *Arizona*'s Greatest Escape
Along With Viewing Rare Photos of the Attack by Visiting:
USS*Arizona*sGreatestEscape.com

Alvin Albert Dvorak, BM 2/c

USS *Arizona*

KIA

Chapter 20
MORPHINE DREAMS

Aboard USS *Solace*
7 December, 1941

"You'd think I'd gotten over my recurring dreams by now," said Lauren. "Even after all these years. I still call 'em Morphine Dreams."

"Sounds kinda' crazy, I know. But if you've never had one or, much less countless recurring dreams, like I had… Jesus… wouldn't wish them on anyone."

"Mine began aboard the hospital ship, *Solace,* after nearly every inch of me was toasted aboard *Arizona."*

"Shit that hurt."

Lauren described a morphine dream to be "…like a train wreck, where two locomotives run head on into each other, at full speed… using the same track. No brakes."

His dreams began within minutes after he and Dvorak were taken aboard.

Unscathed by the attack, *Solace,* still lay moored off the tip of Ford Island.

"Alvin Dvorak and I had finally made it up the gangway steps," said Lauren. "Pretty much on our own power, although Corpsman Underwood was helping Alvin. It took every ounce of energy I could muster, to climb them steps."

They reached the landing, at the main deck, and were met by another corpsman "…shorter than I was," said Lauren, "and skinnier… dressed in white pants and white t-shirt."

A tall Navy doctor in khakis gave orders. And a Navy nurse stood by, dressed all in white.

"Like I said before, I'll always think of her as an angel in white. And how she shimmered in the morning light."

For a moment, I thought she might even fly away.

"Dvorak had stepped forward, and I watched the angel mark his forehead with some kind of… I think maybe lipstick. Bright red. Same time, the doctor gave him a shot of morphine."

"Seemed to me… because Alvin was hurt so bad, he passed out right away. He was laid on a stretcher. As two corpsmen tagged him and carried him off, I wondered if the same fate awaited me."

"At that moment… didn't even care."

Lauren's extreme burns took him past the point of exhaustion.

"I glanced at my right arm. The skin was falling off; my fingers were blacker than burnt toast."

The skinny corpsman yelled, "Come on, sailor, you're next."

It was all Lauren could do to muster enough strength to turn over his scorched body to these people he'd never met.

"Then, the doctor asked the name of my ship. I'm certain I answered, but have no memory of it."

"I recall, though, the angel touched an arm to help steady me as she marked my forehead. And she smelled so good."

"The doctor stuck me with a big needle, somewhere in my side or ass…. Don't recall the shot hurting. All of a sudden I just couldn't keep my eyes open."

"Hands grabbed me as I began to fall. Last thing, before the dreams started, was their lifting me onto a stretcher, tagging my toe… then hearing—more than feeling—the sound of scissors cutting away what little was left of my clothes. That's all."

Because every hospital room was filled beyond capacity, the stretcher-bearers carried Lauren to a long, dimly lit corridor—outside the wards on the main deck. Lauren would have to reside in the ship's hallway, until someone died inside to create additional space.

Suddenly, on 7 December, 1941—aboard USS *Solace*—Lauren felt frightened. Extreme anxiety set in, and he slipped ever so quickly into a recurring morphine dreamland.

"The lights went out," he said, "...and the trains started crashing into each other."

"Imagine what the apocalypse might be like.... Fire and brimstone, wicked people and evil monsters chasing after you."

"Then imagine these things mixed all together," he said, "with your mother holding you as a child... rocking you gently, while telling your favorite bedtime story. It was like the first time you kissed a girl, or climbed naked into bed to make love... but was scared, beyond belief, at either thought."

"Those dreams," said Lauren, "were similar to all these things, and a hundred more. They collided into each other, without me knowing what would come next. Enough to scare the hell out of me, one minute, while the next... caused me to believe I was in the safest place I'd ever been."

Although the pain was left behind, the morphine dreams wasted no time taking over his mind.

"And they were goddamned awful, and have stayed with me all my life."

"One of my most vivid first dreams was of some crazy guy, not too far away, on *Solace's* deck... yelling, cussing and throwing what appeared to be rocks at the enemy fighters as they flew over the ship."

"In reality," said Lauren, The fighters did continue to fly over… strafing everything except for *Solace*. They must've known what the big Red Cross, on each side, meant."

Nice of the bastards.

"I mentioned the rock-throwing dream to a corpsman, when I was more coherent… a few days later. He told me, the story was real. The sailor I saw in my morphine state was actually on deck, throwing potatoes… not rocks, at the enemy."

"According to the corpsman, several days before the attack… this sailor was sent to the brig for something… can't remember what… and was let out, the morning of the seventh, to skin potatoes up on deck."

"He was doing just that before the attack started. By the time I saw him, the guy was already going crazy. Hell, we all were. We all thought this might be the first day of the last day of our lives."

"One of my most often recurring dreams featured devils in flying machines. Hobgoblins who sat on their planes' wings… as the contraptions chased me all over the harbor."

"You may think I'm pulling your leg… but I'm not. I just knew, at that time, I was dying. And the world was ending."

"Following pretty dammed close, to that dream, was a vision of my mother. But I couldn't figure out why she hated me, so much, that she'd given me away, and kept my older brother Clarence, after Dad died. Despite all that hurt, and that dream… I still loved her. Figured, in the dream, maybe I'd see her again… if Heaven really existed."

Eerily, as Lauren's initial shot of morphine began to wear off, he awoke to sensations of pain—and of movement. It was a temporary balm from the nightmares. But, while he drifted in and out of sleep, the pain and ship's movement continued.

Between his altered states of consciousness, he imagined he'd heard an announcement repeated over the PA system.

"Man your lifeboat stations… be prepared to abandon ship."

Incapacitated by the morphine, "….I was deathly afraid I'd be forgotten by staff and left alone, to drown."

He questioned his mind. And he began to panic.

Is this another dream? Was the announcement real or imagined? What if the ship goes down? There'll be no one to help me.

He drifted in and out of consciousness. The feeling of motion persisted. And the pain wouldn't let up.

"I must've been moaning, in agony, because an angel in white came by to quickly administer another dose of morphine. Any memory of motion left me, at the time, and I quickly drifted off into a different world."

"It might have been a day or so later, early in the morning... when I was awakened by a corpsman, to prepare me for my first skin peel and bath."

Lauren recalled the sensation of movement, he'd felt, and asked the young corpsman if the ship had been moved to another mooring.

The corpsman was surprised to hear he'd felt the ship's motion while in a morphine dreamland. He explained how, soon after *Solace* had reached full capacity, the ship's sonarman noticed an anomaly on the radar screen. It indicated an object appeared to be directly underneath the ship.

"Captain Pearlman sent a diver over the side," the corpsman said, "to look below the *Solace*'s hull."

The diver resurfaced, and it was confirmed. A Japanese Ko-class midget-submarine had nested squarely below.

"As the story goes," said Lauren, "the *Solace's* captain ordered his ship moved over to the harbor's mud flats, in an attempt to get her away from the sub… and to expose it.

"But the midget-sub continued to hug the bottom of *Solace,* probably because the entire harbor seemed to be in search mode for anything that resembled an enemy submarine."

"Realizing what was happening," Lauren continued, "the captain apparently ordered a shut down of all engines. A tug was brought in to tow it quietly away from the mud flats, so that the sub wouldn't detect the *Solace's* engines, and continue to follow their sound."

With stealth, the tug pulled *Solace*—engines off—back, from the mud flats, to its original mooring point, just off Ford Island. This maneuver prevented the sub from knowing where *Solace* had been moved to, and exposed it to targeting by other ships.

If the sub would attack directly, hospital staff and crew needed to be forewarned—to assist patients in abandoning ship. It was at that point the captain issued the "be prepared" warning, over the PA.

"Shortly after *Solace* was towed to its original mooring, depth-charges were released directly over the submarine's last known position. The rest, history."

"That might explain," said Lauren, "why *Solace* had remained unscathed throughout the surprise attack. The Japanese may have intentionally avoided the hospital ship… not because it was considered a mercy ship, rather that it may have been pre-planned that one of their midget-subs would use it for cover."

"At least, the corpsman gave me some comfort from my original fears. Now I knew I hadn't imagined what I thought I'd heard… and felt, as the captain of *Solace* performed his evasion tactics."

For years, it was difficult for Lauren to recall much of anything else that happened, those next few days.

And for equally as many years, his nights were filled with angels in white—and gargoyles wearing leather helmets and goggles.

— —

USS *Arizona* Following the Attack

"This artwork captures the view that I looked at every day after the attack, first from my bed on the outside corridor of USS Solace looking down at the channel and then from my wheelchair at Hospital Point. As much as I didn't want to look I couldn't help myself. Looking through a pair of old binoculars I must have cried a million tears.

Most often during the days following the attack I think that I was looking to the ruins for my best friend Billy, expecting to see him standing on the deck." **On the day of the Attack on Pearl Harbor, the Great Battleship and American icon USS *Arizona* was 25 years, 5 months, and 18 days old.**

"Recently, I was honored by the University of Arizona, where the tattered American flag flying in this artwork now rests. It was a great honor for me to recently hold it, and as I did memories of my friends, my buddies, and my fellow crew members came flooding back. It was very emotional for me."

Chapter 21
THE WHITE WALKER

"Sailor, you awake?"

Lauren opened his eyes. But, in the dimly lit passageway, where his bed was positioned, he could only see a fuzzy image of a tall man, wearing a khaki uniform.

At first Lauren thought the image was something not real. Then the man spoke again.

"You're Fire Controlman Bruner aren't you? Off *Arizona*?"

Lauren forced a nod, somewhat confused.

"I'm Dr. Erik Hakansson. Just wanted to drop by, meet you, and shake your hand."

My hand? Lauren panicked.

The doctor noticed the concern on Lauren's face.

"You're not my patient," he explained. "My ward is forward. I asked a corpsman to notify me when you started to come around."

Lauren relaxed.

"Just wanted to tell you… you're one lucky son of a gun. Your crew's escape from *Arizona* was a miracle, if you believe in those kind of things. As far as I have been able to determine, you and your crew were the last to leave *Arizona*."

Lauren's voice was still gravelly, having not fully recovered from the effects of the searing flames, ingested fumes, and from smoke inhalation. "How… do you know… about it?"

"I was outside on *Solace's* deck filming the harbor to send my family—when the attack began. I have a sixteen millimeter camera, and it was shooting in color."

"You… you kept filming?"

"Yes."

"Then *Arizona* was hit. I guess I just froze and kept my camera going and caught the whole darned thing, including the explosion and fireball. Think I have it all on film."

Lauren absorbed the doctor's message, though still too drugged to react.

"Yesterday, I ran across your name, on the ship's roster, and that of another sailor named Dvorak. Notes on your records indicated you were the last two from *Arizona* to be brought aboard. It's almost impossible to believe you survived. Even with the extent your injuries."

Dvorak... Dvorak... Had he heard Alvin's name?

Lauren perked up. "How... how is... Dvorak?"

"Pretty bad shape, I'm afraid. Like you, but even worse. Charts indicate you both were burned over most of your body. You're covered in this white powder because it stops infection."

"Sailor, an infection will kill you even faster than burns, if we don't catch it in time."

Adrenaline began to pump.

Lauren forcefully cleared his throat and willed his head to face the doctor. "Doc... the rest of the crew? What about..."

"Sorry. Not many sailors on your ship survived. *Arizona's* totally gone."

The air was sucked from Lauren, and he sank back into the sheet. Tears clouded his eyes. No longer could he see the doctor's face.

"Bruner," he continued, "do you remember where you were when *Arizona* blew? Was Dvorak a part of your crew? How the hell did you get off, anyway?"

Shaking his head, slightly, Lauren couldn't answer.

"Just would like to know... for the history books. In order to go along with whatever my film captured."

Lauren understood what he needed, but his only wish was to push those memories as far into the back of his mind as possible.

"Bruner? At least tell me where you were, onboard."

Lauren struggled to get it out. In a whisper, he answered, "At the tip of the explosion."

The expression on Doctor Hakansson's face said it all... he didn't get it.

A long silence ensued.

"Look," Lauren grappled for the strength to speak. "The only reason… my crew escaped and I survived… is because of Alvin Dvorak and… a another sailor on *Vestal* named George. They're the heroes. My crew and I owe both of them our lives. If I don't make it, make sure that this goes along with your film."

"I understand," the doctor said, still not completely comprehending what he was being told.

Lauren changed the subject, "We fighting back… yet?"

"About to. The United States declared war on Japan yesterday. President Roosevelt gave a powerful speech. Called the attack a 'date which will live in infamy.' I think the Japs will regret their actions."

Both remained quiet, digesting what the war would mean for the country, and what was to come.

"Good luck," said the doctor, "Gotta' get back to my patients. But I wanted to stop by and shake your hand."

Lauren watched him check his right hand. The doctor chewed his lower lip.

"I'll check up on Dvorak when I can. I'd still like to shake your hand … once it's healed enough." Then he walked away.

Lauren closed his eyes. He was tired, and knew what would come next. Enough nightmares to last a lifetime. Decades later, he would remark, "And they did."

The following day, another doctor stopped by to examine Lauren's burns. He examined his hands.

"I'm afraid we'll have to amputate some fingers, sailor," he said, not unkindly. "Your hands and fingers are just too far gone to heal."

"No, sir," Lauren abruptly shot back.

"Has to be done. I'll have to remove the third, fourth, and fifth finger… from each hand. But you'll still be able to get by. You'll still be able to hold."

"You're not going to take my fingers, Doc. I won't let you."

If Lauren could have sat on his hands to keep the doctor away from them, he would have.

The doctor searched his mind for the right words.

"Look, son, there's no way those fingers can heal and be anywhere close to useful again. Gangrene's sure to set in."

"Don't take my fingers, Doc. I'll take my chances."

"You certain?"

"Yes, sir."

Frustrated, but having no time to argue, the doctor yielded to Lauren's resolve.

"All right, sailor. They're your fingers and your life. I'll honor your decision."

But Lauren didn't believe him. Every time he awakened from a morphine dream, the first thing he'd do was check his fingers. "I'd actually count them," he said.

If there was anything that Lauren thought would drive him crazy, more than his burns, and the hobgoblins from his dreams, it was the constant moans and screams of fellow patients, twenty-four hours a day. Even more than that, the sounds were interspersed with heart-wrenching sobs. With his bed located in a passageway, and several hundred burned andwounded on board, "…the cacophony echoed through the corridors, and got so bad, at times, I could hardly stand it."

"Then, a corpsman took pity on me after I complained about the sounds. He later brought me a roll of toilet paper."

"Here," he said, "Tear this up and use it for earplugs."

"I did. And it cut down on the cries of the dying."

Amidst the morphine and slowly passing time, his assigned doctor stopped by to see Lauren. "Thought he'd cheer me up," he said, "by encouraging me with news about my future.

"Once your burns heal," the doctor said, "you'll be out of the Navy and back home, to sit out the rest of the war. Then you'll have your whole life before you, to start over."

Over my dead body, Lauren thought.

"Look, Doc. Burns won't stop me from getting back into this fight."

Lauren had vowed to get back at the enemy "…for what they did to me, to my crew, and to my best friend Billy, so help me God." And he meant it.

The doctor thought he was delusional. And Lauren suspected his diagnosis would be written into his medical records.

The next day began what a severe burn victim might interpret as "real torture."

Burn treatment commenced when a medical team pulled off the large scabs that covered Lauren's burns. It was especially painful because, simultaneously, they pulled away all the attached hair.

"Then they bathed me with some kind of alcohol solution and recoated my body with that white powder." He learned, later, that the powder was called Tannic Acid. This was the beginning of routine procedures—a bi-weekly ritual, which would "…totally wear me out to the point that I'd beg for my next shot of morphine.

"That procedure was really bad stuff," Lauren said. "Something I never want to go through again."

He often thought, *Almost better to die than this*. It hurt that bad, and they seemed to do it only when the morphine was wearing off.

One morning, coming out of a deep sleep, Lauren was visited by what he thought was an angel. Officially, she was a student nurse from the university. "A pretty angel, at that," he said, "who'd volunteered to help out on *Solace*."

"I liked thinking of her better as an angel than a nurse, but she was what she was, and she was nice to me." The only problem, Lauren determined, was that she kept calling him "Mister Bruner."

"This attractive young lady gave me sponge baths. At first I wasn't too sure about the arrangement. I was naked, after all. But I grew to enjoy the baths a lot and looked forward to her daily visits."

Several days later, she showed up with a clipboard. "Would you like to send a postcard home? Let your family know you're alive?"

"Sure. Can I do that?"

"Well, all I can do is check a box on the postcard to let them know you're all right. Not much elseallowed."

"Can I ask about Bozo… my dog?"

"We can try," she said. "It seems harmless enough. Maybe the censors will let it pass." And they did.

Lauren believed this one thing would tell his mother he was truly still alive. He supplied the nurse with his mother's address. And just before she moved on to another patient, he asked her a question. "Do you think on your way home, could you do me a favor?"

The nurse wasn't prepared for his next request.

"I had a date for Sunday… uh, the seventh… with a girl name Nikki. Works at a bar called the Broadway Inn on Fort Street. Could you please stop off, there? Tell her I'm still alive?"

She smiled. "Your girlfriend?"

Nodding, I said, "Yeah..."

"Jeez, it felt good to tell someone that."

The nurse nodded, smiled, and before moving on, she said she would try.

"Unfortunately, this angel came by the next day to inform me that the Broadway Inn had been closed."

"A posted sign on the door," she reported, "said the closing was due to it being owned by Japanese."

"Maybe it'll open again someday. Sorry to have to bring you such bad news, Mister Bruner." Then, she left.

After she had gone, Lauren quietly cried for what-might-have-been. But if anyone had asked about his tears, he had planned to just say it was his burns that brought the tears.

"You know, I never thought of Nikki, Shigeo, or Kinuyo as the enemy. Never even thought of them as Japanese. To me, they were just good people, and always nice to me."

At the beginning of his fifth day, aboard *Solace,* Lauren awakened, feeling worse than when he'd first arrived. "I remember closing my eyes, while waiting for my next shot of morphine. I felt a tight knot in my gut."

This feeling was something new to Lauren. As far as he was concerned, he'd just been afflicted with "...one damn more pain too many."

"I asked the corpsmen for something that might help. Anything. But they were all too busy to worry about my stomach problems." Then, perhaps for the first time, uncertain thoughts crept into his mind. *Maybe I'm not going to make it.*

Cramps persisted most of the day and finally he understood the problem.

"I had to go to the can or I was going to burst. I could've asked for a bedpan, but pissing into one and shitting in one were two different worlds. And there was no way I wanted an angel to have to help me do that. What a vision that would have been."

With so many patients and so few to take care of them, no one noticed as Lauren shimmied down his bed, under the canopy that covered it, and down its length, to the end. No one appeared to care. As he crawled out from the sheets "…still hooked up to my drip system. And I dragged that damned wheeled stand after me, as I headed down the deck—intent on finding a head and taking a crap."

"I know I musta' looked pretty funny, but I didn't give a damn at that point. There I was… stark naked… powdered in white. But my problem had reached the point where I damned well didn't care. I had to relieve myself before I'd burst… all over the deck."

He passed a corpsman and asked directions to the head.

"The man didn't so much as blink. Just pointed and said, 'Follow the deck to the sixth door on the left.' "

"What's the word? Surreal? I think surreal describes that moment in my life."

"Here I was, dragging my tubes, attached to a rolling stand behind me. Dressed head-to-toe in white, not a stitch on. Hah! All I needed was a bow tie, one a' those cummerbunds, and black tuxedo shoes."

Lauren finally located the head … much to his relief. However, following that effort, he found himself suddenly tired, and not certain he could make it back to his bed without assistance.

Especially since he was now lost.

"Hard to believe I could get so lost going such a short distance." But he'd managed to do just that. And he kept thinking, *All I want now is another shot of morphine … or even better, a couple of Nikki's rum and cokes.*

Having turned down the wrong corridor, Lauren found himself "...in a room filled with survivors... most sailors, and maybe a couple of Marines."

Someone in a bed called out, "Hey! What ship were you on?"

"*Arizona*," he answered.

The man tried to whistle, but he couldn't get it past his lips.

Someone, nearby, piped up, "Hey, fella', there's another guy from *Arizona* over there."

He pointed to a far corner of the room. "Maybe you know 'im. Nurses said he's one of the last to come aboard. Not doing too good."

Instantly, Lauren was filled with a mixture of joy and dread, and a renewed determination that put aside any thoughts about challenges he faced.

Pulling his rolling hospital after him, with a renewed energy and speed even he didn't know he still had, Lauren quickly skirted beds and medical devices, as he made his way to the indicated corner.

"I looked down at the naked, powder-white guy lying there... and immediately knew. It *was* Alvin."

Tears streaked trails down Lauren's white-powdered cheeks.

"Alvin, it's me... Lauren. Hey, buddy... look, we're twins. All dressed in white and ready for the dance!"

Dvorak gave no sign he'd heard Lauren.

Moving up as close to Alvin's head, as he could, he talked softly, so that only Alvin might hear what he was saying.

"Come on, man. Ya' gotta be strong. It's me... Lauren. We're gonna' get better. We're gonna' make it. Both of us. We'll get back into this fight together, I promise."

Again, Dvorak showed no sign he'd heard what was said.

"I wanted to say more to him, but just then a nurse and corpsman entered the ward."

A corpsman saw Lauren and crossed the room—dodging things in his way. He grabbed Lauren by an arm.

"What in hell are you doing, sailor?"

Lauren didn't answer.

He asked again.

Attempting not to look at the nurse, he responded, "I needed to take a shit. You understand?"

Lauren could feel his face turn red, but he didn't care anymore. Reality had finally set in. All he wanted, right then, was another shot of morphine—and to forget that Alvin didn't have any ears.

— —

SECOND TO THE LAST TO LEAVE

Dr. Erik G. Hakansson

Dr. Erik G. Hakansson was born on 5 September 1886, **and on the day of the Attack on Pearl Harbor, he was 55 years, 3 months, and 2 days old.**

At the time he was aboard USS *Solace, Dr. Hakansson* was a Navy Captain and the ship's Chief Medical Services Officer. On the morning of 7 December 1941, USS *Solace* was moored off the northern tip of Ford Island, and it was at this moment in history that Dr. Hakansson filmed USS *Arizona* exploding. His film even captured the enemies' bom as it hit its mark.

"Dr. Hakansson was one of the Navy doctors who treated me when Alvin Dvorak and I were first brought aboard the hospital ship in the midst of battle. I met with him for the last time on 30 January 1941, on the day I was transferred off the ship to Pearl Harbor Naval Hospital at Hospital Point.

I have only seen Dr. Hakansson's film once because it was too painful for me to watch. As I viewed his film that one time all I could see in my mind's eye was the memory of Alvin Dvorak with his ears burnt off. It was damned awful, and I don't ever want to see the film again. I don't need to. I lived the nightmare."

Erik G. Hakansson, M.D.

Dr. Erik Hakansson

Navy Doctor USS *Solace* Filmed USS *Arizona* Exploding

Chapter 22
HOSPITAL POINT

December 1941

In the waning days of 1941, Lauren remained aboard *Solace* in total misery. Small remembrances of time and events would slither through his mind—as the morphine began to wear off. Consequently, it was difficult for him to tell the difference between dreams, recollections, nightmares, and side-effects.

There were times, throughout much of his recovery, when it was difficult for Lauren to differentiate between a prickly "pins and needles" feeling, and a crawling itchiness, that moved across his body, "...like bugs feeding on his scabs."

Other morphine side effects produced constant headaches. "....And I'd get dizzy, just tryin' to lift my head. What's the old saying... 'caught between the devil and the deep blue sea?' I was caught between the choice of more morphine, to take away the pain and memories... or to avoid it, and have to worry about dying."

Although administration of morphine doses were spread further apart, a corpsman or nurse would dispense it any time the pain was too great or, as Lauren often suggested, "When I just wanted to forget."

He continued to get peeled every two or three days. "That's when it hurt most," he said. "Felt like being skinned alive."

Following each peel, his open burns would be bathed in a solution of "...what I believe was a combination of water and alcohol," he said. "Of course, whatever it was, it caused throbbing, searing pain. Hurt so much, I often thought I'd die from these treatments that were supposed to make me better."

"Then a nurse or a doctor would come by, and assure me I was slowly healing. Their encouragement must have worked. Seems to have been just enough to coax me through the mental and physical agony I felt.

"Various corpsman, assigned to take care of me, would often ask, 'Bruner, what're you going to do after you get better and get out?' "

"At first, I didn't understand what the hell they were talking about... getting 'discharged'. Finally, one day, the corpsman... named Jim Underwood... stopped by my bed. I recall his name because, early on, while he powdered my burns, he told me how Dvorak and I had arrived on the ship... with enemy aircraft still strafing the harbor."

At the bottom platform of *Solace's* gangway, Underwood—Hospital Assistant 1st Class— was assigned to help arriving victims from a launch onto *Solace*. Nearly 150 hospital corpsmen were aboard to assist with triage, walk with or use stretchers to carry victims to their beds, and otherwise perform any other basic duty that the registered nurses oversaw.

"So, when Underwood asked me the same question, about being discharged, I told him I didn't know what he meant."

"Underwood was a good guy, with the best intentions. But thinking he'd provide a boost to my morale, he assured me that, with my wounds, the Navy would send me home... and I'd be able to sit out the rest of the war."

Lauren couldn't have caught Underwood any more off guard.

"Bullshit. By God, that's not gonna' be me," I told him. "I'm getting back into this fight, soon as I can."

Throughout the remainder of December, time for Lauren seemed to move between slow and slower, aboard *Solace*. Eventually, as more patients were transferred to land-based hospitals, or had died, beds became more readily available in actual hospital rooms.

"As a result," said Lauren, "I was finally moved out of the breezy passageway, into a hospital-like ward. More comfortable than the outside deck. But to me, it just smelled like medicine and death. Would've rather stayed where I was."

Friday, 19 December 1941

Several days after moving inside, a nurse stopped by to let him know his friend, Dvorak, would be transferred back to the states, that very day. The Navy had commandeered the SS *President Coolidge*, a civilian cruise ship, to transport the most severely wounded back to Mare Island Naval Hospital, about twenty-three miles northeast of San Francisco.

The nurse explained the conscripted ocean liner had just arrived in the harbor to pick up the wounded. It had been painted hazy gray, over its traditional white; and the windows blackened out to prevent light escaping from inside— all to help prevent it from being sunk by Japanese subs.

"Everyone's certain the enemy's still lurking outside the harbor," she said. "The *Coolidge* leaves, tonight, just after dark."

The nurse explained how the Willamette University Bearcats football team, that played in the Shrine Bowl on 6 December, were hitching a ride back to the mainland, along with the Spartan football squad from San Jose State.

"The captain's allowing them to sleep in steerage," she said, "as long as they help medical personnel and corpsmen with care of the wounded. Or help evacuate them, in case of an attack, at sea."

"So, your friend will be in good hands," she said, "with all that extra help on board."

Lauren remembered hearing how the Salem Oregon football team had been issued rifles, following the attack. They stood 24-hour guard, for ten days, around an ammunitions storage facility that had been quickly set up at Punahou School, following severe damage to Army facilities during the attack.

Lauren asked if he could see Dvorak, before he left. "Sorry," the nurse had said, "Alvin Dvorak was one of the first transferred. He's already aboard the *Coolidge.*"

"What day of the month is it?"

"Friday," the nurse replied, over her shoulder. "December nineteenth." And she left his bedside.

What a shitty Christmas it's going to be, was his only thought. Then, Lauren remembered walking down Fort Street from Broadway Inn, with Nikki and the Christmas tree lights strung across the street. His eyes filled with tears.

Wednesday, 24 December 1941

Lauren found himself in a place, he thought, without much hope. Mail hadn't arrived from stateside. No family members—or others—seemed to be aware that he was alive, aboard the *Solace.* The holidays would come and go without the traditions most had grown to appreciate.

Only eighteen days prior, he was hopelessly in love with a woman with whom he could share a bright future. His previous youthful thoughts of meeting women on the beach, or on Hotel Street, or even in Chinatown, had become a distant memory after meeting Nikki.

Over nearly three months, Nikki had become the only woman with whom he had bared his soul, and shared some of his secret thoughts. He had given in to the possibilities that might open up for them, as a couple. And he thought he might have been ready to settle down.

But an opportunity to change his life was taken from him. Would he ever see Michiko… Nikki, again? These were the thoughts that clouded his mind, on Christmas Eve, as he wallowed in a drowning-pool of morphine and memories.

— —

Unbeknownst to the patients—and to most of the *Solace's* medical staff and corpsmen—a secret plan had been hatched in the nurse's quarters, below decks. Nurse Lally, and her nursing staff of twelve, had scavenged, cajoled, and coaxed anyone who would listen, in or around Pearl, into her scheme. Together, they would gather and divide 32 pounds of candy to share, and supply a special gift for each of the remaining 327 patients still aboard *Solace*.

Individually wrapped presents ranged from amusing to inspiring.

Peace of mind was in short supply, following the attack of 7 December. But Nurse Lally knew, despite any lack of sleep on their part, there would still have to be a Christmas for these men—these survivors—some with bodies burned so badly, even *she* had to avert her eyes from time to time, to maintain sanity.

"A tree always rides the mast on Christmas," Lally had said.

It was a Navy tradition. She would not be detoured, and dispatched a group of nurses to forage around for anything resembling a holiday tree, for Christmas eve.

"Sure enough," she wrote later, in her diary, "our ladies managed to collect four scraggy cedars, in Honolulu, together with enough tinsel, holly, decorations, toys, and knick-knacks. Every man aboard the *Solace* would have a gift and as much a celebration as we could muster."

"There it was… in the middle of a territorial-mandated blackout," Corpsman Underwood reported, "the remnants of our largest, tinsel-laden cedar tree, ridin' the Solace's mast in the dark."

An occasional string of tinsel picked up ambient light from the half moon that reflected back from channel waters. To gathering staff, on the quarterdeck, and to patients who were ambulatory enough to make it out on deck, that night, the darkened sight was still enough to bolster spirits—and determination.

Lauren couldn't remember if he made it out onto the deck with some of the others. Life was hell at the moment, and he was in no mood to celebrate anything, even if he could.

Nothing would stop them from celebrating Christmas.

As everyone gathered around a second, smaller cedar tree, a "plump, jolly-looking boy" showed up on deck, dressed in a Santa suit—sewn from bunting, at the last minute, by an old salt and sail-maker.

Santa had hoisted "… a bulging seabag on his back" filled with individually wrapped gifts—and candy—for everyone on board.

Nurse Lally wrote of that night:

> (Santa) led our small procession below. We sang Jingle Bells as we went, and out of nowhere the ship's captain appeared. "I'm with you, Miss Lally," he said.

> "He fell into step behind Santa Claus, and I followed him, first to the (Intensive Care) Ward, where, after the Japanese attack, we had placed our most serious burn cases. Behind us came the girls and the corpsmen, all singing. I could not sing right then, being too terribly aware of the eyes that looked at me from some of the burn-blackened faces.
>
> War and Christmas seemed suddenly incongruous. Only several years before, these kids sneaking down the stairs to watch their mothers and dads place the last glimmering icicle on the tree (and) tuck a walnut deep in the toe of a stocking. Pain now made the young faces seem mature. But even eyes that had been almost lifeless brightened miraculously, as the nurses distributed their presents, and Santa Claus his bounty."
>
> *The American Magazine*

Lauren, in his morphine dream-like state, heard the sound of "Jingle Bells" that echoed through the corridors, leading to the I.C.U. A corpsman, with an accordion, accompanied the singers and, as they approached Lauren's ward, it seemed to warm his heart and mind, if only for the moment.

He struggled to open his eyes, to determine if it was all a dream. He imagined several angels in white, but wasn't certain if they'd come bearing presents--or to take him to heaven. He thought his dreams had conjured up a Santa, complete with a beard made of... rope. *No... that had to be the morphine talking.*

But Lauren eventually discovered a bag of candy and a wrapped present, setting on a side table—a bar of "poifumed" soap, as one raspy-voiced patient referred to his own gift. Santa must have, indeed, paid a visit during the night.

Decorations were left up, in the wards, for days, after. And Lauren questioned Corpsman Underwood about it. Little by little, memories of song, laughter, and gentle touches crossed his mind. And he was somehow even able to smile at the thoughtfulness of Nurse Lally and her staff.

Maybe I am getting better, after all.

Still, as the holiday came and passed, Lauren noticed fewer patients aboard the *Solace*. He also noticed that he was still there.

"The others had either died or were transferred," said Lauren. "And most every night I'd go to sleep wondering if *I'd* wake up, the next morning.

When I awoke, I'd still count my fingers."

Tuesday, 30 December 1941

Several days later, Dr. Hakansson dropped by to bring Lauren news.

"It was about mid-morning, when the doc showed up. He wanted to let me know I'd be transferred, later that day... to Pearl Harbor Naval Hospital at Hospital Point."

Before the doctor bid goodbye, Lauren asked him why he was one of the last patients to leave *Solace*. "The doc smiled, slightly. He told me it had been his decision... along with the doctors of my ward, to keep me aboard ship. That way, they could better monitor my progress."

"Bruner," said Hakansson, "if I can ever get my film developed, and it turns out not to have too much of my shaking, you and Dvorak, along with the rest of your crew, will become legends in Naval history. I wanted to do everything I could to make certain you'd get better and history would remember your name."

"You think I'll get better?"

"I think… you're on your way," Hakansson said. "But I won't mislead you. It'll take time… and still be a rough haul."

The doctor studied his patient for a few moments. Lauren reflected on what he'd been told.

"Look, Bruner… depending on how you handle the trauma you've gone through, the Navy may even decide to keep you. The country needs all the heroes it can get, right now."

Lauren stiffened, slightly.

"Doc, I'm no hero and don't want to be called one. In my life, there will always only be two heroes... Joe George and Alvin Dvorak."

Smiling again, the doctor gently took Lauren's hand. And they shook.

"Good luck Bruner." Then Doctor Haakenson was gone, and I never saw him again.

"And so was I," said Lauren. "It wasn't an hour later… two corpsmen placed me on a stretcher… still stark naked and powdered in white. Thank God they threw a sheet over me. I recall being damn cold."

From the *Solace's* deck, he could see the destruction of the harbor. But as his bearers approached the gangway, a new concern came over him. On 7 December, he'd walked up the long gangway under his own power. On this day, however, the stretcher-bearers would have to carry him down the gangway steps, to a waiting launch. And it would be a long drop down, if something went wrong.

To Lauren, the procedure to get him down to water's edge was no less dangerous than when they were being strafed, by the Japanese, three weeks prior.

The corpsmen halted, at gangway's edge, as two more corpsmen joined in to assist with each end of the four poles. They prepared to negotiate the turn to the steps—and adjusted their arms for proper height leverage. The four sailors hefted the stretcher to manageable heights and began—what to Lauren—was a treacherous trip, down the gangway.

The corpsmen on the downward end had a disadvantage over the two at the top. Forced to carry Lauren down the steps, backwards, they'd adjust arms high above shoulders to compensate for incline of the stairs—in their attempt to keep their patient as level as they could.

"This was when I realized how long the fall would be, to the water," said Lauren, "and I was strapped in… with visions of the corpsmen losing their balance and accidentally dropping me *and* the stretcher overboard."

"Immediately, I regretted words I may have said to any of them, in pain, while having my skin peeled."

"Fortunately," said Lauren, "with military precision, they carried me, and three other patients, down the gangway to a waiting motor launch… without incident."

Lauren was certain their group was among the last to leave the *Solace*. It was a melancholy time for him. In reality he had no idea what the future would allow. He glanced back to the ship, while it grew more distant. In three months, it would head for Pago Pago, Samoa, to serve four more years and earn a total of seven battle stars before being decommissioned.

For the moment, he'd attempt to put the past behind.

Aboard the launch, it was obvious the harbor was already changing. Not back to how it was, or the way Lauren had committed it to memory, but… how it would become.

Better. And stronger. He reluctantly turned his head toward Battleship Row. *No one will ever catch us like this again.*

The same corpsmen, including Underwood, stayed with the men for the duration of their ride, as it headed to the dock on its way to Hospital Point— situated where the Harbor Entrance and West Channels meet—nearly two miles south of the *Solace.*

Quietly, without a word between them, their launch headed up Battleship Row and the Southeast Loch.

They motored down, past the berth where *Nevada* had broken for the open sea, before it beached directly across from Hospital Point. It was an eerie scene.

Lauren recalled hearing about *Nevada's* gunners, how as they'd passed *Arizona*—it's fires raging so hot, the gunners used their own bodies to shield their shells to prevent further onboard explosions.

Lauren's stretcher had been laid on the boat's starboard side. From his vantage point, he saw what remained of *Arizona.*

Arizona's bridge had collapsed over where the bow had once been, bent to an angle that looked as if it was searching for the ship's prow—it's Admiral's platform nearly hidden in the rubble. Salvage crews were already working to take away twisted superstructure.

"I didn't want to look. But... for some reason, I couldn't take my eyes away. Immediately, I was drawn to what was left of my director, and could pinpoint exactly where I was... at the center of the fireball... the tip of the candle, as I'd said before."

" 'I was standing right there' …I must've said to myself out loud, 'cause one of the other guys on a stretcher next to me said, 'What'd ya' say?' And I had to think… I turned to the fella', then pointed to the crippled sky platform… 'I was right there,' I repeated to him… 'after the explosion.' "

"Ya' know what? After that…I never said another thing about it for close to seventy-five years."

It was then Lauren realized, tears had made everything go fuzzy. A salty sting tracked down his face.

"Finally, I shut my eyes as our launch passed by… and did my damnedest to retreat into a dream about Nikki… or home… anything other than that moment's reality. Didn't work, though."

Instead, Lauren's mind flashed-back to his first bed, in the *Solace's* corridor. "For three days from where I laid, I could see the cherry-red glow of *Arizona*… at night. I felt its heat on my burned skin… didn't need morphine to give me *that* nightmare. Three damn nights, I watched her burn red-hot… kinda' like what you'd see in a blacksmith's forge. Except it was molten metal… the size of a ship's bridge."

"Sonovabitch. Just about killed me to see that. Even when I closed my eyes, I couldn't escape the glow. It seemed to smolder right through my eyelids."

"Ya' know… everyone had feared the glow from *Arizona* would act like a beacon, for the Japs… to bring them directly into Pearl Harbor for a repeat performance."

Their launch glided by the skeletal remains of USS *West Virginia, Oklahoma,* and *California*—each being salvaged or dismantled for scrap by hundreds of workers aboard tugs, barges and on land. Much of the other wreckage rested in awkward poses—throughout the harbor. No one said a word as they passed.

The launch docked at Ten-Ten landing, and the accompanying corpsmen reloaded the four men into a banged up, battleship-grey Navy ambulance. "By the looks of it," said Lauren, "the ambulance probably took some heavy machine gun rounds, during the attack. There were bullet holes through the painted white cross, on the outside, that climbed up to and across the roof."

Underwood patted Lauren's arm as he left and wished him good luck.

"I just said 'thanks.' "

"At that moment I couldn't help but think... of all the times Billy and I'd catch the last launch back to *Arizona*, from this dock… half drunk after a night out. Now my best friend was gone. I'd never see him smile, or laugh, or hear him sing 'Red Sails In The Sunset,' as he often liked to do… especially after too many drinks." Lauren laughed at the memory, but it just didn't seem right. Suddenly, he was angry, all over again.

Before the ambulance doors closed, Lauren was overtaken by a fetid stench. "What the hell's that stinking odor," he asked a corpsman. "Where's it coming from?"

Another corpsman explained it was the acrid smell from bodies still being pulled from the harbor. "Every day," he said, "scavenger patrols still find bodies and parts after they float to the surface."

Lauren felt a chill. *It's been over three weeks, and they're still…*

"The question on everyone's mind," the attendant continued, "is how many more will the boat crews have to retrieve, before there are none left?"

Okay… Shut up. I don't want to hear anything more.

Lauren was sickened by the thought. *Don't want to hear anymore.* But the words stuck in his throat.

The doors were closed. It was almost dark inside, except for rivulets of sunlight that shot through the trail of bullet holes in the side and across the top of the vehicle.

"The engine started with an uncomfortable jerk, we began to move. It wasn't but a few minutes later, the driver let out the clutch too fast and we jerked to a stop. The ambulance's double doors swung open, and we were greeted with a soft cool breeze."

"I was the third stretcher pulled from that sardine can. My first view of Hospital Point was from that position. I'd seen it from *Arizona* hundreds of times before, as we'd pass by. Coming and going on maneuvers. Like a guiding beacon, the hospital stood at the head of the channel."

Up close, the hospital looked more run down than it had from the ship. Built mostly of wood, and only two stories—though the Navy had attempted to maintain it—the outside looked pretty weather beaten.

"You look like I feel," Lauren spoke out loud to the inanimate, battered hospital. His comment drew a reaction from the others. Each struggled to let out some slight form of laughter. Then I told myself, "No matter how it looks, this will be my next step to getting better."

"And I wondered if a letter from home would be waiting for me, there."

"It wasn't. Just another letdown… thrown onto an already large pile of life's disappointments. Then again, I was certain at least one letter must be on its way."

"It wasn't either. Both my mother and a girl I had dated back on the mainland had sent letters. I found out later, the girl… Marcella Stapleton, had continued to write. But she, and my mother, had no idea as to my whereabouts. So I was feeling pretty damn sorry for myself."

Lauren would not receive a letter, from anyone, until after he was transferred back to the States, to Mare Island Naval Hospital, where his mail would eventually catch up to him. That was still considerably down the road.

"Following my admission to the Naval Hospital at Hospital Point, I don't recall ever seeing again, the other three sailors, transferred from *Solace*. We were all placed in wards, with up to twenty-five beds in each, anywhere there was a vacancy.

"Me... I was placed on the first floor."

"I truly didn't care where they put me since at the time, all I craved was a shot of morphine... and to go to sleep and forget. But it wasn't in the cards."

Shortly after Lauren was assigned a bed, a nurse stepped up with two corpsmen. He was informed they'd be doing a peel, followed by a sponge-off of his burns—with the alcohol solution later that afernoon.

Oh great.

"But I had the foresight to ask if I could get a shot, following my bath. And this particular angel in white must have been at the end of her shift, as she answered sharply, 'We'll see sailor. If it's necessary.' "

"No sooner had I closed my eyes... then they started in on me. I wondered who in the hell was injured here, anyway. Then I felt a breeze blowing down the ward, and heard the engines of a ship pass close by, in the channel."

Occasionally, a volunteer from the Salvation Army would make his rounds through the wards, some guy bearing small gifts.

"He'd come by every bed, in the ward, heartily greet the recovering sailors, offer magazines to read...and later during my stay, gave me an old sleeveless wool sweater."

"He'd sometimes pull a cigarette from his 'own' pack," said Lauren, "to offer each man a smoke… or so we were led to believe."

"Everybody smoked in those days. And after the attack, I smoked, even more. So I looked forward to this guy's bedside visits, where he'd sacrifice his own cigarettes for wounded sailors."

Lauren later discovered that the volunteer was supplied with cases of cigarettes weekly. "Enough to give every man in the hospital a pack every couple of days," said Lauren. "Turns out, they caught him smokin' our cigarettes… and sellin' the rest on the black market."

"Probably just one bad apple."

"Unfair as it might be," Lauren continued, "for years, it left a bad taste in my mouth about the Salvation Army. And I've never forgiven the bastard who stole our cigarettes."

Lauren laughed at the memory.

"I knew smokin' was a nasty habit… and I finally gave it up, cold-turkey, in eighty-six. Took me that long."

"I was workin' at a refrigeration company, back in the day. And there were five of us, in the shop. We were talkin' about how bad smoking was for us… especially for my age."

"Decided to give it up, that very day. All five of us. And each literally nailed his last cigarette pack to the shop's wall."

"We made a bet, amongst ourselves, while each handed over twenty bucks to the company secretary. A hundred bucks for her to keep secure, for the guy who held out the longest… and didn't go back to smoking."

"You might guess… every guy in the shop weakened, over time. 'Cept me. Like always, I was resolved to see this one through."

"Thought I'd have to share the hundred bucks with at least one of the guys. But I walked off with the hundred dollars, and immediately went out and bought a case of cigarettes."

"Naw… just kiddin'. Been nearly thirty years. Never smoked a day, in my life, since."

— —

Father Benito Y. Caraballo

Father Benito Yambo Caraballo was a country priest on the island of Oahu. He was ordained a priest on 9 March 1940. **On the day of the attack on Pearl Harbor, Father Benito, as Lauren would call him, was 28 years, 8 months, and 16 days old.**

He was short and stocky with close cropped black hair, dark brown skin, and brown eyes. His family background was "Poi," as they call it in Hawaii, which means he was a mixture of races. His father was half Spanish and half Italian, and his mother half French, one-fourth Indian, and one-forth Puerto Rican.

"I called him Father Benito because I had a hard time saying his last name. He was a good guy and helped me through a bad time in my life. We met just over three weeks after the sinking of Arizona and I still had a long way to go in my recovery. Father Benito's visits helped give me the strength to heal and get back into the fight.

In the short time we got to know each other we became good friends and much of what we talked about has always remained with me, especially the last thing he said to me on the day we parted."

Rev. Benito Y. Caraballo

Father Benito Caraballo

Hawaii Country Priest

Chapter 23
BACK INTO THE FIGHT

Wednesday, 31 December 1941

A morning storm raced through the leeward side of the islands, accompanied by unusually heavy thunderclaps. Lauren enjoyed the rain, in spite of his constant discomfort. They brought cool breezes through the corridors, on warmer days. And they carried nearby scents of plumeria trees, pikake flowers, and Chinese ginger that surrounded the hospital.

It was on this rainy day, Father Benito Caraballo, a Portuguese Catholic priest from a small country parish, made the rounds of Lauren's ward. During the short time they got to know each other, and because Lauren was never sure how to say the priest's last name, he came to call him just Father Benito.

"The first time Father Benito approached my bed," said Lauren, "he asked to sit and visit for a while. He wanted to wait out the storm and needed a rest, before heading back to Sacred Heart. His church was located at the Waianae Sugar plantation, about 30 miles of rough road, up the coast north from Pearl… not an easy drive any time, but following the rains, especially hard."

"I think he sensed I really didn't want to talk with anyone. Priest or not. But I was starved for news about the war, and nodded for him to stay. He sat, close by, for nearly an hour… and filled me in on the latest stories about the war effort… how we were already out chasing after the enemy… and our progress on rebuilding the harbor."

Eventually, the storm moved past, and Father Benito said he'd better get going. It would be a good hour's drive back home. Leaving, he asked if he could stop by, to visit again, as he had volunteered to say Mass at the hospital, three times a week.

"I made no bones about it," said Lauren, "when I told him I wasn't Catholic. But if he wanted to come by and fill me in on the news, he could."

At that moment, Lauren was caught off guard. Father Benito grinned. "I wasn't Catholic, either," the priest said, "when I first started out."

He began to walk away, then turned back. "Father Benito leaned over… and I'll never forget this…"

"He quietly said 'Son, I'm sorry about the loss of your crew. But try to remember, God has a plan for all of us… including battleship sailors and their ships. Remember,' he continued, 'we *all* have to be strong now, as never before.' "

He turned to leave and, over his shoulder, the priest quickly added, "I'll see you, Friday, after Mass."

Lauren remained still and quietly stared at the ceiling. He didn't know what to make of this short, dark-skinned man. This country priest had taken the time to learn he was a battleship sailor, and was aware most of his crew had been lost.

The New Year—1942—was only hours away. On 1 January, Admiral Nimitz would, with little ceremony, take command of the crippled Pacific Fleet, from acting commander Vice-Admiral William S. Pye. Three weeks earlier, President Roosevelt retired the Commander-in-Chief, Pacific Fleet, Admiral Husband E. Kimmel, following the disastrous surprise attack on Pearl Harbor.

Despite expensive celebrations that would go on in mainland cities, there was little to celebrate in Hawaii, other than just being alive. With the territory of Hawaii now under martial law, following the attack, there would be no champagne or fancy dinners, no party hats or horns to blow. No fireworks.

When the clock struck midnight, there was visible relief among the doctors, nurses, and corpsmen at Hospital Point Hospital, that they'd made it through another year. They, like others, felt lucky to be alive, and quietly celebrated New Year's Eve—as did many who had lost friends and relatives in the battle.

For their patients, still under heavy sedation, the transition into the New Year had been uneventful. If they'd been awake at midnight, they might have heard the traditional old Scottish tune, "Auld Lang Syne"—times gone by.

From somewhere in the hospital, from aboard the *Solace*, and from numerous ships across the harbor, the song quietly drifted through the air, and echoed down the channel and into corridors.

Lauren was awake, due to after-effects of forced withdrawal, initiated by the medical team. As his pain subsided, so had the doses of morphine.

He found himself silently mouthing words to a song he'd never sung before. In the dimly lit ward, Lauren still swears his high school track mate and best friend, Billy Mann, appeared at his bedside.

He recalled their times running track, double dates with pretty girls in Long Beach, practical jokes, and always, laughter. That would take an eternity to forget.

Lost in tears that tracked to his bed sheets, the pain of loss sheltered Lauren from his corporal pain. And he vowed, then and there, "...my lost shipmates and buddies will never be forgotten."

In spite of his wounds, Lauren felt a renewed sense of calm.

Maybe it was Billy's "visit" that made him feel more tranquil.

"Things will get better" Lauren was certain Billy had assured him.

Maybe it had come from the priest's visit, two days earlier.

Friday, 2 January 1942

"True to his word," said Lauren, "a couple days later, Father Benito showed up, after saying mass. The priest carried what appeared to be gifts. It was sorta' like Christmas had come, all over again."

In his arms were a rolled up pair of dungarees, two thick objects, wrapped in a piece of black and white checkered cloth, and something in a brown paper bag.

Father Benito asked Lauren if he'd like to go for a walk. "But I'll be the only one walking," he said.

Lauren's heart lit up for the first time, since before the attack. "I was too emotional to speak. I just nodded, yes."

Lauren was handed the dungarees.

"I purposefully got these large," said Benito, "So they won't chafe at your burns. They're old, but clean."

It didn't take Lauren but a second to jump at the chance to get out of bed. He sat on its edge, while Father Benito commandeered a corpsman to help Lauren pull on the pants.

"Getting dressed was a little awkward," said Lauren. "I had to keep on my hospital gown, with the open back… and cinch up my pants, with an old belt that came with them."

Then almost magically… and rather too coincidentally to Lauren, another corpsman appeared with an old wicker backed wheelchair. "I laughed, and looked to Father Benito, when I realized he had prearranged everything, from the beginning."

The corpsman was amused. He winked at Lauren and helped him into the wheelchair.

Setting the wrapped package and mysterious brown bag on Lauren's lap, Father Benito pushed him the length of the ward, out into a long corridor. The corpsman remained a respectful distance, behind. "As we moved," said Lauren, "the hallway, seemed to stretch on forever. I recall the feeling of a cool breeze on my face and hands."

Near the end of the corridor, they approached a large side door, held open with a brick used as doorstop. "I was nervous as hell… my adrenaline pumping. I couldn't wait to get outside."

Bright golden rays poured into the shadowy hall. "Reminds me of St. Peter Basilica's dome… at the Vatican," said Benito. "It's a stunning view, to see the sunlight streaming through the windows around this time of day."

"You were there…"

Benito stopped to admire the rivulets of light. "A long time ago… after I left Maui, where I was born."

Lauren was moved. Memories were stirred and, at once, he felt more relaxed.

"To me…" said Lauren, "This reminds me of days at sea, while out on maneuvers…or when we used to come into port aboard *Arizona*. If I'd pulled an all-night duty, or couldn't sleep, I'd get up early to watch the sunrise, from the forecastle. The sun would dance through the clouds like thousands of fingers reaching for the water…sort of just like now… I've missed that.."

"Then, let's get out there and enjoy what God's given us," said Benito. He picked up the pace once more. The soothing breeze increased as they emerged through a side door—and crossed from shadows into light.

The sun reflected off channel waters, onto the hospital's façade. It flickered through the plumeria trees and palm fronds, and undulated around Lauren's wheelchair.

Maybe it was due to being his first real day outside, in weeks. Perhaps it was the morning air. But every color of plumeria seemed brighter that day.

"The morning rains bring out the colors and the scent of the plumeria," said Benito. "Look at those yellows…"

"This is really special," Lauren commented to the priest. Everything looks brighter and better."

For Lauren, it just kept getting better. "So, Father Benito…. If I've ever complained about too warm a day," he said, "today will not be one of them."

Benito quietly pushed Lauren's wheelchair down the path, to a large wooden bench near the center of Hospital Point's water's edge.

The scenes before them tempered the mood. From this perspective, Father Benito had allowed Lauren to throw open a new window to the world. Yet, he found himself directly facing the channel's entrance—the only way in and out of Pearl—with all the reminders of the day that took too many lives, and so many of his friends and crew.

Billy would have liked this.

Ambient sounds surrounded the two men from every direction. Ship's engines and horns sounded. Riveters and pile drivers pounded. Dredgers and mud scows scooped and dragged bottom sludge from beached hulls. And myriads of miniature waterfalls flushed foul, mucky seawater from pumps that drained most of the sunken ships.

Aircraft warmed up and took off from Hickam Field, to the left. Across the channel, Ford Island Naval Air Station seemed as active as it had been prior to the Attack. It all heightened the sites and sounds of renewed life.

Lauren was silent as he took it all in. The scene was encouraging to eyes and ears.

Father Benito mentioned that everyone in the harbor—sailors, construction men, divers, and engineers—seemed to be "…all charged up. Their new motto," he said, "is 'Remember *Arizona*'… and they're predicting they'll eventually have every ship in the harbor salvaged or raised in record time."

Slightly to the West, and across the shore was Ford Island, with burned out hangars 6 and 38, standing next to the destroyed seaplane ramp—the site where first bombs had landed.

Nearly straight ahead, in the muck of the South Channel's harbor bottom, undergoing a massive salvage operation, lay the beached USS *Nevada*. Father Benito saw Lauren's eyes begin to water. "They say she's still viable, and the Navy's best hope for returning such a highly damaged battleship to the fight."

A beehive of Navy and civilian workers, and tugs all pulled together in their attempt to get the ship back into the war.

Lauren's mood was galvanized, once more.

He was awash in memories of his and Dvorak's escape to *Solace*, aboard *Vestal's* launch, and how he had witnessed *Nevada's* valiant attempt to race along Battleship Row, out into open waters.

From the ship's stern, *Nevada's* new flag was waving from its staff— the tattered one replaced after it had been shredded in the heat of battle. Despite nearly two-dozen fighter planes and bombers going after *Nevada,* the Japanese had come up short in their attempts to close the channel, by sinking it.

While aboard *Solace,* Lauren was told of *Nevada's* race from entrapment, in their desire to take the war outside the harbor. But one of the ship's quartermasters intentionally beached it, just beyond the entrance to the South Channel, to prevent sinking and blocking the Harbor's entrance to the Pacific.

On 7 December, *Nevada's* stern had been backed into the shoreline and its bow remained in deeper water. By the time flooding of compartments was complete, water was splashing across its decks.

Now, Lauren and Father could see the heavy lines that held her anchors, astern. Divers could be seen alongside its hull, using underwater cutting torches, near the bilge keel.

Father Benito pointed out multiple circles of oil and bottom muck that ringed the hull's surface. "It's like looking inside a tree stump" he said. "With each new line, you can see the progress they've made with re-floating the ship." Just as one might look at a cross-section of a tree's rings, the ship's sides marked every level from which *Nevada* had, so far, recovered its buoyancy.

Lauren recalled, at that moment, how the Friday before the attack—the day the fleet had come in from maneuvers—*Nevada* had originally tied up along side *Arizona,* for the night.

"Ya' know, Father, a lot of us thought it was mighty strange that for... what seemed like the very first time, nearly every ship in the fleet was in port."

"According to Lou Conter, who was in the pilot house on *Arizona,* he heard Admiral Kidd tell the Captain that he was not in favor of what was taking place, with the entire fleet being in the harbor over the same weekend. We'd heard a rumor, later... one of the Marines on board had spotted a ship... leaving port at night. Now, to my knowledge, ships rarely ever left Pearl at night. In the end, though, we didn't give it a second thought."

This was the first time, in weeks, Lauren had carried on a lengthy conversation, with anyone—having been under the influence of morphine, most of the time. Father remained quiet, and just listened.

"So, after we came in from maneuvers, that Friday around noon," continued Lauren, "... *Nevada* first tied up next to *Arizona,* through Saturday morning."

"We were quayed in Fox Seven. Then tugs pulled *Nevada* into its own quay, right behind us."

"The maintenance ship, *Vestal,* then moved alongside and moored next to us, stem to stern. They were supposed to add a counter in the galley, in order to create a new cafeteria-style serving line. I also heard they also had to clean up a mess in the boiler room, created when the pilot brought us in, too fast, around the northern side of Ford Island.

"The way I heard the story from my friend Lou Conter, who was the ship's Channel Helmsman, was that Captain Van Valkenburgh just took over."

"Shit! ...Sorry, Father. We felt the whole ship vibrate like hell. Stirred up the channel bottom. Heard that it ruined our water intake, the boilers, the evaporator filters, and who knows what. We were scheduled to head back to Long Beach on 19 December to pick up six new 1.1 guns for the ship."

"*Vestal*'s crew had shared a movie, on deck, that Saturday night. And my friend, Billy, had grabbed me, that morning, to remind me. Billy wanted to make sure I wouldn't forget. He was star-struck, as hell. In fact, anytime we spent at Waikiki Beach, he always rubbernecked to look for Hollywood stars that might be staying at the Royal Hawaiian or the Moana Hotel."

"Billy loved the movies, and had said that we were in for a good film. 'Dr. Jekyll and Mr. Hyde,' he had said. 'With Claude Raines.' he kept goin'."

"I feel guilty, now, knowin' what I know about the bomb dropping into the powder magazine, and Billy's last moments." Lauren abruptly stopped talking. He could feel the pain, again.

"Go on," said Father.

Lauren struggled to regain his composure. Finally, he spoke.

"…. But I didn't stay aboard and it was the last time I ever saw Billy. I'd had shore patrol duty, Friday night, and had finally gotten up the nerve to ask Nikki out on a date. So now it gave me Saturday and Sunday off, after inspection... to meet my girl at Broadway Inn after she finished work."

"So, missing the movie didn't bother me much. Here it was, getting close to Christmas. I wanted to take the train into town, early, and get some shopping done, before my date."

"Anyway, the thought occurs to me, Father, that it's funny what small unimportant things you sometimes remember… like the name of a movie. And now, here I am... trying to get better... with *Nevada* being in the same predicament."

Father Benito sat on the bench, adjacent to Lauren's wheelchair, and opened up the wrapped package. "Only then," said Lauren, " did he explain to me that it contained two Japanese-style bento box lunches, made by Emily Picadura, one of his parishioners who lived near the church."

The priest had talked to Emily about Lauren, and that he needed something more than Navy chow to regain his health. Like the true Hawaiian she was, she wanted to go to any length to help him heal.

Her traditional, tightly packed lunches were beautifully displayed, and proportionally divided, in handcrafted red, lacquerware containers, wrapped in the traditional checkered furoshiki cloth. Inside each box was a densely packed meal of two rice balls with small strips of nori—black seaweed—and a slight amount of shoyu poured over the rice; teriyaki chicken; fried mullet and shoyu; pickled yellow turnips; and mango, for dessert.

A piece of sugar cane stock and some pineapple topped it off.

"Hawaiian gum," Benito said.

Lauren looked up.

"What we call sugar cane on the plantation… Hawaiian gum. Just chew and suck on it when you want something sweet."

Lauren glanced at the pineapple.

"You know, Father… this reminds me of the train into Honolulu," he said. "You've probably heard how us guys'd jump off the slow moving train… headin' into Honolulu, on liberty. And we'd 'borrow' a pineapple from the fields, to try to impress some girl, in town…"

"Yes," Father Benito laughed, as he made a sign of the cross. "And you're forgiven. "Chopsticks or fork?" Benito held up both.

"Chopsticks. I'll give 'em another try."

Despite his fingers being severely burned, Lauren had recovered enough to slowly navigate their use.

"I ate every bit of the lunch. Father was pretty impressed to see my fledging ability with chopsticks. He asked how I learned to use them, and I immediately thought of June and Nikki. I told him a couple of friends had taught me."

"Pretty good for a haole boy," he had said.

The two men finished lunch. Then Father Benito turned to the mysterious brown paper bag. From it, he pulled out an old, beat up leather case, which he handed to Lauren.

"This is for you," he said. "It's a loan from Jacinth, Emily's husband, while you're here recuperating."

Lauren opened the case, and discovered it contained a pair of well-worn binoculars.

"We both thought you might enjoy watching the harbor's rebuilding and some of the ships coming and going."

Lauren closed its lid, and read the inscription on its flap. Printed in faded ink it read:

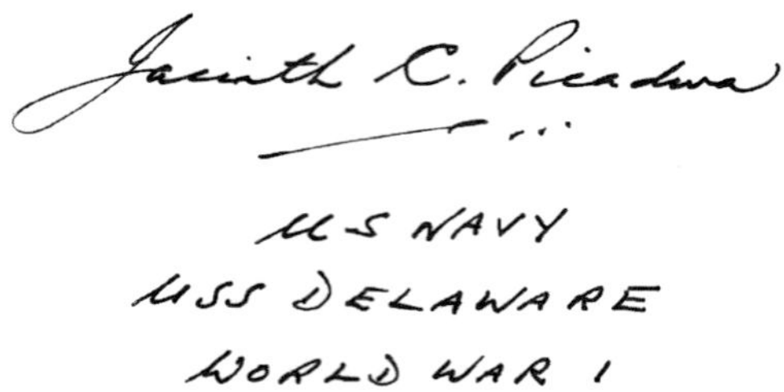

Lauren was quietly moved to tears, as he reflected to the last time he had used binoculars—aboard *Arizona*. Without words, Father Benito understood. He gently placed his hand on Lauren's shoulder, "Enjoy, my friend. Get better."

Over the next two weeks, Father was as good as his word. Every day he was scheduled to say Mass, he'd stop by afterwards to visit, and to take Lauren out to the channel.

Lauren was reserved about any discussion of his past—or events that happened aboard *Arizona*. Still, the two men shared many stories.

Father Benito spoke of what inspired him to become a priest. And Lauren discussed his days growing up in Elma and McCleary, Washington that eventually led to enlistment in the Navy.

"We spoke of nothing important," said Lauren, "Just a couple of friends getting to know each other. And he never brought up *Arizona*. Only once he touched on the morning of the attack. I told him I didn't want to talk about it, and that was fine with him. We never discussed it again."

Lauren had looked forward to the time, outside. Over the next two weeks, whenever Father wasn't around, he'd get a corpsman to push him out to the point. He always brought Jacinth's binoculars along.

"Using them, I could pretty much see all of Pearl. And it seemed, no matter where I aimed the binoculars, without fail... my eyes would drift over to the ruins of my ship, sitting there... now a rusting hulk with only an American flag flying from its twisted deck."

"In all the times I gazed at *Arizona*, I never saw once anyone close to the ship's remains, other than salvage crews . She just sat there silently... and alone. Maybe it was out of respect for the dead. Or... I'd ask myself if they were afraid of the spirits that might reside there."

"Over the years, from school days… and then into the service, Billy and I had spent a lot of time together. I often felt his phantom presence, close by, almost like… protecting me through the rest of the war. Hell, I've never told anybody this."

"But it also bothered me that, when I'd think of Billy, morbid thoughts would creep into my mind. Like what he might have felt as the bomb dropped, and blew him to smithereens. But that was all too painful. And I'd immediately put it out of my mind. After dark, sometimes, back in the ward... my God... with stealth, those thoughts would silently creep back into my head. And I'd hear Billy yell out my name, as clear as the ship's bell. Perhaps it was the morphine playing tricks on my mind. But his voice was as distinct as it had ever been."

Lauren would watch the ships pass through the harbor entrance, as they headed out for maneuvers or returned to port. And a certain melancholy would nag at him. Much of his time was spent trying to sort out his life. The two persistent questions: Would he ever truly get well... enough to get back into the fight? And if he didn't... what would he be able to do, to make a living? He was still short of his first four years, and hadn't given up the idea to repay Uncle Sam for his father's bailing on the Navy. Deep down, he knew his first choice would be to stay the course, and "…remain Navy."

One afternoon, Lauren managed to get up and out to his favorite bench, without the assistance of a corpsman. He sat with only his thoughts, binoculars up, scanning the channel beyond Hospital Point.

His attention was drawn to a heavily armored destroyer, leaving the harbor. It bristled, in the sunlight, with its four 5-inch guns, 20mm guns, and twin-mounted 40mm guns. Along its sides were a dozen torpedo tubes and depth charge projectors.

Lauren was aware destroyers had become a more important asset to the war effort. Placed into service to interrupt and destroy any threats to a fleet, the Navy utilized its modern destroyers mostly for defense against submarines and against air attacks on its larger, but slower, ships—such as the carriers, the new backbone to the Navy.

Suddenly, he wanted to be on a destroyer. He felt an emotional pang that he would not get over, until he found that desire satisfied. "The destroyer slid by, almost silently," he said. "It was sleek, graceful, and looked strong as hell."

"I thought of the difference between that ship and *Arizona*. And I wanted to serve whatever amount of time I had left in the Navy, on a destroyer." Lauren pulled the binoculars from his eyes "...to see that beautiful piece of work in the flesh, so-to-speak."

As the destroyer approached Hospital Point, he noticed one sailor, in particular, watching him. He brought his binoculars back up.

"We were nearly across from each other, when all of a sudden the sailor came to attention and gave me a salute... paying me an honor, for some reason… I don't know why. It was so unexpected, and so sudden, that my reflexes took over, and I somehow... without thinking, braced myself with my left hand on the wheelchair, put down the binoculars... stood up… and returned his salute."

The ship continued to quietly glide out of the channel, toward the open sea.

"The two of us stood that way until his ship had completely passed. Although I never shared this story with anyone... it meant a lot to me. In my heart... I truly believe it was the turning point. That sailor... at the time no older than I, gave me the resolve needed to still make the Navy my career. I'll never forget the name of that destroyer. USS *Reid.* And how that same ship would come back into my life a couple of years down the road, in the South Pacific."

Sunday, 11 January 1942

The day finally arrived for Lauren to be transferred back to the States. Early that morning, he was notified that USS *Henderson* would take him aboard—in the afternoon—to head for Mare Island Naval Hospital, just outside San Francisco. Though it would take decades for his body to entirely heal, at Mare Island, he would go through the final stage of Naval assistance with healing and recuperation—before being assigned to another ship, or sent home.

On this Sunday, Father Benito visited one last time. And they shared their final Bento box together.

"He was a good guy," said Lauren, "...that short little priest. Because he didn't try to pry into my life, he helped me, in no small way, through the most difficult time."

"We finished our lunch, that day, and I handed him back Jacinth's binoculars. I was grateful for the loan, and offered thanks… and for Emily's terrific box lunches."

Father Benito waved his hand and told Lauren that Jacinth had decided to make the binoculars his gift to him. "In that way," he had explained, "I could continue to use them on my next ship... and remember him by it."

"I was pretty choked up and didn't know what to say. Although I'd never met, Emily and Jacinth Picadura, I asked Father to thank them for their friendship and generosity."

With a wide smile, Father said, simply, "It's the Hawaiian way."

"He handed me a pen, and instructed me to write under Jacinth's name. I didn't want to screw up a gift so special, so I asked Father to do it for me."

Lauren picked up the old case and read from it, aloud.

"This is what he wrote... as I read it now, and although it's much faded, I'll always remember what it says, and our friendship:

Lauren F. Bruner
USS Arizona
Pearl Harbor T.H.
World War II

Then Father Benito and I shook hands. He told me he'd keep in contact, and follow my career. Then he said something like... because I can't call to mind exactly, 'Lauren, we can never figure out what God's plans are. So there's no sense beating yourself up. You were dealt one hand. Your ship mates another. Make the best of yours, for *their* sake, and for your own.' "

"I tried to hide the fact that my lower lip was trembling, slightly, and could say nothing in return."

"He was right, of course."

"Then, he pushed my wheelchair back into the ward and turned me over to a corpsman. Once more, he spoke, "Take care Lauren." And with an assurance and confidence that Lauren had rarely seen, Father Benito said, "We'll meet, again... don't worry."

Then he was gone. "And I was moving on… and never saw him again."

"Although I'd receive an occasional letter throughout the rest of the war, I still remember what he told me last, best."

"It only later occurred to me... that, from his perspective... when he said 'We'll meet, again'... He wasn't necessarily referring to a *physical* meeting. And somehow, that gave me comfort."

— —

SECOND TO THE LAST TO LEAVE

Lauren F. Bruner
7 December 1941

Lauren F. Bruner was 21 years, 1 month, and 3 days old on the day of the Attack on Pearl Harbor, and is shown in this artwork as he appeared on 6 December 1941 when he went out on his first date with Nikki.

Lauren is known as the Second to the Last to Leave USS *Arizona,* as the ship slid into her bloody grave, and was one of six sailors, who according to Naval Legend, became *Arizona*'s Greatest Escape.

As one of USS *Arizona*'s last survivors Lauren has dedicated the remainder of his life to working through his nonprofit foundation in order that future generations will always remember USS *Arizona* and her crew, and the great sacrifice they made defending America and freedom.

"In leaving, I would like to thank you for visiting my ship and USS Arizona Memorial at Pearl Harbor whenever you can. To answer one of the questions that you might have as you finish my book, yes, I married that pretty French-Irish brunette Marcella Margaret Stapleton on 25 July 1943."

Read the Full Story of *Arizona*'s Greatest Escape
Along With Viewing Rare Photos of the Attack by Visiting:
USS*Arizona*sGreatestEscape.com

Lauren Fay Bruner, FC 3/c

USS *Arizona*

Survivor

7 December 1941

Lauren Fay Bruner, CFF

USS *Coghlan*
At War's End

EPILOGUE

After the attack on Pearl Harbor, it took seven months in Naval hospitals for Lauren Bruner to heal enough to get back into the fight. The day he left Mare Island Naval Hospital near San Francisco, he became the gun captain aboard the new destroyer USS *Coghlan*.

Throughout the course of the rest of the war, this ship earned eight battle stars, which meant that it fought in eight of the Navy's Greatest Naval Battles, including the Battle of the Komandorski Islands, which has become Naval legend.

A larger and expanded book on Lauren Bruner's life is now in the works, which will share the stories of his entire life throughout WWII. This story will also include being given away by his mother at age six and getting caught running moonshine at eight.

Lauren and the crew of USS *Coghlan* fought throughout the South Pacific, and ended up as Occupation Forces in Nagasaki, Japan, less than six weeks after the atomic bomb was dropped, ending the war.

By visiting the website listed below and leaving your contact information, you will be notified when this next edition becomes available.

LaurensNextChapter.com

HOW THIS BOOK CAME TO BE WRITTEN

A Pearl Harbor Survivor Spent Decades Trying to Forget It. Then One Man Got Him Talking.

By David Montero
Reporting From Honolulu
For the Los Angeles Times
12/07/2016

He walked slowly, an entourage of help ensuring he didn't slip. People in the bar clapped as he moved past. Then Lauren Bruner gave up his cane and settled at a table against the wall where his picture had been hanging for years.

Dwight Lockwood, reed-thin in shorts and flip-flops, darted behind the bar and quickly popped the cap off a Kona Longboard beer. "It's his favorite," he said. The drink was on the house, of course.

Bruner took a swig. Around him, dozens of people waited to shake his hand, share a story or take a picture. The bar was a dive, barely more than the width of a long hallway. He looked around from the stool — his stool — and the decades began to melt away.

No longer was he 96, with a broken heart and a busted back. He was back in Smith's Union Bar, and it was in the exact same place it had been when he was stationed at Pearl Harbor all those years ago. In his mind, he was 21 again — strong from swabbing decks and climbing steep ladders aboard the battleship Arizona.

Then came Dec. 7, 1941 — the day of America's first 9/11, the day the U.S. got drawn into World War II in a hail of fire and fury. The day more than 2,400 men and women died in a surprise attack from a country America wasn't even at war with. The day Bruner has spent most of his life not talking about.

That changed a few years ago, when he met Ed McGrath.

It has been a week of memories all over this tropical Navy town, where survivors are commemorating the day the Imperial Japanese Navy, seeking to keep the U.S. Pacific Fleet out of Southeast Asia, aimed 353 bombers, fighter planes and torpedo planes in a preemptive strike at eight U.S. Navy battleships berthed at Pearl Harbor, including the Arizona, which exploded and sank.

The Arizona, which is the centerpiece of the World War II Valor in the Pacific National Monument, will be the site of a ceremony Wednesday honoring the 1,177 sailors and Marines who were killed on the battleship during the Sunday morning assault.

Bruner worked in fire control, where the ship's guns were aimed. He spent months in the hospital, and in 1942 joined a crew on a destroyer to finish out the war. From there, he settled in La Mirada with his wife and got a job at a plant making industrial-size refrigerators.

His life never included having children, and it also never included talking about what happened that day on the Arizona.
But then, one day in 2011, long after he'd retired, Bruner got a phone call. A man named Ed McGrath said he'd seen his name on a list of Arizona survivors and wondered whether he'd be willing to talk to him about it. Bruner said he wouldn't talk about the attack, but he'd be happy to meet with him.

"I had called 12 Arizona survivors and Lauren was the only one who responded," McGrath said. "I love history and I thought I might try to make a documentary about it."

McGrath, 70, had worked in Hawaii in the early 1970s and fell in love with the history and culture of the islands. Writing a book or making a film about Pearl Harbor wasn't something he'd tried before — but why not?

McGrath showed up at Bruner's house in La Mirada, and the two men sat down in the kitchen. "We started just by talking about his life and his naval career," McGrath said.

The next week, McGrath came back. And the week after that. Every Thursday morning, he'd go through the same routine: Drive from his home in Palos Verdes, drop the dog off at the office in Torrance and make the 42-mile drive to Bruner's house. McGrath would drive in silence, lost in thought. He'd pull up to the modest home with light-green trim and Bruner would let him in. They'd sit at the round, cluttered table in the kitchen over coffee.

Slowly, the memories began to leak out.

Bruner talked about how the crew on the Arizona, which he'd joined in 1939, would make wagers on what time the anchor would drop. Bruner only won that pool once. There were tales of fights he broke up at the bar, scuffles he got into himself, how he met actress Lana Turner on the beach in Hawaii.

He told him about Michiko Takahashi, a bartender he'd met on shore leave and fallen in love with on the spot. Nikki, she told him to call her. They were supposed to have their first official date on the morning of Dec. 7, 1941. He never saw her again.

When it came to the attack itself, though, there was not a word. McGrath would ask around the subject and Bruner wouldn't bite.

Then one day Bruner was talking, and McGrath noticed he'd started to cry.
The old man started with three words: "It was bad," he said.

McGrath listened intently through Bruner's tears. The story was worse than he'd imagined.

"He told me that the ship was listing and he was looking down on the deck and there are bodies everywhere," McGrath said.
"But he said he spotted these two sailors wearing their white uniforms, and the way they were walking, they looked like two friends taking a walk. He said he thought they'd be OK and were going to make it. Then, he said, they turned around and their uniforms were burned off, their hair was burned off and even their peckers were burned off."

McGrath was scribbling down notes quickly as Bruner began to open up more. He began recording everything. It was as if McGrath had poked a hole in a bag of salt and the building pressure around the hole opened the rip wider.

Bruner cried a lot more as he recounted the tales of carnage he'd witnessed — skin separating from flesh under intense heat, bodies ripped apart and hurled into the oily seawater, the searing pain of two bullets ripping through his leg.

Bruner suffered burns over more than two-thirds of his body. He and five other crew members — hands badly burned — managed to escape the burning vessel by sliding along a line tied to a nearby ship.

He spent several months recovering in a hospital before ultimately taking an assignment as a gun captain on a destroyer in the Pacific theater in 1942.

Bruner's brother, Chet Danforth, an Army sniper in the Battle of the Bulge, said he and his brother never talked much about the war. The conversation would end before it started.

How McGrath got his brother to talk, Danforth doesn't know. Bruner does: He realized the more he told, the fewer nightmares he had. And it wasn't just about the war and the attack. He found himself telling McGrath how he had been angry at his mother for giving him and his siblings away when he was 6 years old. It was during the Great Depression and the lumber mill she worked at laid her off and was seizing the house — but he hadn't known that at the time.

He confided details about his marriages and relationships after the war, all of them ending in loss: The first one lasted almost 13 years before she died. The second one he was with for nearly 24 years before she died. The third time around, it was 11 years — and then she died.

His latest girlfriend died in November, the week of Thanksgiving — the same week he hurt his back, which made the flight to Honolulu excruciating. His sister-in-law, Mary Danforth, said his heart hurt more than his back.

After the war, Bruner came home with all that had happened sealed up tight in his brain, and he left it there for seven decades.

Gradually, it began to seem as if the war hadn't happened at all. It was the script of the occasional nightmares of an old man — nothing more.

Then McGrath came along.

"Being able to tell him what happened lifted a great weight from my shoulders," Bruner says now.

McGrath eventually turned their conversations into that book he'd wanted to write, along with photographer Mark Comon. "Second to the Last to Leave" debuted Sunday morning at an autograph session in Honolulu with three other Arizona survivors.

To meet Lauren or order his book, visit SecondToTheLast-ToLeave.com

"I told Ed for the book so I wouldn't have to talk about it again," Bruner said.

Bruner was weary after signing his name hundreds of times, but he took a nap that afternoon so he could be ready to head over that night to Smith's Union Bar, which had been the Arizona's go-to bar before the attacks.

The other three survivors had been invited to come to Smith's, but only Bruner made it.

"Lauren's a sure thing," said Lockwood, the bartender. "I think he'd stay and close the place."

Bruner's face lit up when 88-year-old Virginia Hepper, who knew him from his days at Elma High School near Seattle, planted a kiss on his lips. "Not the first time I've kissed him," she said with a coy laugh.

Teri Mann, another family member of an Arizona veteran, wiped away tears while sitting next to Bruner. Because he'd told his story, she said, she finally knew more about what her uncle — William Mann — experienced aboard the ship and how he'd died. It happened instantly, when a bomb "literally dropped into Billy's lap," Bruner recounted in the book.

"I was always so proud growing up and I'd give these presentations in school about my uncle on the Arizona — it was a big deal," Mann said. "And now … "

She nodded her head, overwhelmed. Openly crying. "I'm so thankful."

As the crowd at Smith's thinned out, McGrath wasn't sure whether he'd make it as long as Bruner — who seemed to have picked up a second wind. But midnight wasn't far off, and finally Bruner gestured for his cane. As he got off the stool, though, his 96-year-old body turned mutinous.

Bruner winced as his bad back twisted. He wasn't going to be able to walk out of the bar this time. Bruner gave up the cane and settled into the wheelchair. The crowd parted as he rolled slowly and carefully out the door, to where his ride was waiting.

Smith's Union Bar
USS *ARIZONA* CREW'S FAVORITE "WATERING HOLE"

Remembering Pearl Harbor at the Oldest Bar in Hawaii

By Clint Lanier & Derek Hembree
Reporting From Honolulu
For the Huffington Post
12/02/2016

There are few places as meaningful to the people of the United States as the Pearl Harbor Memorial. At what is now a quiet, somber National Monument, the course of this country changed on December 7th, 1941. Within the span of a few hours, 2,403 men and women lost their lives when the Japanese staged a sneak-attack on the United States Pacific Fleet and sent this country into war.

Of those who were lost, at least 2,008 were sailors aboard the various ships that were targeted in the attack. And of the ships that lost men, none lost more than the USS Arizona, which was struck by a high-altitude bomb that dropped into the munitions room. The ship violently exploded, quickly sinking and immediately ending the lives of 1,177 men aboard. Only 335 survived.

But none of this was on our minds when we walked through the doorway of **19 North Hotel Street in Honolulu**. We were here to visit Smith's Union Bar, the oldest bar left in all the Hawaiian Islands. Here we hoped to not only learn about the history of the bar, but to also gain a different perspective about the Islands' past. Boy, were we in for an education.

During our mid-morning visit, Hotel Street, running diagonally northwest and southeast through Honolulu's downtown district, was quiet, with little traffic and a few pedestrians wandering in and out of the shops. With a cool breeze and music wafting out of the open doors of small shops, the landmark Iolani Palace just a few blocks to the east and the Aloha Tower to the south, it seemed almost quaint.

But we knew this scene only belied the history of this section of town. You see, for as far back as Westerners had been visiting the Hawaiian Islands, this part of Honolulu had always been known as the Red Light District. Chinatown is a stone's throw away and the docks and ports that have delivered hundreds of thousands of sailors to the island over the past two centuries are just a 10-minute stroll or a short bus ride to Pearl Harbor. So the district was a convenient distraction after months at sea.

Smith's Union Bar was just one of dozens of bars in the area, and all of them chock full of the pursuits a lonely, bored sailor with money in his pocket might want. There were gambling halls, opium dens and, of course, many, many brothels.

The Red Light District was seedy, dirty, and dangerous. It was everything you've ever read about – all the bad stuff anyway – about sea ports and villages of the 19th and 20th centuries.

But as just one bar of many, Smith's probably didn't stand out that much at the time. At least that was our impression. It isn't cavernous with a large stage for live music. Instead its small; a long room with enough space for a bar

on the right and tables against the wall on the left. There's no intimacy here, no dark booths for privacy. Just open seating that serves the purpose of drinking.
And from what owner Dwight Lockwood told us, that's pretty much what went on. Named for the next block's cross-street (Smith Street) and cashing the union checks from local workers, Smith's, apparently, never really made a commotion. There aren't any rooms off to the side that could have made it a brothel. No backroom with which to hold illegal poker games. Nope, none of this. Smith's was just a sailor's bar.

And it may stand to reason that's why it's survived. Chances are the police were too busy raiding other more nefarious places to bother with Smith's. There weren't any rival opium dens to burn it down or gangsters coming around to collect a take from the gambling. Nope, it was just a sailor's bar.

And when you walk in today, that's what you get – a bar. You sit down at a table and order a drink and settle in to a cozy, yet comfortable space just right for throwing one back. You can hear the conversations around you – mostly now from locals during the day talking about neighborhood characters, the weather, recent events and what have you.

Dwight told us the crowd, and therefore the conversation, changed throughout the day. In the morning until the mid-afternoon it's filled with the people we were surrounded by – aged locals. In the late afternoon they shuffle out and are replaced by business people. These stay for maybe a couple of hours, wandering in before or after dinner, and then finally go home. The last shift is owned by the college crowd, who migrate to the downtown area well after sunset and are still found here in the early morning. No longer are there any classic bars left in the area, save

Smith's Union, although there are still numerous lounges and pubs.

Dwight also tells us about Smith's staying power. He tells us that he has customers coming in who've been drinking here for decades. They talk to other customers who likewise have been here for years. They ask about each other's families, about each other's lives. They know each other - truly know each other. We witness this ourselves as they crack jokes and carry on.

But then Dwight tells us about one customer in particular, perhaps the longest running regular any bar has ever had. His name is Lauren Bruner and he is one of the last Crew Members of the famed battleship USS Arizona and for whom the Arizona Memorial was named. As Dwight tells us about Lauren, the importance of Smith's Union suddenly dawns on us, and our perspective completely changes. This isn't just a bar anymore. This was the Arizona Crew's Favorite "Watering Hole."

When the USS Arizona was transferred to the Pacific Fleet in 1939, and subsequently to Pearl Harbor, Lauren Bruner was a crew member. He was a young Fire Controlman whose job was to call out the coordinates of the enemy to the plotting room down in the ship. The plotting room then entered those coordinates into a computer (which they called "Bertha"), aiming the guns, and then firing.

A stressful job no doubt, especially for a young 20-year-old. And like most other 20-year-olds, Lauren liked going out with his friends and fellow Crew Members after hours to relieve some of that stress. For Lauren, and for the crew of the USS Arizona, their go-to spot was Smith's Union.

According to Ed McGrath, Lauren's close friend and his co-author of a newly released memoir about him, every ship's crew had a regular watering hole. The crew of the USS Nevada would frequent Shanghai Bill's Bar on North Pauahi Street. The Crew of the USS Maryland preferred the Four Aces Bar on Alakea Street. But for the crew of the USS Arizona it was always Smith's Union.

And for Lauren, even today at 97, Smith's is still special. When the Japanese attacked, Lauren was at his battle station on the Arizona. When the ship exploded, Lauren suffered burns on over 73% of his body and was wounded by two machine gun rounds from an enemy plane.

Few, including his Navy doctors, thought he would survive, but survive he did. And for the last dozen years, he's been coming back to Honolulu for Pearl Harbor Remembrance Ceremonies and to visit Smith's. According to Lauren, in that order.

For us, Smith's Union Bar definitely epitomizes what a historic American bar should be. Sure, it's the oldest in Hawaii, but there's more to it than that. It was the fly on the wall when the underworld of the Red Light District was real, and not the setting for some Hollywood film. It was also a safe harbor for young men from the Arizona who vanished from the earth in the blink of an eye, and according to Lauren, is a memorial, perhaps, to their spirits.

While the true memorial is only a few miles away and pays tribute to America's sacrifice, a place like Smith's Union pays tribute to the Sailors and Marines of Pearl Harbor's love of life and to their youth. What a glorious way to remember them.

Whenever you are in Hawaii, be sure to stop by if you are visiting the area. Have a beer here and take a look at the USS Arizona artifacts hanging on the walls, most of which have been signed by Lauren. Try to connect with a different side of Hawaii's complicated history.

According to Lauren, Smith's Union is his favorite bar.

"It's where I grew up with my crew before the Attack on Pearl Harbor and where I most like to return to. It's never changed."

SECOND TO THE LAST TO LEAVE

Lauren Bruner's
DREAM GIFT TO AMERICA

As you read the Deck Log of USS *Arizona* on the Shrine Wall at the USS *Arizona* Memorial, know that these men, *Arizona's* Sailors and Marines, are those to whom Lauren has dedicated this book.

In reading each man's name, think for a moment of what it would be like if in addition to visiting the Memorial, you would be able to view a portrait of each crew member, all 1512, as they looked on the day of the attack on Pearl Harbor, much like the portraits in this book.

Please visit **DreamGiftToAmerica.com** to learn how you can help in this research. Once completed, this entire collection will be offered to the National Park Service at Pearl Harbor to share with visitors.

What Lauren has undertaken through the non-profit foundation that he has established will be a gift to America in which every *Arizona* Crew Member can be honored by future generations who will be able to meet the man by seeing what he looked like on 7 December 1941, along with viewing his personal story.

DreamGiftToAmerica.com

USS *Arizona* Collectables
TRADING CARD COLLECTION

Lauren Bruner invites you to consider what may be the single most treasured Trading Card Collection ever created. This collection of American Heroes are the crew members of USS *Arizona* who fought together as brothers in arms at the start of World War II and who have become American history and legend.

Each card shows a Crew Member as they appeared on the morning of the Attack on Pearl Harbor in the uniform of the day. On the back of each card, you will be able to learn the story of that crew member, which will include the day he was born, the day he joined the crew of USS *Arizona*, and his age to the day on 7 December, 1941.

The introduction of the USS Arizona Collectable Collection is titled *Arizona*'s Greatest Escape and is available now, only through the retailer offering this book or at:

USS*Arizona*Collectables.org

Edward J. McGrath, Jr.

Ed McGrath considers himself a storyteller first, as far as his writing carreer. Second To The Last To Leave USS *Arizona* is his first novel, although he has written other histories. He considers himself Irish-Hawaiian, as after he moved to the Islands early in life, he was adopted into the Hawaiian family of Jay Silva.

Although Ed and his wife live in Los Angeles, both consider the Islands of Hawaii their hearts' home, and return several times each year. He is married to Dyanne Y. McGrath, a nationally recognized designer of women's clothing, and together, they have nine children, four of whom are "hanai," and thirteen grandchildren. Ed's family is the most important thing in his life, and he considers Lauren Bruner family.

Together, Lauren and Ed have co-founded the Lauren F. Bruner USS *Arizona* Memorial Foundation, which is nonprofit and has been established to pay honor to USS *Arizona* and its crew for all time.

As part of this undertaking, along with the Board of Directors of the foundation, they plan to build the USS Arizona World War II National Experience – Honolulu, and continue to work with the state of Hawaii to make this possible.

Edward J. McGrath Jr.

Storyteller ▪ Historian ▪ Novelist

Craig O. Thompson

Craig O. Thompson is an international duo-award-winning author of the suspense-thriller, OMAR: A Novel. A keynote speaker and counter-terrorism / business disaster recovery planning consultant, Craig also serves as communications director for the International Association for Counterterrorism & Security Professionals (IACSP).

Mr. Thompson holds a B.S. and M.A. in Education from Northern Arizona University. He has been writing for more than forty years—from professional journal articles about al-Qaeda, evolving terrorism, and biological warfare, to lighter fare such as poetry, lyrical pieces, and ad campaigns for corporate clients.

As a member of the International Platform Association, on August 9th (Washington, DC / on C-Span) and September 10th, 2001 (KFI Radio, Los Angeles), he publicly warned of horrific terrorist attacks that would occur on our own homeland. Currently, Craig is working on a novel, a non-fiction book, and two screenplays.

Craig O. Thompson

Novelist

Ed Mell

*"**Ed Mell** is an Internationally-known fine artist who has painted the cover of my book, and I want to take this opportunity to thank him. He has captured as a painting, USS Arizona along with my battle station shortly after my escape while the battle of Pearl Harbor still raged. From my memory Ed's painting reminds me of my Escape From Hell.*

When I first met Ed Mell and asked him to consider painting my book's cover, he shared with me that as a young boy of 12, he visited Hawaii and Pearl Harbor with his parents before the Memorial as we know it today was ever built. He told me that of all the things his family did on this trip, the most exciting and meaningful thing to him was visiting Pearl Harbor and USS Arizona, and it was for this reason that he wanted to create this painting.

I can't thank him enough for his kindness and for allowing his painting to become the poster that will be used for the National Fundraising Campaign to build USS Arizona World War II Experience – Honolulu, of which my foundation is working with the State of Hawaii to build.

To view other works by my friend Ed Mell, I would like to invite you to visit his website and gallery."f

edmellgallery.com

Ed Mell

Cover Artist

Karin M. Andrino

Karin Mavely Andrino is a professional portrait artist, painter, illustrator and teacher of art living in the Los Angeles area and teaching school on the Palos Verdes Peninsula.

Karin was born in Guatemala City, Guatemala and came to America at a young age. She graduated with a Bachelor's in Studio Arts from California State University in Los Angeles and has worked as a fine artist ever since.

Second to the Last to Leave is her first book to illustrate. She is also the National Director of Art for Lauren Bruner's Dream Gift to America, and is a member of The Portrait Society of America. Karin lives in Los Angeles with her husband, Samnuel Dammett, and three cats.

"I cannot thank Karin enough for all her work in helping to bring my book alive through her portaits of my crew and those I love. It was because of her incredibly beautiful portaits that Ed McGrath and I created Dream Gift to America with the goal of one day completing a portrait of each of Arizona's 1512 crew members. To visit Karin's website that shows more of her work, I suggest you visit karinandrino.com."

karinandrino.com

Karin Andrino

Portrait Artist

MAHALO & THANK YOU

The authors would like to take this opportunity to sincerely thank those listed below for their individual efforts in helping to tell this story of an extraordinary man and an American Hero.

Due to these individual contributions, a classic piece of American Literature has been written in order for it to be passed along from one generation to another.

Dyanne Y. McGrath
Edward J. McGrath III
Iesha Saldana
Mark Comon
Sheryl Comon
Bob Basche
Karey Basche
Hunter Ryland
Desiree Ryland
Ulrich Krauer
Halekulani
Richard Faulkner
Erin Farr
Marcie Kagawa
Paul Hewitt

Continued on next page...

Margaret Ambroson
Karin Andrino
Tammy Antilla
Tom Aslakson
Raf Bacani
Dennis Ballard
Bengie Barin
Tom Bartlett
Ed Bendet
Brian Bryans
Greg Byrne
Taffy Cannon
Donny Chambers
William Cole
Lou Conter
Sharon Craig-Insalata
Louann Daley
Chet Danforth
Mary Danforth
Charles Fattig
James Francis
Tim Gray
Hawaiian Airlines
Jessie Higa
Percy Higashia
Eddie Hoeschen
Kelsea Holbrook
Robert Hopper
Stephen J. Hussman
Jeffrey W. James
Captain, USN (Retired)
Lyn Johnson
Al Johnson
John Paul Jones, III
Mickey Kaisaki
Eric Kilgore
Sam Kong
Dwight Lockwood
Ben Lum
Mona Lum
Joe Mamola
Lorraine Marks-Haislip
Daniel Martinez
Barin McGrath
Aaron Metzler
Lori Miller
Victoria Miller
David Montero
Roger J. Myers
Aubria Niemi
North Texas State
University
Jaclyn Ostrowski
Jeff Pantaleo
Lori Peterson
Carol Ponds
Rear Admiral
Frank Ponds (Retired)
Trent S. Purdy
Bob Puttock
Delys Recca
Elan Recca
Joe Recca
Shirley Recca

Carol Reid
Carol Reiley
Iesha Saldana
Larry Sather
Ronald Schreiner
Ryan Sebring
David Seckman
Pat Sexton
Miyuki Sohara
Sakura Productions
Don Stratton
Kaitlynn Sullivan
Joe Switzer
Joe Ann George Taylor
Mark Terrell
Janette L. Thompson
Jordan Tucker
Jim Underwood
University of Arizona
Rich Weathers
Linda Wenzel
Rich Wenzel